# Too Darn Soulful

## The Story of Northern Soul

David Nowell

 Robson Books

*To my mum and dad, Winifred and Tom.*
*Thanks for tolerating my strange nocturnal habits all those*
*years ago!*

Published in Great Britain in 1999 by Robson Books Ltd,
10 Blenheim Court, Brewery Road, London N7 9NT

A member of the Chrysalis Group plc

Copyright © David Nowell 1999
The right of David Nowell to be identified as author of this work
has been asserted by him in accordance with the Copyright,
Designs and Patents Act 1988

'Not You' – Words and music by Cynthia Weil and Barry Mann
© 1966, Screen Gems – EMI Music Inc, USA.
Reproduced by permission of Screen Gems – EMI Music Ltd,
London WC2H 0EA

**British Library Cataloguing in Publication Data**
A catalogue record for this title is available from the British
Library

ISBN 1 86105 270 7

Typeset by SX Composing DTP, Rayleigh, Essex
Printed and bound in Great Britain by Butler & Tanner Ltd.,
London and Frome

# Contents

# Acknowledgements

The author would like to thank the scores of people who have happily given up their time and knowledge to help with this mammoth project. They are too numerous to mention individually, but special mention must be given to soul guru Richard Searling, Nick Mattingley of Granada TV, the *Wigan Observer*, the *Stoke Evening Sentinel*, *Blues and Soul*, the *Blackpool Evening Gazette*, and Ian Palmer of *Manifesto*.

# Introduction

Indulge me one moment while I tell you about the first time I heard Walter Jackson's 'Not You'. This 1966 beat ballad, recorded for the Chicago-based Okeh label, is something of a connoisseur's item among rare soul fans. It is not a dance record, it is not even a Northern Soul record in the true sense of the word, but it has all the haunting qualities that lovers of 1960s black American music yearn for.

I am ashamed to say that until relatively recently Walter's classic recording was utterly unknown in the author's household, but that's the beauty of being a fan of rare soul. Just when you think you are on the brink of becoming a leading authority on soul music, a gem like this leaps up from the bottomless pit of treasures from the 1960s and bites you. Hard.

And so it was that at 7.30 am on a normal workday I'm driving along the A-roads from Blackpool to Preston with the motorway in sight and the car cassette player on maximum volume as usual. (A welcome lift for the spirits before beginning the daily grind.) Now Walter has had his critics over the years for veering towards middle-of-the-road material more suited to the smart lounges of Las Vegas than the sweaty cellar bars of the British Northern Soul scene. Sure enough, his smooth cabaret-style delivery and schmaltzy strings that bring in the intro to 'Not You' make me fear the worst.

Girl now I know
But still I can't believe it's true
If there's one person I believed in, baby, it was you.

His warm, dark voice is perfect. And then the orchestra comes in with the most delicious backdrop to the words.

> From the day I found you
> I built my whole world around you
> Someone else might be untrue
> But not you, no, not you girl, not you.
> I can't believe it's true.

His voice is quivering with emotion and I'm stunned. I'm no longer concentrating on the road. I'm inside the music, living every word, loving the passion, loving the sensation that this masterpiece is creating inside my brain. And the schmaltzy strings suddenly return tenfold, suddenly sounding so right, cascading brilliantly as Walter builds up the emotion.

> I thought we shared so very much
> But now I see.
> I gave my heart and soul to you.
> But you just gave your lips to me.

Now I'm in raptures, and the car is slowing down to a crawl. And Walter is shouting:

> Girl, the way my heart saw you
> Yes, you were everything good and more.
> You were so sweet, girl you were mine.
> And I swore on my LIFE,
> YES, you were mine.

And the orchestra is in full flow. And I've pulled over to the side of the road because I can't concentrate on the road any more. Nothing else matters, right at this moment, other than listening to Walter baring his soul. His pain is almost tangible, the effect of music and vocals combining to grab you by the throat, bringing tears close to the surface.

Someone else, baby, maybe might be untrue.
But not you.
NOT YOU.

Walter isn't singing the words, he is living them. He sounds like his heart is breaking. And I'm sitting in the car, a grown man, with tears filling my eyes with the sheer beauty of what I'm hearing. The hairs on the back of my neck are tingling and I'm totally transfixed by the sounds coming out of the stereo.

Then the piano break comes in with one of the most wonderful arrangements of strings, keyboards and horns ever put on vinyl. Walter's voice returns, rises and falls and he continues his exquisitely pitched delivery right to the fade-out. The instant it finishes I hit the rewind button, my heart pumping like mad. And I play the track again. And again. And again. It's a few minutes before I feel able to drive off, feeling slightly dazed and elated and moved. As a consequence I'm ten minutes late for work.

There is no doubt that this kind of behaviour is just a touch eccentric for a man approaching middle age. I recount this slightly embarrassing tale with some trepidation, because you, dear reader, will probably be feeling one or two reactions: a) What a sad bastard, or b) My God, I've been there myself.

My Walter Jackson experience merely illustrates the power that music has over thousands of people like me. I could have given a dozen examples of more out and out Northern Soul recordings that have reduced me to an equally quivering wreck over the years, but this is the most vivid recent experience at the time of writing.

I cite this somewhat bizarre behaviour purely to illustrate how even after twenty-four years of being a rare soul fan, the unheard-of gems, the underrated oldies, the unreleased master tapes, the little-known album tracks keep turning up to enrich my life. Music either strikes deep into your heart or it doesn't. If rock, blues, reggae or classical music do it for you, then good luck to you. If you have never felt the whirl of emotions that music can bring, whatever your tastes, then I feel genuinely sorry for you. Soul music, you see, is *real* music, made by real people playing real instruments and using words that reach into the soul of its listener. Soul music has a depth, such texture and such passion that it demands to be listened to. Once it gets a grip, it will grab you, hurl you around and leave you breathless for more.

Soul is something within all of us. Something that transcends music, race and age. A feeling that starts deep within you and builds up to create warmth and happiness, or misery and despair. Soul is the humanity and the emotion in all of us. It is what is lacking in modern techno dance music. Rhythm and clever riffs alone are not enough to give a recording soul. The lyrics, the voice and the delivery bring the complete article.

Black artists do not have a monopoly on soul music. Bono of U2 pouring his heart into the Irish supergroup's rock-oriented output and George Michael through his wistful ballads and poignant lyrics could teach some of the modern so-called soul artists a thing or two. Similarly, there are many on the soul scene who would say that hugely successful black artists like Whitney Houston have never made a decent *soul* record in their lives.

If you are reading this and feeling perplexed at how music can evoke such passion in the listener, then this book is not for you. If you can associate with some of the emotions listed above, but your musical tastes are somewhat different from mine, then I wish you many hours of enjoyment of your CD and vinyl collection. If you are reading this and nodding your head, or mentally compiling your own list of tracks that give you goosebumps as you drive along, then welcome to the club.

Anyway, this book is not about me. It's about the greatest underground scene in the world and the all-consuming passion that it demands from its devotees. This is the world of Northern Soul. Yes, my wife thinks I'm mad (but she likes Mariah Carey, for God's sake, so there is no hope). Yes, the kids think I'm stranger than other dads because I often stay out all night and come home clutching vinyl, CDs and tapes which I force them to listen to and approve.

On the other hand, if all Northern Soul fans were totally rational, we wouldn't leave our families at home to drive two hours or more down the motorway to spend eight hours immersed in music with like-minded souls. We wouldn't get excited about totally obscure tracks that the rest of the world has never even known, let alone rejected. We wouldn't want to dance with an enthusiasm or agility normally associated with teen-agers.

Northern Soul is a culture, a hobby, a lifestyle, an obsession. The all-nighter experience begins the moment you wake up on the fateful day. The first thoughts are always the same: 'How have I slept?' 'How do I feel?' 'Damn, it will be twenty-four hours or more before I see my bed again.'

Then the first pangs of excitement creep in – you try to banish them to the back of your mind and go back to sleep. But it's no good – your mind is already buzzing with images of packed dancefloors, a headful of songs, and handshakes and hugs with the fellow soul fans you will meet later that night some distance down the motorway.

Work is a godsend – it helps to occupy your mind as the clock ticks towards the fateful hours when you will embark on another all-nighter adventure. No work and an empty day without a family means a seemingly interminable wait for darkness. Every-one has their own pre-all-nighter ritual they have honed to perfection over maybe two or three decades: a good workout; a lazy afternoon reading; an attempted tea-time nap (usually futile); a few beers; whatever gets you in the mood physically and mentally.

Checking the right clothes are ready; ringing around to arrange transport; sorting out babysitters; making peace with your loved one who will stay at home awaiting your return at breakfast-time. And, yes, even ringing around to arrange the drugs to sustain you through the long night ahead. These are, and always have been, part of the essential pre-all-nighter ritual which so many tens of thousands of Northern Soul fans have enjoyed over the last three decades.

Let's get this straight. The Northern Soul scene even today is not populated entirely with angelic, clean-living men and women. All human life is there. All the venues over the years have attracted the good, the bad and the downright criminal. Nowadays many of us are in our thirties and forties, and have children. Age has brought maturity and wisdom and a sense of responsibility. Despite that, some of us still make the same mistakes of old, and that is what makes the scene what it is.

The Northern Soul scene is *real*. Populated by *real* people listening to *real* music. No pretence, no bullshit, no plastic, sugary smiles and flash suits. No competing against each other with personalized number plates in the car park. The moment you walk through the doors into the all-nighter you are immediately accepted for what you are – a soul fan. Small, tall, black, white, male, female, wealthy, poor, it makes no difference. You are on the scene now, and the scene will look after you and treat you like a member of the family.

Yes, we are a little bit eccentric. Yes, we like being different. Yes, our families and work colleagues think we are barmy. But if our obsession with Northern Soul constitutes madness, then long may we remain insane.

*Dave Nowell*

# Part I

# THE TWISTED WHEEL CLUB

**6 WHITWORTH STREET, MANCHESTER 1**

Tel. CENtral 1179          (Opposite Fire Station)

---

## ✶ GRAND OPENING ✶

of New Twisted Wheel Club Premises on

### SATURDAY, 18th SEPTEMBER, 1965

### THE SPENCER DAVIS GROUP

---

The Club in Brazennose Street will Close on

SATURDAY, 11th SEPTEMBER, 1965

with

### *JOHN MAYALL BLUES BREAKERS*

PLUS

### *GUEST ARTISTS*

---

ADVANCE TICKETS ARE NOW
AVAILABLE FOR BOTH
DATES

# THE TWISTED WHEEL
# MANCHESTER

## FORTHCOMING SATURDAY ATTRACTIONS
### 11.00 pm – 7.30 am

**21st FEB.** — **Edwin Starr**

**FEB. 28th** — **The Bandwagon**

**MARCH 7th**    **The Ferris Wheel**

**14th MARCH** — **Jimmy Ruffin**

**MARCH 21st** — **Junior Walker** AND THE ALL STARS

**28th MARCH**    **SPECIAL AMERICAN ATTRACTION**

COMING APRIL/MAY

BEN-E-KING – INNEZ & CHARLIE FOX
THE TAMS, & THE STEAM

# 1

# I Can't Help Myself

*'Motown basically formulated the disco scene. Without Motown we wouldn't have been able to keep the dance floor going . . .'*

Mojo paused for breath, sweat running down his face, and ran his hand through his close-cropped hair. Around him the legions of other dancers ground to a halt and spontaneously applauded the DJ as the record faded out.

'This place is amazing,' gasped Mojo for the tenth time that night. And then the bassline and driving beat started again and he vanished back into the darkness of the dance floor, gone again, lost in a Northern Soul heaven.

Mojo, alias Blackpool Pleasure Beach worker Wayne Morris, is enjoying his first all-nighter for twenty years; the first all-nighter since the heady days of Wigan Casino, which he frequented with the Blackpool lads for several years. Now in his forties, he finds himself in the late 1990s moving and grooving once more in the company of a thousand like-minded souls.

His sense of disbelief is shared by everyone else who has been away from the Northern Soul scene for two decades or so. Just when you thought you had said goodbye to the ridiculous demands of an all-nighter, the anti-social hours, strained domestic relationships, obsessive record collecting, the heart-thumping anticipation, the legs-turning-to-jelly ordeal of dancing for hour after hour, marathon motorway journeys, the naughty substances and the sheer exhilaration of being part of *your* scene, Northern Soul jumps back up and bites you.

Tonight the venue is the glorious King's Hall in Stoke-on-Trent. Its vast oblong dance floor, raised stage and balcony ensure that stepping inside is like entering a timewarp for former Wigan Casino-goers. Twenty years, marriage, children, hard work at a career, a more mature outlook on life, a whole succession of hobbies and interests, and what happens?

You're back on the dance floor in the middle of the night while the rest of the world sleeps, surrounded by gyrating, spinning, jumping and shuffling bodies that, like yours, don't seem to move quite as quickly as they did in 1975. And do you care? Do you hell! Northern Soul fans are getting what most people can only dream about – a chance to relive the music, the company and the magic of their youth.

The cavernous King's Hall is tonight hosting the 25th anniversary of the long-gone Torch all-nighters. A quarter of a century! The whole world is a radically different place and so much has happened to its inhabitants both collectively and individually. But tonight, in Stoke, from 9 pm to 7 am, Northern Soul fans are converging to celebrate their music and their lifestyle which has remained virtually unchanged.

No other underground music scene has survived for so long and demands such dedication and commitment from its followers. No other music scene can inspire men and women in their thirties and forties to embark on marathon car and train journeys to reach an event they feel they simply can't afford to miss. No other music scene can turn otherwise sensible and mature people into latter-day versions of the excitable teenagers they used to be.

The Northern Soul scene did not start with the Torch all-nighters. Ex-regulars at the Twisted Wheel in Manchester will tell you they did it first. As, probably, would ex-customers of the Flamingo in London.

The heritage of the Northern Soul scene as we approach the millennium is a long and chequered one indeed . . .

Northern Soul by its very name must have been created, moulded and sparked into life by the clubs and music enthusiasts of the North of England, right? If only it was so simple. To look at the roots of what became known as Northern Soul one has to acknowledge the trends, style and sub-culture of the late 1950s and early 1960s, and the 'in' scene in London.

It is impossible for those of us who came into the world during a later era to fully appreciate the tremendous social changes that happened during that momentous period. It took the advent of rock'n'roll, or 'the devil's music', depending on your age or your point of view, to bring about a chain of events which led to that dreaded creation, The Teenager.

Pre-1950s, youngsters were basically younger mirror images of their parents. The austere post-war years, rationing, and the social and class structure of British life in particular all had a profound impact on the way families thought and acted. Young fashion was non-existent. Young people dressed and styled themselves as their parents did. The pop charts of the time reflected the 'grown-up' tastes of the record-buying public.

Enter the rock'n'roll years, which hit Western society with the force of an atom bomb. Young people had money in their pockets, for the first time, something to say and were becoming a force to be reckoned with. The record, film and clothes industries were awakened from their slumbers and realized that here was a vast untapped market.

In 1955 pent-up teenage frustrations and aspirations towards setting their own identity were sparked into life by the unlikely figure of Bill Haley. The 29-year-old former hillbilly singer hit gold dust with a fusion of country and western and rhythm and blues that was becoming known as rock'n'roll.

'Rock Around the Clock' and 'Shake, Rattle and Roll' catapulted Haley and The Comets to international stardom. Here was an exciting, unique youthful-sounding music that teenagers could call their own. Meanwhile Black American rhythm and blues artists were already experiencing mixed feelings about their music proving so popular with white teenage audiences. For every original black recording finding a niche market and healthy sales promoted by plays on black-only radio stations, there were several more which were overlooked in favour of cover versions by white artists which then stormed up the national pop charts. The then top-selling R & B label, Atlantic, was the first to complain about the raw deal meted out to black artists, a cry that would often be heard in ensuing years. Small, black-owned independent labels simply could not compete with the major, white-owned labels in terms of promotion and exposure and distribution to a mass audience.

One man who championed the cause of black R & B artists was the 'King of rock'n'roll', American DJ Alan Freed. As well as playing the 'new' music to ever growing audiences on his radio show in Cleveland, Ohio, he was also promoting tours of R & B artists. He wasn't without his critics. 'All rhythm and blues records are dirty and as bad for the kids as dope,' one sniped. Freed snapped back: 'As in the past, the shrill outraged cries of critics will be lost beneath the excitement of a new generation seeking to let off steam. There's nothing they can do to stop this new solid beat of American music from sweeping across the land in a gigantic tidal wave of happiness.'

In 1956 a former Memphis truck driver called Elvis Aaron Presley was signed to RCA Victor. This young upstart was bound to upset the status quo right from the start. Not only was he young and darkly good-looking, he made riotous dance music that got the pulse racing. But even that was forgivable compared to his most heinous sins that would drive strait-laced parents all around the western hemisphere to apoplexy: he had SEX APPEAL and he SOUNDED BLACK. Together with Bill Haley, Buddy Holly, Little Richard, Jerry Lee Lewis, et al., Elvis would personify the rock'n'roll revolution.

Suddenly here was a young guy with attitude, slicked-back hair, tight jeans, and who moved his body on stage in such a way that led some TV stations to show him from the waist up. Together with movie icons James Dean and Marlon Brando, he helped the youth of America to forge their own identity, one far removed from that of their parents.

Many white middle-class American and British parents openly despised rock'n'roll. It was unchristian, unwholesome and the jiving, gyrations and mass hysteria it brought from youngsters would lead to the end of the world as we know it. At least that's what opponents of this musical revolution would spout from the pulpit, on TV and in newspapers at every opportunity. As every teenager knows, this only increased the attraction of 'their' music and 'their' scene.

Across the Atlantic, Britain was avidly following this social and musical upheaval. Rock'n'roll groups and Elvis imitators sprang up and suddenly the British pop charts were taking on a more youthful look. Teddy boys appeared, with their slicked-back hair, flamboyant jackets, drainpipe trousers and arrogance. Phrases like 'the generation gap' and remarks about how teen-agers were dressing and behaving confirmed that youngsters now had a different outlook and different needs from their parents.

Coffee bars became places for teenagers to meet, chat, listen to their favourite 45s on the recently invented juke box, fight, seek members of the opposite sex, and plan the downfall of the civilized adult world. By the early 60s there was no going back, and fashion, pop music, politics, and social change were on the agenda.

For many, the mainstream rock'n'roll offerings of Elvis, Cliff Richard, Jerry Lee Lewis, The Big Bopper, etc., provided more than enough musical satisfaction. But for others, those exciting recordings merely whetted their appetite for more American recordings. There was a growing fan base in Britain of black American blues and rhythm and blues artists. The fledgling Beatles and Rolling Stones were among those turned on by Chuck Berry, Fats Domino, Bo Diddley, Muddy Waters, Howlin' Wolf and John Lee Hooker.

Guitarist Alexis Korner is often credited with forming the first British R & B group, Blues Inc, in 1961. His famous clubland 'jamming' sessions would bring on stage a veritable *Who's Who* of future rock stars, like Mick Jagger, Charlie Watts and Brian Jones of the Rolling Stones and John Mayall and Paul Jones of Manfred Mann.

Many R & B fans were forming local groups all over Britain and bashing out cover versions of their American idols, and among them were the young Paul McCartney, John Lennon and George Harrison. It was in October 1962 that The Beatles had their first hit with 'Love Me Do', starting a spiral of success that had never been seen previously, or since. By the time 'She Loves

You' hit number one for four weeks in September 1963, Beatlemania was in full swing. It has been argued that this one record was the trigger for the swinging 60s, moptop hairdos, free love, and hedonism on a large scale. What is beyond dispute is that the Lennon-McCartney composition sold over a million copies in the UK alone, and showed their talent for writing original material, and that there was a market for it.

The Rolling Stones and others, meanwhile, were slower in putting their faith in their own compositions. Mick Jagger, acknowledging that in the early days his band like many others was primarily an R & B cover band, once remarked memorably: 'We do not use any original material. After all, can you imagine a British composed R & B number? It just wouldn't make it.'

Both supergroups would find success with cover versions of black American artists' songs. The Detroit-based Motown label, founded by ex-boxer Berry Gordy, was having a major say on the American charts, but was hitherto little known among the general music-buying British public. This would be rapidly rectified (as we will see later), as a result of the Beatles recording three Motown songs on their second album, 'Please Mr Postman' (originally cut by the Marvelettes), 'Money' (Barrett Strong) and 'You've Really Got a Hold On Me' (The Miracles).

The Rolling Stones would the following year find chart success with cover versions of Bobby Womack's 'It's All Over Now' (which they cut at Chess Records in Chicago) and Irma Thomas's 'Time Is On My Side'. A further look at just some of the cover versions that stormed the British charts in the early 1960s shows how much influence black America was already having on the UK.

The Beatles and the Tremeloes covered 'Twist and Shout' (previously done by the Isley Brothers). The Tremeloes also covered the Contours' 'Do You Love Me'; the Hollies did Maurice Williams's 'Stay' and Doris Troy's 'Just One Look'; Sandi Shaw covered Lou Johnson's 'There's Always Something There to Remind Me'.

More and more British bands were modifying the American R & B sound and calling themselves beat groups. The British pop-buying public went mad, snapping up the 'Merseybeat' releases with gusto. For every few pop fans there was a purist in the background shouting: 'Hang on a minute, these are R & B recordings. Let's see what else the original artists have to offer.' It suddenly became hip to know, or own, records by the American R & B and soul artists whose success on the other side of the Atlantic had not yet translated into British pop sales.

One of the forerunners of the underground soul scene in Britain was the Flamingo Club in London. Long before the term soul was even coined, the Flamingo Club was at the heart of the capital's jazz and rhythm and blues scene in the late 1950s and early 60s. Starting life as a Jewish social club, moving on to modern jazz and later staging live jazz gigs, the Wardour Street club gained a reputation second to none. Its weekend all-nighters, running from midnight to 6 am, attracted a wide following among the local music cognoscenti, black American servicemen based around the capital, and recently-arrived West Indian immigrants. Fashion-conscious youngsters – more than a few of whom were gay – and increasing numbers of black music fanatics were attracted out of the coffee and jazz bars to sample the Flamingo's unique atmosphere.

The American Forces Radio Network, set up to cater for visiting servicemen, was also gathering a cult following among the indigenous population. The BBC in the early 60s was still entrenched in classical and easy-listening music. The musicians' union had a stranglehold over the amount of BBC air time given to playing recordings. This did much to protect the livelihood of professional musicians but little to promote popular music. Jazz, rhythm and blues, or beat music had even less chance of finding its way on to Auntie's airwaves.

Oddly enough, certain types of music, such as classical or 'songs from the shows' were exempt from such restrictions. (With the benefit of hindsight, a knowledgeable DJ could, for instance, have played April Stevens' 'Wanting You' without fear of being castigated because the original song derived from a show.)

In the pre-Radio 1 days of 1962, the more adventurous teenagers found music more to their liking on the American Forces Network, which could be easily picked up on their portable radios. Radio Luxembourg was also essential listening under the bedcovers at night when your parents thought you were asleep.

AFN in particular featured a heavy sprinkling of blues, jazz, R & B, and current material by black artists like the Coasters and the Drifters. One of the many people drawn to this style of music was veteran Northern Soul DJ Brian Rae. 'I just preferred that sort of music,' he said. 'It never entered my head that it was soul or R & B, or whatever. The first record I ever bought myself was "Charlie Brown" by the Coasters.'

Warrington-based Brian was at the time attending college in Manchester, and won himself a scholarship to a one-year course in food studies at the College of Distributive Trades in London. So, aged sixteen, he found himself living in the capital and soaking up the different culture and experiences of big city life. Armed with the American Forces Network, Radio Luxembourg and the American charts courtesy of *Record Mirror*, he gradually learned more and more about the wonderful black music he was listening to. His record collection was also growing and an invitation, which he accepted, to play them at a function for a group of Kensington College students gave him a liking for DJing.

Then one night Brian found himself in the West End near the Flamingo, watching streams of suit-wearing young Mods coming off trains and buses and frequenting the all-night clubs and café bars. He was fascinated by the fashions and the 'cool' but slightly glazed look that the Mods had as they passed him by. He was particularly fascinated by the amount of business a hot dog stand appeared to be doing. The owner had two separate lines of bottles of Coca-Cola, and the Mods were showing great interest in one particular row. Brian was later told by a friend that the hot dog seller was actually pushing bottles of SKF 'blueys' – amphetamine pills used by Mods to keep them going at all-nighters.

Finding himself a £12-a-week job in Tottenham Court Road with a wallpaper and paint distributors, Brian made friends with colleague Chris Lorimer, who went to the Flamingo and shared his love of black music. Chris explained to a naive Brian the illegal trade the hot dog seller was doing. It also turned out that he was living next door to an up-and-coming singer called Rod Stewart who, with his group Steam Packet and other R & B acts like Long John Baldry, was playing at the Marquee.

Monday night became a regular Marquee night out for Brian and Chris, and the young northerner even managed to land a job as a roadie helping out the Marquee acts. Back at the Flamingo, the R & B diet of live music was dished out by the resident band, Georgie Fame and the Blue Flames, who did many cover versions of black American recordings. In the interval, the records maintained the jazz/R & B format that was pulling in an ever more enthusiastic crowd.

One Friday night, Brian made his debut at the Flamingo all-nighter (a less than wise decision as he was working the following day) and slightly apprehensively spent most of the night sitting in the theatre seats in front of the stage while people danced all around him. 'I found it all very seedy but yet very exciting,' he confessed. Through Chris he found a whole new circle of friends, including one Dave Godin, who would later become a columnist for *Blues and Soul* magazine. Dave had founded the Tamla Motown Appreciation Society and during a visit to his flat in Camden Town, Brian was handed an honorary membership card.

Dave's presence and influence immediately captivated Brian. 'There was the guy in this room with all these records. He played the Little Eva album and talked about Doris Troy and "Just One Look".'

Brian also became aware that his circle of friends included a number of homosexuals. 'I once found two blokes in bed together in this house. I had no idea they were gay. I was really naive. It was all a hush hush thing then. Nobody talked about being gay. It made me feel a bit uncomfortable.'

Returning to the north older and wiser about the ways of the world, Brian continued to develop his DJing career. An early highlight had already been DJing at a function at Northwich Memorial Hall where the Beatles were crowning the May Queen. Their first hit single, 'Love Me Do', had just been released and Brian was witnessing their transformation from a decent local band into rulers of the pop world.

By now his material included items like Len Barry's '1-2-3', Phil Spector productions and the ever-reliable Tamla Motown current releases. He recalled: 'I was playing mainly soul-influenced material. Some of it charted, but only after it had been played for a while. All we were trying to do was find our own way and a musical direction.

'I loved DJing. I had a million jobs in the 60s. I was fired left, right and centre for not turning up because I had been up late the night before!'

By 1964, with the Tamla Motown hit factory in full operation and labels like Stax, Atlantic and Chess all producing quality material, the hip DJs knew they had to have all the new release material in order to keep ahead of the game. So Brian placed a regular order with his local record shop to reserve his copies of all the UK Tamla Motown releases. They were almost without exception guaranteed floor fillers wherever Brian worked: 'It was a form of dance music that worked well and was very playable. It was a bit more earthy and had such a wide appeal. Motown basically formulated the disco scene. Motown was responsible for people being able to dance to records all the time.

'If you were playing, say, Billy J Kramer, or a lot of the chart stuff you never got a constant dance beat. Motown became so popular because it was so danceable. Before long there were disco juke boxes in pubs. Without Motown we wouldn't have been able to keep the dance floor going for hours.'

Without Motown it is debatable whether there would have been such a groundswell of followers to sustain the future Northern Soul scene. What Motown did, via its irresistible dance riffs, catchy choruses and memorable melodies, was popularize soul music in an unprecedented way, and almost single-handedly bring about the discotheque phenomenon.

The story of the Motown empire is the kind of rags-to-riches tale that is the stuff of fiction.

Motown founder Berry Gordy's dream of a musical empire and a 'family' of recording artists that would help, inspire, nurture and fight for each other, came so spectacularly true that his accomplishment surpassed all before it and has never been equalled since. Berry Gordy set out to make music that would strike a chord in the hearts of everyone across America, and later the world, and that is exactly what he achieved.

Is there anyone over the age of thirty who hasn't got at least one Tamla Motown record in their collection? Is there any adult, of any age, who hasn't sung along to 'Tracks of My Tears', 'My Girl', or 'This Old Heart of Mine' on the radio? The appeal of Motown in many ways reflects the enduring appeal of Northern Soul. Regardless of race, age, or class, there are always delights to be found in the Tamla Motown catalogue, just as there are always delights to be found in the more obscure output of the American soul labels of the 1960s.

Berry Gordy billed his empire as 'The Sound of Young America'. Not 'The Sound of Young Black America' or 'The Sound of Young Black Americans for White America'. He wanted to create music that appealed to young people regardless of their background or colour. He dreamed of a record label where young talented singers and musicians could walk into Motown as unknowns and emerge as polished, hit-making performers. The Motown legend surely changed the face of popular music for ever.

Berry Gordy Jnr was born in 1930, the son of a small Detroit businessman and one of eight children. Always creative and innovative, Gordy discovered a talent for music and songwriting that for years did not necessarily translate into a steady income. Scorned by his family at times for 'not getting a proper job', he persevered and in 1957 wrote a song with his friend Roquel Billy Davis that was to prove the launching pad of his career.

That song was 'Reet Petite', which the already-popular Jackie Wilson recorded and took to number one across America. Learning fast about the realities of royalties and profits from recordings, Gordy formed his own song-publishing company, Jobete (an anagram of his children's names, Joy, Betty, and Terry).

In 1959 he borrowed $800 from the family savings to set up his own record label, figuring that as writer, publisher and label owner he would have complete control (and maximum income) over all future releases.

Toying with a name for his new label, Gordy wanted something familiar and thought of Tammy – the title of the number one pop hit at the time by Debbie Reynolds. But, on going to register the name, he found to his dismay that someone had already beaten him to it. So he dropped the last two letters and came up with Tamla. In 1959 Tamla's first release was 'Come to Me', which he co-wrote and produced with the performer Marv Johnson.

It was a big hit regionally, and when United Artists picked it up for national release it became an American best-seller. Gordy and his Tamla label had arrived.

A young songwriter and singer called William 'Smokey' Robinson had by this time become friends with Gordy. When he rushed in excitedly and told Gordy to listen to his song 'Bad Girl', his friend recognized another hit.

Gordy also recognized that he needed another label, and cash to manufacture and distribute the new pressing. He recalled in his autobiography, *To Be Loved* 'The Tamla name was commercial enough but it had been more of a gimmick. Now I wanted something that meant more to me, something that would capture the feeling of my roots – my home town.

'Because of its thriving car industry, Detroit had long been known as the Motor City. In tribute to what I had always felt was the down-home quality of the warm, soulful, country-hearted people I grew up around, I used "town" in place of "city".

'A contraction of Motor Town gave me the perfect name – Motown. Now I had two labels. My original plan was to put out all the solo artists on the Tamla label and the groups on the new Motown label. But this plan, like some others, turned out not to be practical.'

Gordy made test pressings of 'Bad Girl' by the Miracles using the famed United Sound Studios in Detroit, but found he could not afford to put it out nationally. (After much haggling and hawking the tape around music moguls, the Chicago-based Chess label took the master from him and the Miracles had a hit.)

Fired with his success as a songwriter and producer, and bolstered by the belief in his own talents and those of the people around him, Gordy bought a two-storey house at 2648 West Grand Boulevard in 1959 from which to launch his music empire. The building – which became known as Hitsville – was converted to meet its new identity. The garage became a recording studio, the first floor became a lobby and control room. Living quarters were located between the basement and the first and second floor.

Singer Barrett Strong literally ran into the studio one day as Berry Gordy was going through a raw version of 'Money (That's What I Want)' on the piano. Barrett took up the tune, 'Money' became Tamla recording 54027 and Gordy had another hit, via his sister Gwen's label, Anna. (He could not press and distribute enough to meet national demand.)

By now he had assembled a wealth of talent. The cramped basement studio became the territory of the musicians subsequently known as the Funk Brothers. Many musicians were used by Motown, but the core group who generated the 'Motown sound' were Benny Benjamin (drums), James Jamerson (bass), Earl Van Dyke (piano), and Robert White (guitar).

Some of these fine musicians would later earn Gordy's wrath by doing freelance sessions at Ed Wingate's Ric Tic and Golden World labels, which themselves became sought-after Northern Soul labels. (Edwin Starr and J J Barnes were just some of the artists who graced Wingate's labels. Ironically, Gordy later bought both labels and incorporated both acts into the Motown family.)

'Way Over There' by the Miracles became Tamla 54028 in 1960 and went on to sell 60,000 copies. Yet bigger success came with 'Shop Around', which soared to number two in the pop charts and shipped around 1,000,000 copies.

The Motown empire never looked back and generated hit after hit for artists who became household names – Mary Wells, Marvin Gaye, the Four Tops, the Temptations and Stevie Wonder, to name but a few.

Oh yes, there was also the 'No Hit' Supremes. They were so-called because for three years they failed to emulate the success of their peers. Yet when they finally made the breakthrough with 'Where Did Our Love Go' in 1964, giving Motown its first ever USA and UK number one, Diana Ross, Mary Wilson and Florence Ballard went on to become the most successful girl group ever.

A major driving force behind the Motown empire was the songwriting and producing team of Brian and Eddie Holland and Lamont Dozier. The latter told Northern Soul DJ Ian Levine that the Motown sound was born during the recording of Martha and the Vandellas' 'Come And Get These Memories'.

Lamont Dozier, said Ian, 'went to Berry Gordy and said he wanted to put jazz chords on a stomping rock beat. That created the Motown sound and the Northern Soul sound.

'Northern Soul is basically the Motown sound that other people tried to imitate. Motown was the Detroit sound and when the recordings came out of other cities like Washington and Chicago they often ended up with a fuller, blacker edge than Motown did. Personally I hated the Memphis stuff, Otis Redding, and all that, but I loved many others.'

In October 1964, the Supremes visited Britain for the first time to promote their single 'Where Did Our Love Go'. That same year, pirate radio station Radio Caroline started broadcasting from a ship in the North Sea. The conservative BBC Radio service had still not woken up to the interest in black music, so it was left to Caroline DJs like Tony Blackburn to unleash current soul recordings to the listening public. Tony Blackburn himself, often the butt of many jokes, is credited by many soul fans for helping to make some of the more commercial-sounding Tamla Motown productions into hits in Britain.

In March 1965 Gordy sent a specially-assembled package of Motown stars to Britain. Billed as the Motortown Revue, it included a mouthwatering line-up of stars: the Supremes, Martha and the Vandellas, Stevie Wonder, the Miracles, Earl Van Dyke, the Contours, Marv Johnson, and the Temptations. British R & B keyboards maestro Georgie Fame completed the bill of what turned out to be a financial flop. Although Motown artists had a large fan base in Britain, their following in Beatlemania-dominated times was not sufficient to ensure sell-out shows from city to city.

Ex-Supreme Mary Wilson recalled in Sharon Davis's *The Motown Story*: 'The audiences were good but kinda thin . . . in my opinion the show was too specialized for British audiences. We should have had a few more British bands with us.' The author related how one promoter's theory for the small audiences was that 'By the time people got to know how good the show was, the revue had moved to another town. I didn't make any money at all, but I have to admit those Motown people know how to put on a very good show.'

Newspaper critics were equally enthusiastic but baffled by the low turnout for each show. 'What's the matter with the British public when they won't support such brilliant artists?' questioned one writer.

The tour, however, served to reinforce the growing reputation of the Motown artists. The Tamla Motown Appreciation Society, headed by journalist Dave Godin from his home in Bexleyheath, Kent, ensured a hero's welcome for the visiting acts from Detroit. When the revue touched down at Heathrow Airport, they were met by Godin and company bearing banners proclaiming: 'Welcome to all from Hitsville. We Love You',and 'Welcome the Supremes'.

What sealed Motown's invasion of Britain was the Beatles' recording of three Motown songs for their second album. 'Please Mr Postman', 'Money', and 'You've Really Got a Hold On Me' all found a totally new European audience.

Gordy consolidated his output in the UK on the Tamla-Motown label and the classic black label sold by the shipload to teenagers, pop fans, R & B fans, and mums and dads. Motown's musical output had achieved exactly what Gordy had dreamt of. Gone were the racial divides that had existed for so long in American music: no longer was it white music for white folks, black music for black folks; no longer radio stations that only played songs by white artists and black music ratio stations that only played songs by black artists.

The Sound of Young America was uniting audiences of all

colours, creeds and backgrounds in a way that nothing had ever done before. The worldwide hits went on and on, Martha Reeves and the Vandellas, the Contours, the Velvelettes, the Isley Brothers, and David Ruffin were just some of the artists who enjoyed worldwide hits via the Detroit music factory.

By 1966 the hits were so prolific that Berry Gordy decided at his make-or-break quality-control Friday meetings – at which all the new material was heard and evaluated – that no singles would be released that weren't guaranteed Top Ten hits!

In the case of the Supremes, nothing less than number one would do.

This ensured that only the most commercial-sounding recordings were released, while thousands of superb-quality master tapes never saw the light of day. At least it gave the Northern Soul fans of the future something to hunt for (a certain Frank Wilson record springs to mind), and provided some legal and illegal 'from the vaults' type compilations in years to come.

By the time Berry Gordy sold his Motown empire in 1988 to MCA, virtually all of his hit acts were long gone and the ever-faithful and creative Stevie Wonder and Lionel Ritchie were holding the fort. The asking price was a cool 61 million dollars.

Of course, Mr Gordy and company did not have a monopoly on American soul music output. The Chess, Atlantic and Stax labels, to name but three, had their fair share of talent. Ike and Tina Turner, Ben E King, The Drifters, Aretha Franklin, Wilson Pickett, James Brown, and of course the legendary Otis Redding were just a few of the fine artists who were no strangers to the Top Twenties on both sides of the Atlantic by the mid-60s.

Hundreds of labels sprang up all over the States trying to emulate Motown's success, sometimes even cheekily recording in Detroit using Motown's own musicians. Others brought their own personalized sound to soul recordings. These labels would form the basis of Mod culture in Britain and later become an integral part of the phenomenon that would become known as Northern Soul.

Ex-Twisted Wheel DJ Rob Bellars said: 'The Motown sound was the base of Northern Soul. It got you interested. If you then saw a label like Ric Tic and saw the names Edwin Starr and

J J Barnes or the likes of them, you knew you were on to a winner.'

What has puzzled Northern Soul fans over the years is how some of the most instantly-likeable records which have become dance floor anthems could have been such commercial flops at the time of their release. How could a classic Northern Soul discovery like Gloria Jones's 'Tainted Love', recorded for the tiny Champion label in 1965, fail so utterly at the time of its release? It would later sell in vast quantities when reissued in Britain and in the 1980s it became a worldwide hit after being covered by Soft Cell.

One possible explanation is the actual quality – some of the obscure labels like Shrine made some pretty poor recordings – but this was not always the case. Another is distribution and promotion – the small, independent labels might only have been able to afford to press 1,000 copies and circulate them to local DJs and shops in their part of the city. Another possibility is that they simply got overlooked in the avalanche of material put out by the major players like Motown, Atlantic, Stax and RCA. Whatever the reason, many very commercial-sounding soul records failed to sell enough copies in America to keep the artists, writers, producers and label owners in work. Many Northern Soul icons would quit the music business and end up as office janitors, cab drivers or just plain broke.

Northern Soul DJ and Motown specialist Chris King said: 'Northern Soul is basically an off-shoot of people trying to copy Motown records. When you listen to something like Larry Clinton doing "She's Wanted In Three States" you wonder who on earth it was recorded for. Who were they hoping to sell it to? How on earth did they expect someone to dance to a 100 mph stomper?

'The records that we love did nothing – the odd one crossed over but most were commercial failures. Thank God that they did get it wrong – the music has given us so much pleasure over the last thirty years or so.'

# 2

# Boogaloo Party

*'Being a Mod was always about having a good time, every time, in style. At the heart of this passion for fashion was music, dancing and all-nighters usually heavily fuelled by amphetamines...'*

By 1963 the viewing highlight for Britain's younger generation was the TV show *Ready, Steady, Go*, the forerunner of the long-running *Top of the Pops*. Youngsters could tune in, check out the songs and pick up dancing and fashion tips all at once.

Teenagers were growing in confidence and were becoming more aware of their ability in the enlightened 60s not to conform to anyone's stereotypes of how they should behave. Many youngsters, just like today, wanted to belong to one faction or other. They wanted to shock, to rebel, and often to be the exact opposite of what their parents expected. A newspaper article from the time shows the growing recognition of the army known as teenagers. It comes across as somewhat patronizing and hilarious now, but it reflects the way the generation gap was opening up in a way never previously experienced:

More money, more freedom and more opportunities than ever before have really taken the lid off the younger generation.

Perhaps the outspoken and multi-coloured clothes of today's teenager emphasize this point. The freedom to be able to wear the garments without fear of retribution and ridicule; the opportunities to kit oneself out with almost any style under the sun; and, perhaps the most important point, money to be able to buy the clothes in the first place.

Today's 'Teen Scene' is full of exciting new ideas and new faces and new groups of idealists ready to try almost anything in the search for 'something different'.

But even so, teenagers are no longer prepared to accept just anything that comes along. Gone are the days when they would rush out in their thousands to buy that 'fab disc' or that 'way-out dress' just because the rest were wearing one. Today's real teenager is fast becoming an individual in his or her own right – a right that allows them to dress as they please and, in many cases, go where they please . . .

Part of the welcome to Great Britain for the Supremes given them by the Tamla-Motown Appreciation Society on a recent visit

**Tamla-Motown Appreciation Society**
Organising Secretary: DAVE GODIN, 139 CHURCH RD., BEXLEYHEATH, KENT, ENGLAND Tel: Danson Park 2021

The Mods already knew what they wanted from life – to dress differently, live differently and create their own sub-culture that would keep them ahead of the pack. Made-to-measure suits, crisp shirts, Lambretta and Vespa scooters and the best-looking girls were all part of the Mod designer chic. As was their hatred of other youth cults like the motorbiking Greasers, or the dwindling Teddy Boys.

Soul fan Mick Taylor, formerly of Doncaster, Yorkshire, and now living in Canada, sums up his 60s youth as a Mod thus: 'I think that we all wanted to be different. To get away from the council estates, the pits and factories, all that cloth-capped bullshit. Spending two weeks' wages on a made-to-measure shirt or an import LP would do it!

'The influence of the Beatles can never be understated, not only for leading the musical way, but socially – they showed us that even with a thick Northern accent and working-class background, we could cross those barriers. I don't know one mate who still lives in a council house!

'The 60s *was* a great time to be a kid. As with all teenage years there was so much going on, so many people going in different directions all at the same time and I think I was extremely fortunate to have been there – especially with the music aspect. Discovering all that "new" music was a blast!'

DJ Brian Rae said of his Mod roots: 'In the early days we regarded ourselves as the "in" crowd. We were different to the average punter. We had our own sounds and our own way of clothing ourselves. It was something that a tremendous number of people lived by. It gave us our social link. By the end of the 60s the suits and all that had gone. Flower Power and jeans and all that appeared and it became more a case of being individual than being a Mod.'

But during their heyday, the Mods set standards for the 'right' look and the 'right' attitude that few youth groups since have equalled. Long-time soul fan and DJ John Knight, of Meltham, West Yorkshire, sums it up: 'Being a Mod was always about having a good time every time in style. At the heart of this passion for fashion was music, dancing, and all-nighters usually heavily fuelled by amphetamines.'

The Mods' leisure pursuits were funded by a work-hard play-hard ethic. Work was plentiful in the early to mid-60s and the Mods' wages – or benevolent parents – were needed in order to keep up the credibility and style which they craved so much.

According to John Knight, 'Mods invented the designer label mystique long before the present generation of youngsters were the proverbial twinkles in their parents' eyes.' He explained: 'Ben Sherman shirts, Wranglers and Levi jeans, Levi sta-press trousers, Pierre Cardin mohair suits, Crombie coats with silk hankies in breast pockets, SX Lambretta and GS Vespa scooters were all mod designer chic and mystique. Suit vent lengths changed almost every month. A conservative 8-inch suit vent progressed to a single 15-inch vent, only to see pleated vents become the in thing.

'A first-rate supply of quality suit lengths and a good tailor were essential prerequisites for staying the course. It was all about having a unique tribal identity. An identity that distinctly contrasted Mods from mainstream popular fashion and culture but equally alienated other tribal groups like the Grease and the Teds.'

Alan Fletcher, a story consultant on the 1970s Mod film *Quadrophenia*, says: 'The Mods could and would change "the look" overnight, in a manner which bordered on telepathy. The catwalks were the streets, the clubs, the proms and piers of the coastal resorts of England in the mid-60s. It was just amazing how this cult of youth, normally scattered across the shires, could find a shared confluence on the coast, displaying a dress code which had at its centre a strict conformity in style and cut of cloth.'

If the Mods were passionate about 'the look', they were also very discerning about that other essential accessory – the music. Although many were ardent fans of the Small Faces, the Who, the Rolling Stones, etc, it was almost inevitable that legions of Mods would seek something more musically exclusive. That was where the latest Motown, Stax and Atlantic releases came in. Sweaty clubs would echo to the sounds of Otis Redding's anguished vocals, Marvin Gaye's smooth delivery and Wilson Pickett's hollerings. Ska and Blue Beat were also popular.

But as the Motown empire grew and the hits started to come thick and fast for Otis, Aretha Franklin, the Four Tops and their like, the Mods felt they were losing 'their' exclusive sounds to the British pop-buying public. Showing the contrariness that would always be displayed by Northern Soul fans, the 'in crowd' began to jettison the better-known music and search for more elusive items.

The burgeoning R & B and soul club scene in the north of England recognized this, and the DJs – sometimes willingly, sometimes reluctantly – became more open-minded about their playlists. Many short-lived clubs in northern towns had loyal and passionate followers. It was these clubs and enterprising DJs and record collectors that often 'fed' the larger clubs the latest cult sounds.

John Knight recalls how one such club, The Plebs in Halifax, was considered the best in West Yorkshire and drew the Mod crowd from Burnley, Oldham, Rochdale, Leeds, Bradford and Dewsbury. Dozens of chrome- and mirror-clad scooters would be seen in the town centre whenever a Saturday all-nighter featured a good act. Artists like Inez and Charlie Foxx, Jimmy Cliff, and the Drifters would pack the venue to capacity.

John, who DJ'd at venues like Bradford's String O'Beads in 1968 using various pseudonyms like J W East and Lord Jim, studied the musical press and singles reviews avidly. By then, English labels were putting out the cream of American soul recordings on labels like Stateside and London, and of course, Tamla Motown and Atlantic. But connoisseurs also knew about Cameo Parkway, Liberty, President, Beacon, Direction, and others. A trawl through the latest releases on those labels could throw up a gem or two for soul-hungry clubgoers.

A quick play of a new 45 in your friendly local record shop could be all it took to convince the budding DJ or collector that the vinyl offering he was holding had what it took to become a dance-floor favourite. In this way, Darrell Banks's timeless 'Open the Door to Your Heart' (flip it over and 'Our Love is in the Pocket' was another stormer), Bobby Wells's 'Let's Cop a Groove' and Homer Banks's double-sider 'A Lot of Love/60 Minutes of Your Love' found their way on to the discerning club's playlist.

The other essential route to impressing your peers was via a network of contacts on second-hand market stalls and shops. American imports were almost unheard-of, but occasionally items would surface that would have the Mods drooling.

John explains: 'The genuine small American soul label was for the most part a dream unless you struck lucky in London's Portobello market or had connections in Liverpool with the merchant navy. Acquiring that elusive copy of Chubby Checker's "At the Discotheque", Bunny Sigler's "Let the Good Times Roll", or the Anglos' "Incense" could be as difficult as the search for any present-day equivalent. Suddenly the 6 shilling (30p) single could have a street value of £5 or £10. That might not seem much by today's standards but with weekly wages of £16–£20 a week it gives some kind of perspective on collecting records then. DJs who possessed rarities were treated like royalty at clubs like The Plebs. The buzz was unbelievable when word spread that some well-known DJ like King Arthur would be making an appearance at the all-nighter with his copies of "At the Discotheque" or "Let the Good Times Roll".'

By 1965 Brian Rae had become aware of a number of all-night cafés and clubs in the north-west. The first venue in the area to try the format was the Cavern Club in Liverpool (the legendary home of the Beatles). Brian's then girlfriend was also visiting a club called the Twisted Wheel in Manchester. Unlicensed, basic, and with a small maze of rooms, the Wheel was a haven for teenagers seeking R & B music. It first opened its doors in Brazennose Street in 1963 as a no-frills club with no licensed bar in which teenagers could 'hang out' and dance to both live and recorded music. By 1965, the club had outlived its 'starter home' in Brazennose Street and moved to its more familiar base in 6 Whitworth Street (right opposite a fire station and a police station, a factor which would later not help its longevity one iota). The Brazennose Street club closed on Saturday, 11 September 1965, with a live appearance by the John Mayall Blues Breakers.

The following week the Spencer Davis Group (who had hits with 'Gimme Some Lovin', 'Keep On Running', etc.) were the main attraction at the grand opening of the Whitworth Street venue. It was there that the Saturday all-nighters attracted youngsters from all over the north-west and further.

The Wheel's amphetamine-aided mixture of noise, sweat, black music and basic ambience reminded Brian of why he had loved the Flamingo. 'It was seedy, but I like seedy places,' he reflected. The club, owned by the Abadi brothers, was the ultimate teenage venue of its time. It was dark, atmospheric and its rabbit warren of rooms played host to some of the most upfront R & B and soul music played anywhere in Britain. The weekly all-nighters which were so loved by youngsters and hated by parents and the authorities ran from 11 pm to 7.30 am every Saturday.

Entering the Wheel at street level, youngsters found themselves in a dimly-lit reception area with a soft-drinks bar on the left. A few tables scattered around acted as a magnet for record collectors with their boxes. Speakers on the walls relayed the music being played by the DJ the floor below.

Following the crowds into the back of the building there was a second room which no one can ever remember being used for anything in particular. Its stone floor, however, provided a spare dancing area for those too desperate to wait for the walk downstairs. Also nearby were the gents' toilets, which in time-honoured fashion both stank and flooded regularly. They also acted as changing rooms, a meeting place and a dubious base from which unscrupulous dealers could sell drugs.

Downstairs was where the real action was. The basement area was the domain of the DJs, the innovative dancers and the live artists. It was effectively two rooms: to one side there was the main dance floor, which by today's standards would be considered tiny, and along one wall the DJ was literally caged in behind a wall of twisted wheels. The Wheel's own valuable record library was contained in this section and the barrier was probably to protect the club's own investment as much as the guest DJ's rarities.

On the other side of the cellar area was the live-act arena. Again it was compact and intimate, and it was frequently so crowded that the audience could barely move.

And what a line-up of live acts! Looked at now, the roster of artists that appeared at the Wheel during just a twelve-month period resembles a *Who's Who* of the soul hall of fame: Junior Walker and the All-Stars, Stevie Wonder, Ben E King, Jimmy Ruffin, Bo Diddley, Oscar Toney Junior, Edwin Starr, James and Bobby Purify, Ike and Tina Turner, Inez and Charlie Foxx … the list is endless.

American soul singer Solomon Burke appeared live on stage during Brian Rae's first visit, and Brian was impressed by the original mixture of blues, R & B and soul being spun by resident DJ, Roger Eagle. Roger's tall lean figure ruled the decks during the Wheel's formative years and many people cite the former Oxfordshire man as one of the pioneers of what became known as Northern Soul.

Roger, who died age fifty-six in May 1999, after a long illness, would have none of it. He saw himself as playing merely whatever he felt most appropriate at the time – rare, chartbound, or not. What is certain is that his individual style and willingness to hunt around for the records that had the Wheel sound, influenced many DJs both then and ever since. His musical tastes deeply entrenched in the blues, Roger expanded his repertoire, and therefore, the repertoire of hundreds of Wheel-goers, to include the latest American soul releases. His favourites like Muddy Waters would always get an airing at the Wheel, along with the likes of Chuck Berry and then something like 'On Broadway' by the Drifters. Motown's latest releases might be closely followed by James Brown's material. It was a diverse mix, but if it was black and danceable, it kept the crowd happy.

'The term Northern Soul turned him off,' Brian said of him. 'He hated putting clichés and labels on things, he thought it detracted from what's in the grooves. What he did was introduce people to black music in all its forms. Without Roger being such an influence the Wheel would not have become what it was.

'He doesn't realize now, and we didn't realize at the time, just how good he was. Roger was my biggest influence as a DJ. He would play what he thought were the most relevant releases as they came out. The ones that he particularly liked he would continue to play as long as the crowd danced to them. Mind you, it was pretty hard to clear the floor at the Wheel, but I did it once.'

Roger travelled up from his Oxfordshire home to Manchester on a weekend motorbike trip, and liked the city and its musical tastes so much he stayed. Editing the magazine *R & B Scene* and treating the Twisted Wheel regulars to the whole spectrum of black music became his passion. Refusing to be strait-jacketed into one style of music, he became a little disillusioned as the Wheel crowd demanded out-and-out soul dancers. In a reference to the growing drugs culture, he told former Northern Soul DJ Ian Levine for his video documentary *The Strange World of Northern Soul*: 'I got very, very fed up of having to call ambulances, and not being able to play the full range of music.'

Ex-Wheel regular Tony James, of Bolton, is very clear about Roger Eagle's importance in the Northern Soul scheme of things. 'Roger was playing stuff in 1965 like Darrell Banks's "Open the Door to Your Heart", "Sapphires" "Gotta Have Your Love", "Boogaloo Party" by the Flamingos, and James Carr's "That's What I Want to Know". Roger was way ahead of his time. If there was a "big bang" when Northern Soul was created, it was then.'

Roger would later move on to promote rock and pop concerts and, in 1976, he opened Eric's club in Liverpool, and later the International Club in Manchester. He became a mentor to future stars like Mick Hucknall of Simply Red, who sought him out for his vast knowledge of black music.

Ex-Wigan Casino DJ John Vincent was also among Roger's disciples: 'He was such an influence on me. It was him who got me into record collecting when I was just sixteen. After talking to him you just had to go out and start collecting Chess recordings or whatever. He was light years ahead of his time.'

Back at the Wheel, the club's music policy and reputation spread far and wide, and at least one sister club opened in another town. The Blackpool version of the club operated from Coronation Street about a quarter of a mile inland from the Golden Mile, and, like its Whitworth Street counterpart, ran into trouble with the authorities. The owner Mr Ivor Abadi found himself summoned to appear in court after neighbouring boarding houses complained about noise from the teenage dance club.

To represent him in court, Mr Abadi hired no less a figure than George Carman – who would go on to become a famous defence QC for Ken Dodd and others. The West Lancashire *Evening Gazette* reported on 19 August 1965 that the case was adjourned indefinitely after Mr Abadi had given an undertaking to have further remedial measures taken at the club.

'The source of the noise appeared to be a beat group and, until the remedial measures were taken, the group would not play the club,' the newspaper reported.

Five hundred pounds' worth of noise-insulating work was carried out at the Blackpool club, but it could not prevent Mr Abadi facing further summonses the following year.

Two summonses against the club were dismissed and on the

# THE TWISTED WHEEL CLUB

**6 WHITWORTH STREET, MANCHESTER 1**
**Tel. CENtral 1179**

✦

## 'SPOT DRAW'

MEMBERS NOTICE

From April 4th, 1970 we will be
holding a 'SPOT DRAW' Cash Prize
Competition Every Saturday.

## The Prize is £10 £15

Every members' number goes into
the draw each week. The winning
member must be present at the
time of the draw (approx. 2 a.m.). If
the prize is not won it increases by £5
each Saturday until it is won.

third, the Abadis were given an absolute discharge. Its 6,000-strong membership was free to carry on dancing.

Problems in Blackpool continued to be minimal, but there again there were no all-nighters and the club only opened in the summer. Under the Private Places of Entertainment Act 1967, which required coffee bars and similar places to be licensed for Sunday opening, the Wheel was granted a music and dancing licence. In early 1969, the licence was renewed and the authorities were happy with the way the club was run. But back in Manchester, the Twisted Wheel story was spiralling towards a very different conclusion.

By the time Brian Rae managed to get himself on the Wheel's DJ rota, Roger Eagle had moved on to the nearby Blue Note club, but the musical agenda had then been set and the Wheel was becoming more and more a specialist venue for soul enthusiasts. Brian had managed to impress the DJs' supervisor Bobby Derbyshire at a Tuesday night audition, and landed a job entertaining the crowd at the Saturday all-nighter from 3 am to 7 am. By then he had a solid record collection, and like the others had access to the Wheel's own record library behind the decks.

The vast riches of Motown, coupled with Stax, Chess, Atlantic and Sue productions kept Brian in plentiful supply of current release material to play at the Wheel. His regular record scouting trips would end in him taking his new finds into a handy pub, where he would produce a small record player and listen swiftly to each 45. By the time he left the pub he had the basis of his Saturday night spot at the Wheel. Brian describes his selection process thus: 'I used to judge them by the start. If the first 15 seconds didn't sell the record to me, I would put it to one side and try it later. Something like "The Same Old Song" (Four Tops) or "Dr Love" (Bobby Sheen) grabbed you straight away.'

The Wheel's music policy was probably unique, seeing that access to the American soul charts was very limited, and the DJs were interested in breaking new ground rather than emulating other clubs. The good old reliable American Forces Network was often their only guide to what was going on in the States. It was obvious, however, when the DJs latched on to a winner which would later hit the UK pop charts. One such record was Arthur Conley's anthemic 'Sweet Soul Music', which Brian remembers was played seventeen times in one night at the Wheel!

'Records like "Sweet Soul Music" were at the time as much underground records as, for instance, Robby Lawson's "Burning Sensation", would be in later years. Subsequently it would pass into the mainstream, but when we played it, it was a cult sound.'

Live acts were also a big part of the Wheel experience, and Brian recalls the heady atmosphere as hundreds of bodies were crammed into the basement room as acts like Junior Walker, Jimmy Ruffin, Edwin Starr, and others took to the stage. It was so packed that the crowd waited with their arms in the air as their American heroes appeared (if you kept your arms by your side it was impossible to raise them to applaud later owing to the crush).

Said Brian: 'The artists used to be brought in from the side and had to fight their way through the crowd to get to the stage. The first time Junior Walker appeared, they couldn't get him off the stage when he had finished his act. They passed him across the room over people's heads on his back, still playing his sax.'

After two years, Brian took an enforced break from his residency at the Wheel, and when he returned as a customer in 1969, he found the club's legendary atmosphere was still the same, but times had changed. 'The music was totally different. I wasn't aware of a lot of the records and I didn't know the DJs.'

One of the main factors in the emergence of the Northern Soul scene, as it would shortly be christened, was the arrival of American imports in 1969. Now the DJs and collectors had access to many brightly coloured and fascinating American labels. Some, like the Motown stable of Tamla, VIP, Soul and Gordy, were already known. Others were obscure and gave the clubs of the North a goldmine of material for their playlists. Specialist shops would stock imports and deletions at giveaway prices, and it was not unknown for supermarkets to have stacks of future Northern Soul collectors' items on sale for just a few shillings.

Brian remembers how his import copies of 'Walking the Dog' by Rufus Thomas (Stax) and 'How Sweet It Is' by Junior Walker (Tamla) stood him in good stead with the soul crowd. Similarly, a US copy of 'I'll Always Love You' (Detroit Spinners), which Motown had deleted in the UK, was a prized item.

A copy of Frances Nero's 'Keep On Lovin' Me' on Soul was the first unknown import that Brian came across. 'I was amazed. I had never heard of her,' he reflects.

More and more record shops started importing American releases; the Contempo label started doing bumper soul packs of material which collectors bought 'blind', as did major dealers like John Anderson's Soul Bowl in King's Lynn.

The Wheel's ever more adventurous DJs, like Rob Bellars, Phil Saxe, Carl Deane, Brian '45' Phillips, Paul Davis and Les Cockell, were turning the crowd on to more and more esoteric and rare American imports. This brought in more and more out-and-out soul fans and alienated some of the customers with more mainstream tastes. While there were thousands of soul fanatics eager to try out the Wheel's unique atmosphere, there were others who believed the rare music policy had gone too far.

The summer of love captivated many Mods, and including Roger Eagle, who had moved on to open the Stax Club in Fountain Street, Manchester. Brian Rae noticed that the Mod uniform, which for many was part of the attraction of the soul scene, was fizzling out by the late 60s as flower power got a grip on youths on both sides of the Atlantic.

Meanwhile, the music which would soon be termed Northern Soul by *Blues and Soul* journalist Dave Godin was captivating an audience that would effectively remain for the next thirty years. Jerry O's 'Karate Boogaloo', 'Shotgun and the Duck' by Jackie Lee, Mitch Ryder and the Detroit Wheels with 'Breakout' and 'You Get Your Kicks', the Incredibles' 'There's Nothing Else to Say', Bill Black's Combo with 'Little Queenie', Willie Mitchell's 'That Driving Beat', Bob and Earl's 'Harlem Shuffle', were just some of the favourites that can still fill Northern Soul dance floors today.

But by 1969, a few enterprising DJs realized that there was still a vast untapped goldmine of American imports. The men that DJ-turned-record-producer Ian Levine now credits with creating the Northern Soul scene as we know it are Rob Bellars, Phil Saxe, and Carl Deane. Rob took a chance while working in California and bought 'blind' an interesting-looking single on the Okeh label by Sandi Sheldon. 'You're Gonna Make Me Love You' was to become a stunning 100 mph dancer that would be the epitome of a rare, fast, powerful Northern Soul rarity.

Among other early Northern Soul import discoveries aired at the Wheel were Bob Brady and the Concords' 'More, More, More of Your Love' and Leon Hayward's 'Baby Reconsider'.

According to Ian Levine, 'Nobody shaped the scene like Rob Bellars. Everybody up to then was playing a mixture of stuff, R & B, blues, soul, whatever. These three DJs, and particularly Rob, shaped the future.' Rob Bellars himself is modest about his part in the Northern Soul genesis: 'I'm a bit embarrassed by that description,' he said. 'I was a catalyst perhaps but I don't think inventor is the word.'

Rob joined the DJ line-up in 1969 after a spell on the sidelines shaping the sounds that were played at the Wheel. A record collector and wheeler-dealer in rare vinyl, he helped provide his friend DJ Phil Saxe with rare items.

Then one day he decided to cast his net wider than the UK releases. He had always been a fan of Major Lance, and noticed that the UK Columbia label on which his material was issued stated the song was 'an Okeh recording'. So Rob wrote to America and asked for a catalogue of records on the Chicago-based label. Apart from the expected Major Lance material, he also spotted recordings by groups like the Vibrations and one Sandi Sheldon. Rob thought the Sandi Sheldon title sounded interesting so he decided to take a chance and included it in his next order.

When the record arrived on a white Okeh demo, Rob loved it, but incredibly it did not have the same impact at the Wheel. 'The first time I played it, people stopped dancing. Maybe it was the wrong time – it was a bit fast,' said Rob. However, it wouldn't be long before the record passed into Northern Soul folklore and would light up the dance floors at the Torch, Wigan Casino and every all-nighter ever since. It is still cited in many people's top tens thirty years later.

Rob then placed a regular order of records from the States and would go down to Liverpool docks to collect them. His packages turned up more and more interesting imports – like Jackie Lee's 'Darkest Days' on an ABC promo. Again Rob loved it, but the initial response was discouraging. 'People didn't dance to that, either,' he said. Soon, like the Sandi Sheldon, it took on cult status and when Rob sold it for £25 it was at the time the most money ever paid for a single.

Soon, businessmen on both sides of the Atlantic started to get wise to the English record collectors, and Rob found his unique personal supply of imports was not so unique. Major importers began to get in on the act and US singles started to turn up in English shops in ever-increasing numbers. 'Once the word got around there was a lot of bandwagon-jumpers,' said Rob. 'When you wrote to a company for a record and they said it was out of stock you knew there were a lot of people getting in on the act.'

Rob would often buy records on a hunch, and they usually paid off. Brunswick material was another rich source. 'I would look for the writers' and producers' names and if it said Carl

Davis or Eugene Record you knew it was going to be there or thereabouts,' he explained.

Competition among the DJs, and to even get a spot DJing at the Wheel, was fierce. DJs would spend midweek desperately hunting down rare discs that no one else had in order to get such a spot. One source was the chain of Co-op stores, which had started to stock deleted records and imports and giveaway prices. Rob remembers finding 'Fife Pier' by the Dynatones in the Co-op in Stretford. Stateside, Capitol, Pye and other labels formed a large part of the Co-op cheapie stock. However, more than one manager would twig that there was a great demand among those strange Wheel-goers, and a shilling record one week might be marked up to a pound the next.

The pressure and friendly rivalry among the DJs to come up with more and more exclusive items led to the practice of 'covering up' a record to hide its true identity. Rob is believed to have been the first ever DJ to cover up a record, although he says today: 'I don't really know why I did it. It must have been to protect its identity, I'm sure it was nothing to do with the bootleggers. I think it was more of a joke.' Whatever his motives, in 1969 the Bobby Patterson track 'What a Wonderful Night for Love' was given a false identity and the craze which would later be adopted by many DJs to protect their 'exclusives' and thwart the bootleggers was born.

Rob said the desire among soul fans to have their records played at the Wheel or even get a DJ spot was intense. 'I suppose it was a big ego thing,' he says. Reputations could be quickly made or broken, and the DJs would keep a portable disc player handy to listen to a record a dancer was pushing them to play.

Another aspect of the Northern Soul scene that was fast developing was the dancing style. The side-to-side shuffle was being supplemented by spins and backdrops as dancers became more and more adventurous. The acknowledged king of the dancers at the Wheel was Frank Booper. He would request his favourite records – including 'Back Streets' by Edwin Starr and Earl Van Dyke's 'Six by Six' – and then go into an acrobatic routine which would practically stop the club.

'Frank was the best,' said Rob. 'I suppose he was a bit of a show-off. People stopped dancing and formed a circle when he danced. The Wheel was the first place I ever saw people doing backdrops. There was even a lad who used to do a forward roll in mid-air. It was great to watch.'

As other venues were to find out when Wigan Casino came along, the Wheel was the venue that could 'break' a record on the Northern Soul scene. An obscure track might have a cult following in the Catacombs in Wolverhampton or the String o' Beads in Bradford, but if it became big at the Wheel, that was the moment it went to a higher level on the underground grapevine. As Ian Levine said, 'The Catacombs didn't have the ability to break records. It was basically a record collectors' club that held about 350–400 people. But when the same records reached the Wheel and went big, they created the Northern Soul scene.'

Rob said the Wheel was never taken for granted, and everyone involved realized it would be remembered for a long time. 'We knew it was special. It was unique because it was open all night and there were no other clubs playing the kind of music we had. People came from all over. There were very few Mancunians – people were coming from all over the place.'

The night the Twisted Wheel had its record library stolen was a turning point in its musical direction. Hundreds of British-issued soul and R & B records went missing when burglars broke into the Whitworth Street club over the Christmas period in 1968.

The DJs' own collections suddenly became the focal point of the Wheel playlists. And many non-DJing local teenagers had rare imports and oddities in their collections which surpassed some of the resident DJs'. One such youngster was Brian Phillips. Wheel DJ Paul Davis recommended the 17-year-old Middleton record collector as a DJ and Brian happily joined the line-up. He was already an obsessive record collector, scouring junk shops, second-hand shops and stores all around the city looking for elusive soul records. Many he would buy blind, going by the label, or the names of the songwriters or producers.

Said Brian: 'I remember at the time no one had really heard of Major Lance. I could go into a shop and find twenty-five copies of a Major Lance record and think it was worth a go. I got so many "doubles" in this way I was able to sell them and more than get my money back. I was buying about fifty records a day. I was always skint and borrowed money all the time, then I would sell the "doubles" at the Wheel on the Saturday night. Records were my currency in those days.'

Brian was hired as a DJ in 1969 and regularly did the all-nighter from 2.30 am to 8 am until his nocturnal activities started to interfere with his weekend football matches. He left the Wheel in 1970, but continued to import and sell rare records. Even the Wheel crowd, he recalled, were not too quick to pick up on certain 'new' records. 'There was always a certain element who unless the stuff was fast and furious they used to pull at the wheels like they were wild animals,' he said. 'They wanted the same old stuff all the time. It was hard work sometimes. You had to drop your new stuff in once a week and hope that it would take off.

'A lot of the Manchester lot were more into the pills and back-drops and wanted fast and furious stompers, whereas the travellers seemed to be more appreciative of other stuff. I remember playing Gene Chandler and Barbara Acklin's "From the Teacher to the Preacher" and the locals thought it wasn't quick enough. It was frustrating but eventually we won them over.'

The imports started turning up with more regularity – 'Changes' by Johnny Taylor; Major Lance with 'Everybody Loves a Good Time'; Dobie Gray with 'Out on the Floor'; Jerry Cook and 'I Hurt on the Other Side'.

After finishing his Wheel stint, in September 1970, Brian was still in demand as a record source. Many established and up-and-coming DJs like Keith Minshull, Ian Levine, Soul Sam, and Colin Curtis bought items from him. Brian sold a demo copy of Moses Smith's 'Girl Across the Street' to Colin Curtis for a then mind-boggling £40. 'I used to come home from the pub and find people sitting on the wall outside my house waiting to buy stuff from me,' said Brian.

When Dave Godin visited the Wheel in 1970, its lasting reputation on a national scale was secure. He wrote in his *Blues and Soul* column:

Somewhere out in that black dim night gloom – in this city of what looked like perpetual night – there was an oasis known as the Wheel. It was as if all the life energy of the great city was channelled into this spot and hidden away under the ground for fear of disturbing the 'respectable' citizenry, because looking out of the cab windows on this dank and murky night, Manchester looked like a ghost town. How wrong first impressions can be was to be shown by later events and happenings. Soon the cab drove up a side street and I saw a young man running down a garden path in the miserable night air stripped to the waist and waving! Being a simple-lifer I much admired such Spartan fortitude, and I thought such exuberant behaviour could only come from a raving lunatic or a Soul brother!

Sure enough it was the latter, and for the first time I was meeting Francisco O'Brien (or Fran Francisco as I stubbornly persist in calling him) whom I felt I had known for ages through correspondence, but it is always a great experience to finally meet someone face to face who you have up till then only known through letters and the odd phone call.

Soon we were all in Jackie's place getting to know one another. There was Les Cockell, one of the DJs at the Wheel, who I hardly recognized since in a picture I'd seen of him he had had really long hair, but had now transformed himself into a suede-head. Boly from Earby was there (whose pash is Jackie, hence her being persuaded to put up with so many of us using her place as a central gathering point), and young Tim from Skipton, and Boly's cousin Alan. We were soon talking like we'd known each other for years (a common experience amongst Soul people since we always have so much to talk about which bores the pants off your average non-Soul fan), and the time flew by.

Soon we were joined by Tommy Barclay who was in town on a special visit, and everyone was busy getting themselves together for the evening which to all intents and purposes was going to be the last all-nighter at the Wheel since it has pleased the City Fathers to put a ban on such activities.

The fellows in their mohair suits and 'right on now' black

gloves, and Jackie looking as splendid as Brigitte Bardot, and we somehow managed to squeeze all of us into Les's van and we were off.

Before going to the Wheel, however, we stopped by the pub next door where all the brothers and sisters gather for a few bevvies before going in, since the Wheel would please the strictest teetotaller in being only able to serve Cokes, coffee, flings and milk. The pub was crammed to the doors, and nearly everybody seemed to be young and together. Boly, Fran and the others knew almost everyone, for there is none of the social stand-off-ishness in the North that plagues human relationships in the South!

Crazy rumours were flying round that the last all-nighter at the Wheel would be honoured by a police raid, and I was told that special wire mesh pens had been constructed out the back to herd various people into. The prospect of this imminent drama added to the general elation that I felt, but I was relieved that as events turned out it was only an empty rumour. Young people have become too much a target for police harassment in Britain these days and one gets the impression that we are at times returning to the dark days of Victorian 'morality' when all pleasure was considered improper and wrong, and one slips into a club to dance the night away with the furtiveness that people dropped into speakeasies in America during prohibition. Since the police station is directly across the street from the Wheel I could only hope that at least I'd not die of exposure in a pen before being put into a cell a few yards away!

I was reminded of how London's Tiles Club was virtually closed because of continued police activity which entailed people undergoing the indignity of a strip search for drugs, and all I could hope if the worst happened was that my

Y-fronts would be as spotless as when I first put them on!

Soon it was time for the pub to close, and when they call time in Manchester they mean it. Not like lax London where you can still buy drinks up to about fifteen minutes after the official closing time, and by three minutes past eleven the pub had emptied itself of brothers and sisters who by this time had joined the seemingly endless queue which had formed outside the Wheel. The club itself is in what appears to be an ex-warehouse or church mission. I like to think it the latter since it can at least be said it is carrying on a tradition of spreading the faith as well as doubling as a meetinghouse for the faithful.

The Wheel itself is on two levels. When one enters there is a cloakroom and drinks bar which is always crowded, and music from down below is relayed through speakers at this level. The lighting is subdued but not so dark that you can't see where you are going! Naturally such scarcity of illumination tends to have a widening effect on the pupils of the eyes. Being amongst the first in, I thought it would take a time for things to warm up, but on going down to the lower level I was surprised to see that already people were swinging out and doing their thing. The walls on the lower level are painted red, white and black, and the original arches which divided the various rooms have been left in place to act both as natural crush barriers, and also provide separate areas for groups of friends to form their own circles of dancers. Not that there is any suggestion of clannishness or of cliques forming. Anyone is welcome to get up and join in, and soon the place was alive with sounds and movement!

All over, the Wheel motif is repeated; rows of disused bicycle wheels line the ceiling in one place, and the whole of the DJ's area is a cage built of spokes and wheel frames, and is one of few places that *is* brightly lit. The light here spills out on to the floor, and the continual rhythmic movement of the dancers is only interrupted by the cheers of recognition that greet known favourites. There is no fashion as such, but naturally people tend to follow certain styles which have found favour and popularity. Never have so many Ben Shermans been gathered in one place at one time, and I noticed a style that I have not yet seen in London (but which, I am sure will eventually drift down this way) in that very many young fellows wore black 'right on now' racing gloves. Apart from looking cool and groovy they also serve a utilitarian purpose, for the dancing there is of such a high standard that a certain degree of acrobatic skill is incorporated, and when really carried away whole rows of lithe young bodies bend over backwards and touch the floor with their hands!

The dancing is without a doubt the finest I have ever seen outside of the USA – in fact I never thought I'd live to see the day where people could so relate the rhythmic content of Soul music to bodily movement to such a skilled degree in these rigid and armoured Isles! And, unbelievable as it seems, everybody there was an expert in Soul clapping! In the right places, and with a clipped sharp quality that only adds an extra something to appreciation of Soul music. And what a selection of Sounds there were to dance to. I had taken four treasures from my own collection which I thought would go down well, and sure enough, even on first hearing, the Wheelites were able to fall immediately into the rhythm and mood of them, and were moving and grooving out as if they had all week to rehearse to them.

It is an irony that groups like Pan's People, The Young Generation, and the grotesque automatons on *Top of the Pops*, are employed to combine bodily movements to Soul records, and yet even the most average dancer of The Wheel could show them how it should be done. It could be that one needs a certain amount of affection for the music in order to penetrate the unique peculiarity of its rhythms, but the people at The Wheel have done this, and have done it to brilliant effect. I estimated that there were about 750 people crammed into the premises, but at no time did it seem so crowded that one couldn't move or breathe properly, and with the minimum of chat Les kept the records coming one after the other, each a Soul classic, and each loved and respected by the crowd.

Between records one would hear the occasional cry of 'Right on now!' or see a clenched gloved fist rise over the tops of the heads of the dancers. Every style of dress and lifestyle was there – hair to the shoulders as well as hair like a five-o'clock shadow. Muttonchops and potential Santa Clauses (in which category I fell), and the completely cleanshaven. The tang of after-shaves and the girls' perfumes scented the hot air. The young ladies at The Wheel must be some of the most attractive in Britain, cute as buttons, and as mean as they want to be, but in the nicest possible ways. And imaginative enough to bring a change of clothes with them, so that halfway through the night the young girl you were chatting with in the white suit to begin with, was now dancing the night away in an entirely different outfit! And talk! I thought I'd never stop! Everyone was so friendly and kind, and I truly felt quite humbled that so many people knew who I was, and came up and introduced themselves and had a kind word to say about my writings. I must mention a few of them by name.

There was young Zan who really knows all about Soul, but who still retains a soft spot for the Blues, and people like Bobby Bland and John Lee Hooker. He comes originally from Scotland, and has paid his dues one way or another, but explained how in some ways Soul has played such a big part in his life that it helped reform it. He is one of The Wheel's guardians (which I am told are hardly ever needed), and he will look after any strangers or newcomers and see that they settle in OK and no hustler who might slip in can take advantage of them. Everybody there certainly knew how to conduct themselves. There was no undercurrent of tension or aggression that one sometimes finds in London clubs, but rather a benevolent atmosphere of benign friendship and camaraderie. Everyone seems to know everyone else, and if they don't, then they don't stand on ceremony about getting to know each other, for one thing they know they all have in common is a love and dedication to Soul music, and it is this common factor that links everyone there, and makes everyone a potential friend of the other.

Some of the brothers and sisters had travelled miles to be there, and although they couldn't make it, Viv and Radio were thoughtful and kind enough to send a message to me via a friend. There was Tony from Cheltenham, and Rod (as imposing as Goliath and a DJ at other clubs in the North), and Flash who is not in the least flash, but very hip and very much into Soul.

And then there was Ivor Abadi, who is the owner of The Wheel, and who couldn't have been more welcoming and friendly, and who expressed gratitude for the efforts that *Blues & Soul* has made to draw attention to The Wheel scene, and the struggle that is going on to keep it open for swingers at the weekends. And there was one record that sticks in my mind, as one always will on these occasions, which was the great 'Darkest Days' by Jackie Lee.

I do most sincerely hope that The Wheel is able to carry on its traditional all-night sessions, and at the time of writing the appeal to the Crown Court has yet to be heard, and so they will continue until a final ruling is given, but win or lose, The Wheel has succeeded in becoming a legend in its lifetime, and a focal point for that aware and elite minority who are not content with the lifeless pulp that constitutes the bulk of the manipulated 'hit' parade, but rather use their own taste and judgement to determine what sounds best related to their own ways of looking at things. Live and let live is a rather worn-out well-intentioned cliché these days when life seems to be becoming more and more restricted and uniform, but you would have to search a long way to find a setting where that theory was put into such real practice as Manchester's Twisted Wheel club, and I shall always remember with gratitude that I was taken to its heart, and allowed to be part of that scene even if I could only stay for such a short time.

They are my kind of people, and as I went to the station to get the train back home the faint sounds of Soul music reminded me that the Sunday afternoon session had already begun, and no matter what obstacles are placed in its way, Soul music, like life itself, goes on and on. Because each and every one of us keeps the faith – right on now!

It was around the time of this visit that Dave coined the phrase Northern Soul. He would later explain he was merely trying to describe the rare Motownesque type of music being enjoyed in the north of England while the 'trendier' southerners were getting on down to the funkier new releases from the American charts.

It went further than that, as Dave was involved with the Soul City record label and shop and wanted a convenient shorthand pigeonhole for that musical style. He explained: 'Black American music underwent quite a change and switched over to what we subsequently called funk. I noticed that every Saturday we got a lot of football fans in the shop from the north who were following their teams in the south and their tastes weren't changing. They were still sticking with the type of soul which had been popular shortly before. When records came into the shop, in order to help my team sell them, the term Northern Soul was used to make us aware that this record would be the type of record that people in the north would like. The term just stuck.'

In the 1960s, Lancashire businessman Steve Curry was a typical teenager looking for a 'scene' and a crowd to call his own. He found exactly what he was looking for in the Wheel and its followers.

Steve, from Eccleston, near Chorley, Lancs, discovered soul at the tiny Stax Club in Preston. The name reflected the style of music played there – Arthur Conley, Otis Redding etc. Not Northern or rare soul, but a step beyond the Tamla Motown chart hits of the time.

Burnley Mecca followed, along with new friends who were asking each other if they had tried the Twisted Wheel in Manchester. No, Steve hadn't, but he put that right in 1968. By then he had adopted the carefully cultured Mod look of the time – Cromby coat, made-to-measure suits, Ben Sherman shirts, Levi sta-press pants and brogues. Suits would be custom-made with 18-inch side vents, six or eight buttons on the sleeve, two ticket pockets, and 20-inch parallels with a one and a half inch turn-up. There was only one problem with Ben Shermans, the short-sleeved style was in and Steve and his friends could only ever find long-sleeved versions. The area's soulies found a solution in Eric Passey's shop in Preston. There, for a fee, the owner's mother would hack the sleeves off the newly-arrived shirts and expertly turn them into short-sleeved versions for the Wheel dancers.

Steve soon found that the Wheel was so popular there was no guarantee of gaining admission. The sight of a massive queue in Whitworth Street at 11 pm gave soul fans a sinking feeling as they contemplated having to settle for the city's other all-nighter at the Blue Note, a reggae and ska venue that catered for different musical tastes. 'We went to the Blue Note a couple of times, but the atmosphere wasn't the same and it was hard work listening to the stuff they played all night,' recalled Steve. 'The Wheel was a dump. There was no finesse about the place. But the atmosphere and the crowd was brilliant.'

Steve and his mates found a great scam to save them ten shillings (50p) on their train fare from Preston to Manchester. They would buy platform tickets at Preston, but no train ticket. A friend would go on ahead to Manchester and buy platform tickets there, and then hand them to the arriving soul fans as they disembarked. So the rail authorities sold lots of cheap platform tickets, but lost out on fares.

Steve soon found out that amphetamines were widely used and available at the Wheel and clubs like it. Purple hearts, black bombers, Dexedrine, green and clears were all part of the vocabulary among soul fans at the time. Bombers, a powerful slimming pill called Durophet, were often sold on to soul fans by overweight women who found it easy to get plentiful supplies on prescription.

By the late 60s, bombers were changing hands at two shillings and sixpence, or eight for a pound. 'You always allowed a pound for your gear,' said an ex-regular. Steve recalled: 'In those days the police couldn't do you for internal possession. If you had stuff on you, they would nick you, but if you had already had it, it was too late. Then they changed the law so they could do you for internal possession, so the drug squad would just come into the Wheel and look around for the ones who had their eyes popping out and chewing away, and take them off to the police station. It was a lottery every week whether you would get done or not. It happened all the time. I suppose as far as the club was concerned it kept the peace between them and the police. There always seemed to be someone going down for three months or so.'

None of this detracted from the exclusive music and friendly atmosphere for which the Wheel was famed. As time went by, the DJs switched from current release items to older and often overlooked soul gems. Steve remembers the impact that American imports had on the scene when they appeared in around 1969.

'We were so used to seeing British labels, like Tamla Motown, which were usually black or dark blue and pretty boring colours. When someone brought an import like Motown with the colourful map on it, we all went "wow". We all wanted to see these colourful labels. It was great just to hold them.'

The more adventurous music policy brought with it a problem for collectors, as Steve recalls: 'Some of the records were four or five years old by the time they became big at the Wheel. You couldn't go into a record shop and ask for them. They were deleted pretty quickly.' Then Soul Sounds appeared, probably the first bootleg label. Now collectors could own an utterly illegal disc with an in-demand song by a different artist on each side.

Steve says the Flamingos' 'Boogaloo Party', Frank Valli's 'You're Ready Now' and Hoagy Lands' 'The Next in Line' were guaranteed floor fillers on the concrete dance floors, ensuring that the walls ran with condensation in the energy-charged atmosphere. He remembers vividly seeing Junior Walker, the Showstoppers, Ben E King and Edwin Starr appear live at the club.

Jimmy Radcliffe's 'Long After Tonight Is All Over' would herald the end of another all-nighter, the top and bottom floor exit doors would open and the soul fans would disgorge into the Manchester morning light. Carrying small bags with a change of clothes or a towel, Steve and his mates would make their way to Stephensons Square toilets for a wash and brush-up. Since sleep was usually not an option, they would often head off by bus or train to the Top 20 Club in Oldham until mid-afternoon.

Steve looks back on his two years or so at the Wheel with great fondness: 'It was our secret scene, and we loved it. I didn't realize at the time that it would turn into what it has become since. It was something that only a select number of people went to. If you told people you were into soul music, they would say, "Oh, you mean Tamla Motown?" You couldn't explain to them the difference.'

He remembers watching admiringly great dancers like Kev O'Mara from Wigan, and his pal Jed Rudd from Preston, who perfected their spins, backdrops and fast legs at the Wheel. 'Jed was a really great dancer, and a bit of a hard lad. He was big on backdrops and spins and people would stop and watch.' Later Frank 'Booper' would become a legend among his peers. Jed would later die tragically young aged twenty-five.

The handy flyers that the club produced of forthcoming acts at the club helped fans plan their visits. In Steve's case he went every two or three weeks, depending on who was appearing live. But he is more than aware that the drugs culture proved fatal for several of his former friends. Some overindulged week in, week out and went on to try harder drugs like heroin. 'A lot of the guys couldn't get out of the habit of speeding. They didn't want to come down; they would start doing it during the week. We were young and free and foolish. When I look back I suppose I was lucky.'

When the Wheel all-nighters closed in early 1971, soul fans were left with a void in their lives. Blackpool Mecca filled it, as did fairly short-lived all-nighters like Harrisons Hoist in Earby, Lancashire. Monday nights at Wigan Casino (still two years away from launching its own all-nighter), also provided nomadic soul fans with a treat of music.

Steve and others then discovered the Torch in Stoke-on-Trent, 'a great venue, but a drag getting there'. Blackpool Mecca's Highland Room was gathering a major reputation, and the free coaches put on by the Mecca drew customers from all over the north-west.

'The music was different to the Wheel,' he said, 'there was new stuff coming out all the time. I was in my twenties by then, I was getting older and I got married in 1972.' Some years later, having settled down to family life, he took his records to Wigan Casino to sell them. As he lugged his record box through the streets he was hit by a sense of déjà vu. Two plainclothes police officers stopped him and searched him for drugs. He then realized that the Northern Soul scene hadn't changed so much after all.

Liverpool-born Vince Peach was introduced to the soul scene in the mid-60s as a teenager. And he even has the honour of having been to Wigan's first all-nighter, many years before the Casino was even a twinkle in Russ Winstanley's eye. The club in question was called the Room At The Top. 'I only went a couple of times, around 1965; it was a bit grotty and the main attenders were also a bit rough. Some soul was played but mostly Top Twenty stuff. I stopped going there when I found out about the Wheel.'

The Wheel was a different kettle of fish. The in place to be seen, and people cared about how they looked. Sharp haircuts and smart suits were the order of the day amongst the many Mods who frequented the Manchester club. Said Vince: 'When I first went to the Wheel I was a Mod, and so were 90 per cent of the people there. The first records I bought to learn to dance to. I used to practise at home or round at mates' places. Four of us from Liverpool always travelled together to Manchester on Friday nights to do a few of the clubs . . . Mr Smith's, Time and Place, Roundtrees Sound, etc. All these clubs had a high Mod population, and the Mod crowd was friendly. We always managed to get a bed off someone for the night, as at that time no all-nighters existed on Friday nights, though the Majestic in Manchester did try but not too successfully.

'In the early years the Wheel regulars were mostly Mods, and most people weren't there for the music, though, by 1967, I would say most regulars had started getting into the sounds as well. It must be remembered the Wheel was a dance club, so the music was uptempo and mainly black and in the main on UK record labels.' Vince recalls, however, that American imports became more common after a certain young Blackpool DJ called Ian Levine appeared on the scene with his Stateside rarities. Suddenly the rarity and exclusivity of the tracks being played, whether UK or American releases, became an issue. 'I remember

Keith Minshull followed myself and John Reid all the way to Colwyn Bay after a night at the Wheel one August Bank Holiday weekend in 1968 or '69 so he could get a UK copy of the Tymes' "So Much In Love". I can't remember what I swapped for it,' said Vince.

His love for the music grew and he even managed to secure two spots DJing at the Wheel. That gave him the bug for DJing and by 1972 he had his own mobile disco. Despite going to the Torch and Blackpool Mecca, he never made it to Wigan Casino as he had a contract with Watney Mann for ten years, DJing every weekend at various clubs and pubs.

Teenager Dave Scutt felt the pull and passion of black music from the minute he first saw old black-and-white TV clips of jazz and blues artists strutting their stuff in smokey inner city bars. 'There was something about the way they looked and the way they moved their feet. As soon as you heard the music you wanted to start dancing in the same way they danced, sliding and shuffling around with great rhythm.'

When he heard the mid-60s rhythm and blues and soul, it was the beginning of a love affair that would last a lifetime. Dave, then a 16-year-old living in Southport, Lancashire, found a circle of friends who were dancing to and collecting Tamla Motown, Atlantic, and Stax current releases. Names like Otis Redding, Aretha Franklin and Wilson Pickett became part of the everyday vocabulary for many 'hip' soulsters who until then may have only followed the British charts. 'Tamla Motown really hit it off,' said Dave. 'People would start going to a Tamla Motown night at a local club and that was the way forward for a lot of people.'

The young Mods were also not averse to supporting white bands like the Spencer Davis Group and John Mayall, as you were guaranteed a sprinkling of cover versions of much-loved black American songs.

'They would always do R & B stuff, Howlin' Wolf and Muddy Waters material, and someone would always do a version of "Smoke Stack Lightning",' said Dave. Another form of black music that was big in the early to mid-60s was ska, and

Prince Buster's 'Al Capone' was de rigueur at most beat clubs.

By 1965 the soul followers were focusing on Tamla Motown, Stateside, London and the choicest British releases. Collecting became an obsession for some, as the fans clamoured to find out more about 'real' soul music that they rarely heard on the radio. The work of the late great Billy Stewart and other Chess releases were particularly popular. Dave got caught up in this quest to know and own every American soul recording that came out on British labels, and would later pass on some of his knowledge to Ian Levine, who became the kingpin of Blackpool Mecca. Ian and Les Cockell and others would often go back to Dave's house in Southport after the Mecca and pour over his collection. 'Ian was always asking, "What's this?" and "What's that?" His passion for soul music was the same as mine,' said Dave.

A trained chef, Dave found a fair chunk of his earnings was going on collecting records, but by buying and selling he could keep the wolf from the door. 'Collecting was a way of life. I used to go everywhere. Once myself and my wife and two friends went to Cornwall surfing, but we spent a lot of time trawling record shops and junk shops.'

By 1967, Dave had discovered the Twisted Wheel and his affair with soul music took a different turn. Records like 'Candy' (the Astors), 'Tired of Being Lonely' (the Sharpees), 'Stay' (Virginia Wolves), 'Tell Her' (Dean Parrish) and 'Scratchy' (Travis Wammack) opened up new avenues to explore. 'I went to the Wheel simply because of the power of the music. I started hearing records that I had never heard before, but I soon got into the swing of things.'

Catching the train to Manchester Victoria, walking past Ralph's Records to scan the window for the latest releases, and on to a late-night bar called Rowntrees became part of Dave's pre-Wheel routine. Then at about midnight they would set off again to walk down to Whitworth Street, anticipation growing with every stride, to join the queue for the Wheel. Once inside, clutching his record box, Dave often found himself unable to make too much progress into the inner reaches of the club as he traded vinyl with other collectors. 'I would usually have a box of records with me and I would get as far as the top of the stairs and then grab a table. It could be two hours before I got downstairs. When you got down there it was just a concrete dance floor, but with your brogues on you could shuffle around and dance on it well enough. You would eventually wear your shoes out but it was OK. It was so hot, you were sweating profusely. You could get a drink of Coke of whatever upstairs, but mostly you just went to the toilets and got a drink of water. And the toilets stank.'

The atmosphere and the music got better and better for Dave. Gladys Knight's 'Just Walk In My Shoes', Earl Van Dyke's 'All For You', and the American Poets 'She Blew a Good Thing' all stick in his mind from that era.

His devotion to the scene and his friends meant that Dave even risked serious illness to make his regular pilgrimages to Manchester. He was diagnosed as suffering from TB and spent many months in hospital. After a while, the doctors allowed him home at weekends 'to convalesce'. What they didn't know was the teenager was actually spending his Saturday nights in a sweaty, noisy and far from wholesome all-night venue.

'When I get into something, I get into it full time,' said Dave. 'It was the same when I got into body building years later.' (He became a champion body builder in the 1980s, and found himself competing against ex-Blackpool Mecca DJ Tony Jebb.) 'The music just stuck with me and people like me. It was different, it was rare, and the music at the Wheel was getting better all the time.'

Live acts were also part of the attraction. British-based R & B band Steam Packet (featuring a young Rod Stewart) and the Spencer Davis Group would share the headlines on the Wheel's incredible roster of live acts with black American stars like Ike and Tina Turner, James and Bobby Purify and Junior Walker.

Dave says the artists were always warmly received, but in the small and packed club they were not fêted as living legends. They were expected to mingle, perform and share the experience with the knowledgeable crowd. (It was almost a case of 'So you're Darrell Banks, are you? Nice to meet you. Now let's hear you sing'!) Nevertheless, 'I think the artists felt that they were being appreciated by a British audience and they loved it. They were never considered gods, they were just there. They mingled with the crowd afterwards. Sometimes it got so full you could hardly hear the band because the crowd were making so much racket,' said Dave.

'The minute I first experienced the Wheel I thought "This is it." There was nowhere else like it. Some of the dancers there would really experiment, and they were brilliant to watch. Some of the girls were excellent. It was basically free interpretation of the music. Sometimes a circle would form. The amphetamines obviously helped, but there were some brilliant dancers around.'

An early escape from the Wheel usually meant a visit to the Express Bongo café (for those who could face breakfast). Often there would be an all-dayer on somewhere, but even without, it could be midday before Dave made it home.

By 1967, Dave was doing guest DJing spots at the Wheel – 'just to fill in while someone had a break' – and discovered a love of that side of the business that has remained with him. Now a father of three and a restaurant owner, he still guests at various north-west venues and runs his own monthly soul night at Southport Sailing Club.

When the end came for the Wheel because of drugs and licensing problems, Dave and other regulars were slightly sceptical when they first heard the news: 'We had had these scares before and we didn't believe that it would actually happen. Quite a few of us from around here went to the final night. It was sad when it closed because I had made friends from all over the place.'

*Ten of the best Wheel sounds, courtesy of Dave Scutt*

'All For You' Earl Van Dyke
'Tell Her' Dean Parrish
'That's What I Want to Know' James Carr
'I'll Be Loving You' Soul Bros Six
'Kick That Little Foot, Sally Ann' Round Robin
'Stay' Virginia Wolves
'Just Walk in My Shoes' Gladys Knight
'I'm the One to Do It' Jackie Wilson
'These Things Will Keep Me Loving You' The Velvelettes
'I Feel So Bad' Jackie Edwards

Mick Taylor, formerly of Doncaster, Yorkshire, and now living in Canada, recalls how his music obsession began in the early 60s:

THE TWISTED WHEEL
MANCHESTER

FORTHCOMING SATURDAY ATTRACTIONS
11.00pm–7.30 am

April 18th•Harry J. and the All Stars
April 25th•Showstoppers
May 9th •Gary U.S. Bond
May 16th •Special American Attraction

May 2nd Ben E. King

May 23rd Marv Johnson

May 30th Inez & Charlie Foxx

'In '65 I started work (only the smarties stayed on at school in those days) as an apprentice gas fitter. About this time, the Mod thing was coming up from London, spread by *Ready, Steady, Go*. The whole idea appealed to me and the mates I hung out with. All the best chicks were Mods, all the best clothes (pin-stripes, trying to look affluent, like John Steed). All this had great appeal to kids who were surrounded by slag heaps and a hundred years of coal dust and constantly skint. I earned £4 5 shillings a week, with 2 quid going to the house, so you can see how long it took to save up the 15 quid for my fourth-hand Vespa 125!

'We would all go into town and sit around one cup of tea, in the Coffee House or the Excel bowling alley. Later we would graduate to the Danum Hotel Leger Bar (home of the in-crowd). Sometime in '66 I was shipped off to Sheffield one day a week to gas board school. I got to hang out with all the other apprentices from all over. One place I found out about was a record store called Violet Mays. Run by this old lady with blue hair. The place was full of black music records. It was about this time that black groups were starting to take off (in fact I recall reading in some music mag that EMI had hooked up with a label run only by black people, featuring only black artists).

'The other place I found was the King Mojo club, which was like a church hall on the back of a row of houses, decorated with pictures of old gangster-type cars. The gangster stuff was big at this time, and we all started buying broad chalked-striped suits, double-breasted – trying to look like Robert Stack. I used to pay

5 bob a week for handmade suits and as soon as I had a few quid left to pay, I would get measured up for another!

'The Mojo was *the* place, more like a party in someone's house and I was constantly up asking the DJ Pete Stringfellow, "What's this?" "What's that?" And then I'd be down Fox's record store in Doncaster getting the LP. (Of course "Stringbean", alias London clubowner Stringfellow, is now BIG TIME). Discs that were played a lot were "Wade in the Water" (Ramsey Lewis), "That Driving Beat" (Willie Mitchell), "Rescue Me" (Fontella Bass), "Nothing Can Stop Me" (Gene Chandler), "Love a go-go" (Stevie Wonder), and lots of Billy Stewart and other stuff like Georgie Fame, Zoot Money, Amen Corner, Small Faces.

'I think the only criteria a record had was that you could dance to it, and if we didn't like a record, we would just stop dancing and Stringbean would take it off and chuck it! There were plenty of live acts that showed up like Zoot Money's big "Roll Band", Root and Jenny Jackson, the Four Tops, Ike and Tina Turner, Wynder K Frogg, Stevie Wonder (a big favourite). About then someone discovered Blue Beat, and this took off.

'Throughout '67 all kinds of things were going on, lots of clubs were opening up and the "in thing" to do was to out-club everyone else. I think that this was when we first went to the Wheel, but it was very far away (no motorways then, only across Snake Pass). Also then, the psychedelic stuff started coming out and it was all-change again. The Mojo was redecorated with flowers and changed its name to the "Beautiful Mojo". This caused a big split, with a part of the crowd going one way, and the rest of us staying in the same place. Late in '67 the Mojo was closed (for the usual reasons) and a lot of folks just stopped going to all-nighters all together.'

Mick and his friends stayed loyal to the soul scene and their trips became more and more adventurous as they sought out the mix they loved. He recalls the Wheel with great affection, but also points out that the changing music policy in the late 60s did not find favour with all. 'One thing about the Wheel – it was always open. Don't ask me how, but when everywhere else was off, the Wheel was on. Lots of good nights were had here, but it was all wearing a bit thin, and the lifts were getting fewer (I went to see Billy Stewart and got there at 4 am – he had been and gone! – I'm still pissed off about that one!)

'The DJs there played stuff that was not played anywhere else, which was a good thing and bad. Also there was no contact with the audience, which was always a huge part of the other clubs (especially Stringfellow). The DJ sat in one room, in a booth-type thing made of wooden wheels, and the stage was in another. As well as this, the music was getting away from the traditional all-nighter material. . . . They played some great stuff – Invitations, O'Jays, Brooks and Jerry, Fascinations, Charlie Rich, Roger Collins, the Dillards, etc., but they also played some right shite!

'I think the DJs were on some ego trip, playing stuff just to be different, even if it was crap! So along with all the other things going on, bit by bit, we all stopped going (my own last memory, was late '68, listening to a mate, Tom Slieght, playing a record he'd just bought – "Wear It On Our Face" – on a disc-a-tron [45 player].'

Mick has a typically down-to-earth Yorkshireman's view of the status of the Wheel and the dewy-eyed nostalgia with which it is viewed. He said: 'All of the articles I've read have been written by people who admit they were never at the Wheel. And there seems to be a great deal of "hype" associated with the legendary visit of God's own soul messenger on earth (Dave Godin) to that hallowed birthplace of Northern Soul deep in the bowels of Manchester (more bollocks).

'The Wheel was just a club, and the things that made it great were the same things that made all the other clubs great – the music and the patrons. Once the familiar faces started to disappear, and the DJs started their ego trip, I stopped going.'

Sandra Taylor of Clayton, Newcastle under Lyme, Staffs, recalls: 'I remember the night the Torch opened, long before the all-nighters, and watched it evolve into the country's second best soul venue. The first being The Twisted Wheel, Manchester. I am so glad I lived through it all and after a break of more years than I care to remember I am very much involved again. The dancing is still as unique and the music gets ever better. Only those who share my fantastic memories and a head full of music that just never stops haunting me will understand why my most treasured possession is my Wheel membership card.

'Whilst a new generation went on to Wigan Casino, I was at home raising a family. Thankfully my husband Les and I are back at as many venues as possible and loving every minute, although nothing could ever replace the Wheel.

'Often, having spent the early evening at the Torch, I'd make my way to Manchester. I'd hitch or meet friends for a lift – Russ from Stoke, who had a crazy van complete with spotlight on the roof, or Keith from Shrewsbury.

'Whenever I could afford it, I'd travel by train, arriving at Manchester Piccadilly. Out of the station's main doors, down the subway steps, under the bridge, across the main road into Whitworth Street, and there it was (and still is, I think) on the right. Opposite was the main police station, would you believe. Once inside the Wheel – which looked a dump even in those days – through the small entrance to the little hatch to pay, round into the bar/coffee area, past the cloakroom, tables and chairs through to toilets (once seen never forgotten) nearby was a large area with benches all around the walls.

'Just before this were the stairs leading down; this was the main area, all of which was the dance floor. To the right in the far corner was a raised stage area beside fire doors, and a small alcove, almost like a loading bay. It was through this exit we left on Sunday morning, often to a café called the Blue Dolphin or a dancehall called Brown's.

'To the left of the stairs another dance area divided by a wall of cartwheels, and at the far end the DJ behind another screen of cartwheels. Everything was very dark. More cartwheels decorated the walls and the floors were cement. No wooden sprung floors here!

'My pride and joy at the time was my bottle-green full-length leather coat with matching weekend case. All the girls carried such a case in those days. We wore black, flat ballet-type shoes for dancing. I usually wore Levi jeans and jacket. Though I always wore a mini skirt when I hitched a lift – for obvious reasons. My legs, I am told, stopped the traffic at Keele Services and outside the Cinebowl at Hanley, but that's another story.

'I'm hopeless at names. Those I remember are Sam, Snowy, Chris and her brother Russ, Ginger, Sparky, John, Alan, Keith, Doc ... some of the Stoke girls worked the summer season of '69 in Torquay, but they travelled back as often as possible for the Wheel all-nighters.

'In fact our lives revolved around getting to the Wheel. Everyone was friendly, I don't remember any fights or trouble at all. We were all equal, without fear, enjoying a unique period of our lives together.

'How can I sum it all up – I can't. But even today when I close my eyes, I'm back there. The dancing, the music, the feelings, they are in the very bones of me. Give me a time machine to return – just one last time!'

*Sandra's List*

'Be Young, Be Foolish, Be Happy' Tams
'Let the Good Times Roll' Bunny Sigler
'Billy's Bag' Billy Preston
'Candy' The Astors
'A Touch of Velvet' Moods Mosaic
'Wade In the Water' Ramsey Lewis

Tony James, of Bolton, was astonished when he was introduced to the Twisted Wheel as a teenager. It was as if someone had opened a door to a whole new world. Tony visited the club when it moved to its Whitworth Street site in 1965. 'We were about sixteen or seventeen and I suppose we had been brought up on the Mersey Mania thing, where groups were usually four good-looking white guys. It was always a British thing.

'When I went to the Wheel one of my first memories was of seeing this poster for the Impressions. Here were this group of black American guys who of course looked totally different to what I had seen up to then. Their song "You've Been Cheating" was being played then. It just opened up a completely new world to us. They were playing records by guys like Sam and Dave. I thought "Who on earth are these guys?" It certainly wasn't the

Beatles or the Rolling Stones. This music was nothing like they were playing in the Oasis or the Jungfrau or on the radio. We were hooked.

'Then of course we had to do the all-nighter. It was amazing. Everyone was so friendly. Some of the guys were older than us, twenty or twenty-one, and there were handshakes and the atmosphere and the music was out of this world.' Tony said there were inevitable brushes with the law, and he recalled one occasion when a friend caught with amphetamines on him was whisked off to the police station opposite the Wheel at 3 am. His friend's highly displeased parents were called from their holiday at Pontin's to bail him out.

But although the police took a close interest in the Wheel all-nighters, Tony cannot recollect any heavy-handedness. 'I can't recall feeling threatened at all in the 60s. Maybe I was just oblivious to it all at such a young age.'

Margaret McKelvie (née Smart), of Corby, Northants, and now Whitstable, Kent, recalls: 'I went to my first all-nighter back in 1970. The Frolicking Kneecap was held in what had once been the local cinema in Market Harborough. Cleared of its rows of seats, it provided ample space for dancing and the area where the screen had once been was perfect for the record deck. Cheap shabby wallpaper and chipped purple paintwork did nothing to improve the aesthetic appearance but this was more than made up for with a magnetic atmosphere that produced an addictive need to return each week.

'Before the birth of the all-nighter soul fans had met in The Tin Hat in Kettering. Its name was derived from the nature of the building which was literally a tin shack within the grounds of the local football club. In 1968 this was the place to be for all self-respecting Mods. This was the exclusive world of parka-clad scooter enthusiasts where Sam and Dave's "soul sister brown sugar" took on a new meaning and the all-time inspiring words of Dobie Gray's "The In Crowd" cultivated a dream. The closure of The Tin Hat led us to The Shades in Northampton, The North Park Club in Kettering, and The George at Wilby. The all-nighters were a natural progression from these clubs and pubs.

'By 1970 skinheads pervaded the all-nighter scene. Sta-press trousers, Ben Sherman or Fred Perry shirts and of course Doc Marten boots were worn impressively. Travera suits were popular too. Skinheads also had their day and by 1971 our hair had grown, we evolved into suedeheads, and later the tousle-headed bag-carrying crowd that became synonymous with the all-nighter scene. The fashion had changed but the attitude was the same as in the early Mod days; it was all to do with identifying with the all-nighter crowd through our way of dress and our music, which made us feel special.

'The popularity of the Frolicking Knee Cap grew, attracting people from all over – Northamptonshire, Bedfordshire, and Cambridgeshire, and eventually word spread further afield to people in Nottingham, Wolverhampton, Manchester and Leeds. In turn we found out about other all-nighters and spread our wings in their pursuit. The Saints and Sinners in Birmingham was one such discovery one night on our travels. Entrance to the Saints was through a door at the back of a café, then down a steep flight of stairs to the basement. The Saints seemed plush after the others. Comfortable seats surrounding a small dance floor, quite a change from Harborough's scruffy old settee and spacious floor. Steps led to a raised area with tables and seats where we could cool down, have a drink or just talk to mates – we did a lot of talking. On the upper floor, it was rumoured, was a brothel, and judging by the clientele that appeared there, it was not hard to believe. All we had on our minds, though, was dancing – it was like two separate worlds coexisting.

'Publicity of the all-nighters spread by word of mouth – no glossy magazine announcements or flyers to tempt the swarms of baggy-trousered supporters. On occasions, news of an all-nighter would result in a trek halfway round the country only to find it had either been cancelled or was the result of someone's imagination. We would go to any lengths to find an all-nighter. On one occasion we hitched a lift in a three-wheel car to Bradford in search of The Hippo Club which was closed when we got there. Another rumour of an all-nighter near Sheffield led us on a journey up the snow-covered Pennine Way on a cold December night. We never found it.

'Soon there was a circuit of well-known all-nighters. We would start the evening at The Catacombs in Wolverhampton – not an all-nighter – whose dungeon-like alcoves provided cooling-down areas where people could swap stories, sell records, or just plan the next weekend's jaunt. Then we would trek to Bedfordshire for the Bletsoe all-nighter, literally a barn with a makeshift floor for dancing and a bar erected in one corner. This became the mainstay all-nighter for most of the people in the Northamptonshire area by 1972 and I suppose became the new Harborough. What it lacked in comfort it made up for in a warm friendly atmosphere and brilliant sounds. Others included Up The Junction at Crewe which had to be experienced to be believed. Spanning several floors it provided different sounds for different tastes including live performers that had not been seen previously at an all-nighter. The music was all-important. The all-nighter gave us incomparable sounds – American imports – later to be known as Northern Soul.

'After the all-nighter, on the Sunday morning, we would generally congregate in a service station somewhere on the M1. In the early days of the Harborough all-nighter we would sometimes go down to Jumbo's Shack. This was a disused railway coach at the bottom of a garden owned by a guy called Jumbo who frequented the all-nighter scene at that time. It was a bit cold and damp but provided us with a place to sit and talk. Occasionally, someone's parents would be away and we would invade their house. Sunday evenings for our local crowd were often spent in the Corby bowling alley where they held a disco. Those of us who still had the energy would show off to the locals and impress them with our dancing.

'Our dancing was extremely competitive. There was an unwritten law that existed at all-nighters which gave an individual the right to dance at the front – a place exclusively for the best dancers. They would impress onlookers with intricate steps, fast spins and back drops. A select few were deemed as the best dancers but there were many who would challenge in unofficial "dance-offs". Judging was done by self-appointment or by the comments made by mates, which was invariably biased.

'Status was also acquired by experience. Having been to The Twisted Wheel in Manchester immediately raised a person up the hierarchy. Of course by 1971 it had closed and those who had been there would tell us how nothing was ever as good and how the all-nighter scene had gone downhill since its closure.

'By the end of 1972 the crowds were increasing as word of the all-nighter scene spread. The Torch became known as the main venue as many of the smaller all-nighters closed. Its large spacious dance floor was excellent for dancing but it lacked the intimacy of the smaller all-nighters. Those were special days that can never be recreated. It was fantastic to be a part of the legend.'

Every dance scene this century has had its darker side, and the soul scene is no exception. The combination of all-night events, pulsating music and energetic dancing made the use of amphetamines (or speed) widespread in the 60s. What is more, for those who hadn't had enough after the Wheel all-nighter, there was the option of going back to the Whitworth Street venue for the Sunday afternoon session (11 am to 4.30 pm for only 4 shillings).

Venues like the Twisted Wheel were unlicensed, so alcohol was not an option inside the all-nighter. But even if it had been, most soul fans will tell you that beer and an all-nighter do not sit particularly well together. Booze would usually only bring about a sluggish feeling or a 4 am snooze.

Speed was different – it made users alert, energetic and euphoric and could have been tailor-made for the all-night dance scene. A regular 1960s soul clubber recalled how amphetamine-based pills and capsules were ridiculously easy to come by. Mums, aunties, friends and underworld characters would be prescribed or illegally obtain amphetamines and would sell them on to the Mods.

The short- and long-term effects and the extent of the abuse of such 'uppers' was not known at the time, and the pharmaceutical companies flooded the market with slimming aids and anti-depressants. One ex-Twisted Wheel regular said: 'The thing about the stuff we took those days was that you knew it had come from a pharmaceutical company, or a chemist's. You knew what you were getting. Nowadays somebody hands you a wrap of powder and you could be getting any old crap.'

One long-term speed user told how in the mid-60s he and his girlfriend would obtain 1,000-strong canisters of SKF 'blueys' for the equivalent of 7d each. Selling them on at 1s 3d represented a good mark-up and a thriving industry. 'On Friday nights we would go out to the shop and buy up as many pay packets as we could find, then we would make the blueys up into packets of ten and sell them. I remember driving through the Mersey tunnel with my girlfriend in the car stuffing all these pills into packets ready for the Saturday all-nighter at the Wheel. On Saturday lunchtime we used to set up in the town centre where we lived. People would come up to me and give me 15s for ten, and I would give them a ticket. They would meet a mate parked in the carpark at the back, give him the ticket and he would give them the gear.

'It was so easy it was comical. I even knew a ticket collector who worked on a railway station who sold the stuff. You would get your ticket and your gear at the same time. There was no drug squad then, and people tended to think that drugs were confined to London. We lived in the country. It wouldn't have entered the head of the average copper at the time that there was a drug problem where we were. We thought we were the untouchables. It was only when people started doing chemist's shops that it became a bit of a problem and the police became more aware of what was going on.'

Another regular speed user said: 'I took the decision very early on to take these pills to stay awake. I use them as a tool. As long as you use them, and they don't use you, you are all right. I would never inject myself. For me, amphetamines equal soul. I would never use them at any other time. I can't imagine getting smashed and just sitting in the house or pratting about. Nowadays on the dance scene, using drugs has become part of the culture. Back in the old days, we thought we were a small crowd of people.'

An ex-Wheel-goer told how his naivety cost him dearly one night. Sitting in his battered car near the Wheel one night, he let it be known that he had some gear for sale. News of a bagful of black and whites, green and clears and red and browns for sale spread like wildfire and the young soul fan retired to his car to wait for customers.

The first one appeared and asked him what he had got. The would-be pusher produced a bag of capsules, whereupon the customer reached in through the open window, grabbed the lot and disappeared. By the time the youngster and his friends had got out of the car in pursuit, they were confronted by nine or ten hard-looking lads and decided they didn't like the odds.

It was a hedonistic lifestyle and the authorities in Manchester did not approve one iota of the bizarre, and often illegal, goings-on at the Wheel and clubs like it. The Chief Constable, Mr J A McKay, tirelessly campaigned to rid the city of the 'beatnicks' and, in his eyes, undesirables who were coming to Manchester to enjoy themselves.

The crusade, which Dave Godin likened to the American prohibition, resulted in the passing of the Manchester Corporation Act 1965, which gave police widespread new powers to shut down clubs. The Twisted Wheel, where the drug squad had practically taken up residence, was an obvious target. Chemist's shops were frequently being raided in and around Manchester, and detectives were convinced, not without foundation, that there might be a link with the all-night sessions.

In the autumn of 1970, the corporation successfully applied to get the all-nighters banned. Effectively, the club could no longer open between midnight and 12 noon. The Abadis appealed and in the run-up to the hearing, a petition was circulated among members. A letter dated 25 November 1970, also called, quite comically, for parents of members to show their support. ('Hilarious, really, because it was the parents who wanted the place shut down,' remarked one former regular.)

In the letter, Mr Ivor Abadi wrote:

The date of the appeal against the restriction by the Corporation, namely that the club cannot open between 12 midnight and 12 noon, has now been set for Monday, December 14.

Whilst the petition of members' signatures has been satisfactory, the number of letters in support of the club from both members and parents has, unfortunately, been disappointing, and we urge you to do your utmost in this matter.

The last date for receiving any correspondence and petition signatures to this effect will be Friday, December 4. Any parent willing to act as a witness in court in support of our appeal, please contact me as soon as possible.

Should the appeal not be successful, the last all-night session of the club would be Saturday, December 12 . . .

A temporary reprieve was won, and Wheel-goers can recall enjoying Christmas events at the famous venue. But by early 1971, the powers that be got their way and the all-nighters came to an end.

Now there were hundreds and hundreds of Northern Soul fans rattling around at weekends looking for the next major venue. The void was pretty much filled by another club 50 miles north of Manchester. Blackpool Mecca's Highland Room became the major focal point after the Wheel, its Saturday soul nights attracting up to 1,000 fans every week.

But then came the Golden Torch all-nighters in Tunstall, Stoke-on-Trent, and the travelling army of soul fans knew they had found their new home.

*Twenty Twisted Wheel floorshakers*

'Boogaloo Party' Flamingos
'At the Discotheque' Chubby Checker
'Open the Door to Your Heart' Darrell Banks
'The Philly Freeze' Alvin Cash
'You Get Your Kicks' Mitch Ryder
'Washed Ashore' The Platters
'All For You' Earl Van Dyke
'Harlem Shuffle' Bob and Earl
'You've Been Cheating' The Impressions
'Sock It to 'Em, JB' Rex Garvin
'A Lot of Love' Homer Banks
'Green Door' Wynder K Frogg
'Candy' The Astors

'More, More, More of Your Love'  Bob Brady
'Six by Six'  Earl Van Dyke
'Barefootin''  Robert Parker
'Darkest Days''  Jackie Lee
'Ain't Nothing but a House Party'  Showstoppers
'Baby Reconsider'  Leon Hayward
'Love Makes a Woman'  Barbara Acklin

## The Twisted Wheel Club

PROPRIETORS: SANDBURNE ENTERPRISES LTD.

**6 WHITWORTH STREET**
**MANCHESTER M1 3QW**
Telephone: CENtral 1179

October 1970

Dear Member,

The hours of opening and closing the Club have been restricted by the Corporation, namely that the Club cannot open between 12 midnight and 12 noon. This would mean the closing of the all-night session at the Club (11 p.m.-7-30 a.m.).

We are appealing against this imposition, and the Club will remain open as usual, pending the appeal.

We have won an appeal before on this issue of the all-night session.

A petition in support of the appeal is being drafted and anyone who sincerely feels they would like to support the petition may sign a copy on their next visit to the Club, which will remain open pending the appeal.

We would also appreciate letters of support from Members and their Parents on the merits of the all-night session.

Looking forward to seeing you at the Club,

Your sincerely,

Ivor Abadi.

# Part II

THE TORCH - TUNSTALL
Stoke-on-Trent

## The only one
## in the Land ..

# TORCH ALL-NIGHTER

**FORTHCOMING DATES—**

Saturday, September 9th
Saturday, September 23rd
Saturday, September 30th
. . . . and then every Saturday . . . .

**October 7th** "THE KINGSPINNERS"
Keith Minshall and Martyn Ellis

**October 14th** At Our Club
"THE DRIFTERS" (on Stage at Midnight)

**October 21st** MAJOR LANCE

**October 28th** A very exclusive Super Soul Scoop
"Betcha by Golly" . . . .
"THE STYLISTICS" (on Stage Midnight)

**ALL-NIGHTERS EVERY SATURDAY FROM SEPTEMBER 23rd**

Advance Tickets for THE DRIFTERS and THE STYLISTICS now on Sale

£1.00 Members  £1.25 Guests  Advance Tickets Secure Admission

Postal Applications must enclose S.A.E., P.O. or Cheque for correct amount
and quoting Membership No.  Guest Tickets must be purchased on the Club
Premises, or through the Post with a Torch Membership Form.

**"FRIDAYS ARE SOULFUL"**

Printed by Ron Whittaker, 93 Hassell Street, Newcastle, Staffs.

# The Torch - Tunstall

## Stoke-on-Trent

# The No. 1
# All-Nighter

## TWELVE SO-FULL SOULFUL HOURS

**NOW OPEN EVERY SATURDAY**
**8-30 p.m. to 8-30 a.m.**

---

## DECEMBER
### Programme Details

---

**THE COUNTRYS GREATEST SOUL SCENE**

---

**SUNDAY, DECEMBER 31st**

**The End of 1972  -  The Start of 1973**

### New Year's Eve
## ALL-NIGHT BALL

**We proudly present . . .**

## ★ Archie Bell
### and The Drells
(On Stage at 1-0 a.m.)

Advance Tickets —  NOW ON SALE
£2.00 — MEMBERS and GUESTS

**Plus**

★ **KEITH MINSHULL**

★ **MARTYN ELLIS**

★ **ALAN DAY**

---

**PLEASE NOTE — ALL-NIGHTER, Saturday,
DECEMBER 30th—Open only 8-0 to 1 a.m.**

Evening Sentinel

Youngsters flocking there from all over England—claim

# TUNSTALL CLUB A DRUG CENTRE JUSTICES TOLD

YOUNG PEOPLE FROM ALL PARTS OF ENGLAND HAD BEEN FLOCKING TO STOKE-ON-TRENT—TO A TUNSTALL CLUB THAT HAD BECOME A DRUG CENTRE, IT WAS CLAIMED TO-DAY.

And Mr David McEvoy told the City Licensing Justices: "The which Torch has a national reputation as a place where drugs can be obtained and for trafficking in drugs."

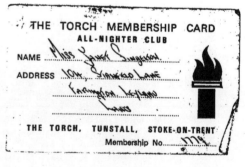

THE TORCH MEMBERSHIP CARD
ALL-NIGHTER CLUB

NAME Miss

ADDRESS

THE TORCH, TUNSTALL, STOKE-ON-TRENT
Membership No

# 3

# A Little Togetherness

*'The Torch sound system was horrific but it hit you right in the heart. The dance floor was like a well. When it was full it was like a sea of human excitement.'*

Midlander Chris Burton is a businessman with a capital B. An entrepreneur and bon viveur who believes passionately in whatever he is doing. He is the man who once promoted the Beatles on a ten-day tour in the early 60s. The man who put together the Mersey Beat Showcase, featuring Jerry and the Pacemakers, Billy J Kramer, et al.

If you saw a live act at the King's Hall in Stoke, it was probably courtesy of Mr Burton. Even more legendary were the parties he threw at his nearby office after these gigs (where you could rub shoulders with the likes of John Lennon and Mick Jagger). By the age of twenty-three, Chris was managing the Hollies and got them their first recording contract on Parlaphone. He owned two E-type Jags and a palatial home and had all the trappings of success.

Mr Burton can tell a tale or two about those heady days of the swinging 60s. But despite all his achievements, he is best remembered by tens of thousands of people for running a nightclub called the Golden Torch. Just the mention of its name is enough to give grown men goosebumps or their faces a faraway, glazed look as they contemplate what many argue was the greatest all-nighter of all time.

The venue that became the Torch was situated, bizarrely, in a quiet residential street in Hose Street, Tunstall, Stoke-on-Trent.

Turning down the side street now, with rows of terraced houses on two sides and a cul-de-sac at the far end, it is difficult to imagine how a nightclub that could become famous throughout Britain could occupy such a small site. The hallowed ground that once held the Torch is now a carpark for an adjoining company's building.

Imagine the horror of grannies living in a previously quiet terraced street when a nightclub appeared right in the middle of their cosy corner of Tunstall. Suddenly there were hundreds and hundreds of youngsters on scooters, in cars and on foot, converging on little Hose Street. And when the all-nighters began, imagine the constant thudding bass line that must have almost shaken them out of their beds as they tossed and turned trying in vain to sleep.

Originally on the site there had been a church, then a roller-skating rink and then the Regent Cinema. Chris bought it in 1963, knocked it down and turned it into a lavishly designed nightclub at a cost of around £25,000. The surrounding houses were at the time due for demolition to make way for a bus station, but that never happened. That would eventually be one of the many factors that ultimately led to the club's downfall.

The brand-new Golden Torch was fashioned on Roman lines and featured an arena of gleaming marble pillars with sculptures and wrought-iron spears. A balcony, bars, a snack bar and a coffee bar gave local Mods plenty of places to wander in between dancing. Outside, there was a tableau of a Roman chariot and horses on the wall. Hardly the stuff of which Northern Soul legends are made, you might think. But all that was to come later.

The Torch's gala opening night on 30 January 1965, featured the Mersey sounds of Billy J Kramer and the Dakotas. Local group Carl Mann and the Candymen were the support group. The club – billed as the greatest teenage rendezvous since 34 BC – charged six shillings (30p) admission and the opening night was a storming success.

Resident DJ was Barmy Barry, a Jimmy Savile-type character with a blond mop of hair and an endless stream of gags. He already had a massive following in the Stoke area and proved a great draw for local crowds in the Torch's early years.

The venue's policy of live bands and chart music continued until the late 60s, with live acts including the Kinks, Dave, Dee, Dozy, Beaky, Mick and Titch, Amen Corner, Wayne Fontana and the Mindbenders and even a young Rod Stewart appearing. Jimmy Savile himself and a certain Peter Stringfellow were among the DJs who later found great fame.

The Torch's music policy always leaned towards soul, ensuring a regular crowd of Mods. In those days, however, where there were Mods there were usually Rockers. And there was usually trouble. Ex-Wigan Casino DJ Dave Evison, a regular at the Torch at the Wednesday and Friday night sessions, said: 'There was a lot of rivalry and fighting in those days between Mod gangs and the greasers. There was often trouble. Even when the all-nighters started there was initially a bit of resentment towards the all-nighter crowd. It was rival gangs from rival towns. Then it all settled down.'

Ex-regular Jon Made, of Audlem, Stoke, recalls: 'On Saturday nights some of us would leave the Torch at closing time and ride up to the Twisted Wheel in Manchester for the all-nighters. We would sleep right through Sunday and then visit The Crystal, Newcastle, in the evening. One lasting memory for me was New Year's Eve 1968 when Johnny Johnson and the Bandwagon were live on stage at the Torch. Lambrettas and Vespas were parked outside, mirrors and chrome glistening under the street lamps.'

Chris Burton himself loved soul music and fondly remembers visiting the Twisted Wheel to see bands like Geno Washington and the Ram Jam Band. But he was still not convinced about what was becoming known as Northern Soul. After some arm-twisting by Torch DJ Keith Minshull, who was rapidly gaining a reputation as a rare soul innovator, Chris however agreed to give Northern Soul a try.

It was a culture shock to Chris to abandon his policy of building a night around a live act or a well-known DJ, but he agreed to give a Northern Soul all-nighter a try. It ran from 8.30 pm to 8.30 am on 11 March 1972. Suddenly the focal point was on local DJs like the aforementioned Mr Minshull and Colin Curtis (The Kingspinners) and the rare soul output of 1960s black America.

Chris said his initial response to Keith's suggestion was that he must be joking. But the night was a huge success and he was hooked. He told the Northern Soul fanzine *Manifesto*: 'I remember turning up at the first one and saying to Keith, "Are these guys for real?" I mean there was no presentation or anything, just a room full of kids dancing to music that I'd never heard of.'

Stoke's Dave Evison was among the local soul fans who made the leap from the 'early' sessions to the all-nighters where the music was rarer and unfamiliar. He said: 'I had already been to the venue about 200 times, but the first all-nighter was different. The atmosphere was great, and the crowd was different. People came from all walks of life, from all areas of the country and were under one roof enjoying this great music. The music was different. It was refreshing. Everything was brand-new to us. I think the fact that it was a weekly all-nighter was crucial, for the sake of continuity. When you look at the great all-nighters like the Wheel and Wigan, they were all weekly events. If somebody had the nerve to do it now and put on a weekly all-nighter it would work.'

A key factor in the Torch success story was the DJing combination of long-time friends Keith Minshull and Colin Curtis. Stoke-born Colin Diamond was only twelve when he decided he wanted to be a professional DJ. So he adopted the stage name of Colin Curtis so his teachers would not find out about his out-of-school activities. His early love of Motown led him into more esoteric forms of soul music. By the age of nine he was a keen pop fan and record collector. Then his grandparents gave him an old Bush radio and he started to retune it to pirate radio stations like Radio Caroline to hear the latest black music. Soul singers like James Carr were already among his idols by the time he was ten.

Soon Colin discovered his love of DJing at local youth clubs. 'I suppose like most DJs there was something egotistical about it,' he said. 'I tried it for a while and people gave me encouragement from there. I loved it. If I hadn't been a DJ I'm sure I would have been something else on stage.'

He recalled how he and Keith were sharing DJing at a youth

club where the decks were hidden from the dance floor. 'We would put on something like the Platters' "Sweet Sweet Loving" and then run around to see if they were dancing, and then run back and put another record on.'

Colin said Keith had been a great influence on him and had done a great deal for the Northern Soul scene. The two became good friends through meeting in local record shops. Colin looked up to the older man – 'Keith had the records and I was a big mouth' – he explained. 'Keith is totally misunderstood. He is a great, great character. Some people get the wrong impression of him. He is totally genuine and has given 100 per cent to the scene for so many years.'

Keith went on to DJ at the Friday night soul nights at the Torch while Colin enhanced his reputation as a mobile DJ. He also found himself compering at major gigs like the Who and Led Zeppelin at Trentham Gardens in Stoke.

The first time Colin went to the Torch – wearing a violet jacket and purple flares – he was flabbergasted at the rare soul sounds.

At the age of eighteen he was spotted by Torch owner Chris Burton and invited to join the DJ line-up at the club. The Friday nights became more and more popular – attracting crowds from Wolverhampton, Birmingham, and Manchester as word spread.

Then Keith talked Chris Burton into trying an all-nighter and the rest is history. Keith and Colin DJ'd the entire first night between them – for which they received £10 each – and the Torch legend was born. Colin soon found that even DJs had to queue up to get into the club. 'If the queue was up to the chip shop you knew it was going to be a full house. The excitement of standing in the queue hearing the music coming from the Torch has never been equalled anywhere. I have never known anything like it.

'The Torch sound system was horrific but it hit you right in the heart. The dance floor was like a well. When it was full it was like a sea of human excitement.'

Colin is in no doubt about the biggest record at the Torch – the instrumental 'Sliced Tomatoes' by Just Brothers. Twenty-six years later it would be reworked into a Top Ten hit by Fatboy

Slim. '"Sliced Tomatoes" was *the* record. When it came on you couldn't get on the dance floor,' he said.

Although the Torch DJs were finding lots of rare imports they played many new and nearly new releases. Colin played First Choice and 'This is the House Where Love Died' three weeks after its release. The very 70s 'Nightlighters' with KayGee was a massively popular instrumental.

The Torch is also where the DJs encountered the now-infamous record collector Simon Soussan. The immaculately dressed Frenchman, whose roots were in America and who also had contacts with French record collectors, amazed soul fans when he appeared with his record box crammed with just about every rarity Northern Soul fans craved.

Simon's sources and ear for music were impeccable and he became a friend of the Torch DJs. Once Colin Curtis went to visit him at his flat in Leeds and was astonished at what he saw. In a white flat with white carpets and a white piano, he had a sideboard crammed full of rare soul 45s in mint condition in cardboard sleeves.

Simon made it clear he did not want to sell – he wanted to swap records with his fellow connoisseurs. To emphasize the point that he did not need the money, he dumped £20,000 in cash on the bed.

Said Colin: 'We were discovering more and more rare records but he was coming up with some other really great stuff. He took it to a different plane.'

The Kingspinners were joined each week by Ian TNT Turner, Alan Day, Martyn Ellis, and Johnny Beggs. Chris Burton recalls: 'Musically I loved the scene, but, more importantly, the energy created by the crowd was incredible.'

Suddenly the Torch acquired a national reputation amongst the Northern Soul fraternity, and the 680-capacity venue was creaking under the weight of far too many punters for its own good. Chris estimates the Torch pulled in up to 1,400 on an exceptional night, which, along with drugs problems, brought the Hose Street club to the attention of the local constabulary.

The DJ rota itself ensured loyal followers came with them from their usual haunts. Alan Day brought fans from the 76

Club in Burton-on-Trent, Martyn Ellis had fans from the Pendulum in Manchester, Pep from the Catacombs in Wolverhampton, Ian Levine from Blackpool Mecca, and so on. At its peak the Torch had more than 5,000 members. For a time it was the country's only all-nighter, and by popular opinion created the template for the Northern Soul scene which has flourished ever since.

US-based live soul bands ensured the Torch stayed at the forefront of the underground Northern Soul scene. The Drifters, Edwin Starr, James and Bobby Purify, Fontella Bass, Oscar Toney Jr, Junior Walker, the Elgins – all graced the stage. Even the smooth falsetto soul of the Stylistics went down brilliantly with the crowd. But to anyone who was a Torch regular, there was one event that surpassed all others.

On 9 December 1972, Chicago label Okeh's legendary soulster Major Lance played a storming set that was captured for posterity on the Contempo label's *Major Lance Live at the Torch* album.

Major was perfect fodder for the Northern Soul fraternity. His silky vocals and the driving beat of the uptempo arrangements were too much for the American and British pop-buying public – only 'Um, Um, Um, Um, Um' and 'It's the Beat' made any impression on the charts. On the other hand, 'Ain't No Soul', 'Investigate', 'Monkey Time', and the powerful 'You Don't Want Me No More' were Okeh anthems in the north of England, very collectable and essential on any Northern Soul venue's playlist. When the artist himself flew over to England with a full backing band, a sell-out at the Torch was assured.

Dave recalled how he spent the daytime prior to the Chicago recording star's famous appearance ferrying cups of coffee from his then girlfriend's nearby house across to the Torch as Major went through his rehearsals.

The night's show left Dave reaching for superlatives. He recalled: 'If like me you were privileged to be there, no amount of words can describe the excitement, atmosphere and pure unadulterated enjoyment of the audience as we screamed, danced, applauded or simply gazed in awe at one of America's great soul heroes.

'Major undoubtedly enjoyed it, as much as if not more than we did. It was a one-off when everything came together in perfect harmony.'

Chris's recollection of that golden era is a little different: 'The Major Lance gig was legendary and Inez and Charlie Foxx were brilliant, but for me the Stylistics were the best. It was as if you had been transported to one of their big live shows in the States. The level of showmanship was absolutely superb. I'm getting goosebumps just remembering it.'

Ex-Torch regular Rod Baker, of Cleckheaton, Yorkshire, was introduced to the wonderful world of Northern Soul after acquiring a taste for Motown and 60s soul. He and his friends Paul (Smithy), Pete (Sid) and Nicky were members of a scooter club, but differed from the others in that their interest in the Mod scene centred on the music.

Rod takes up the story: 'One day back in the early 70s we were approached by a couple of guys who were older than us and used to frequent the Twisted Wheel. Their names were Neil Saville (Sav) and Mick Fitzpatrick. They had seen how we enjoyed our soul music so much and suggested that we tagged along with them to visit this club near Stoke called the Torch. This was going to be our very first foray into the world of Northern Soul all-nighters. You can guess how excited we were.

'Anyway, the day came and we set off on the Friday evening to Southport to stay with one of Mick's friends. We stayed up most of the night listening to all these new sounds. Wow! The following day we caught the train to Tunstall. A lifetime begins here! Getting off the train at our destination I was amazed to see all these people trudging up the road from the station carrying holdalls, wearing what seemed to be very baggy trousers and sunglasses. It was just like going to a football match but this was so much more amazing. Anyway we reached the Torch, queued up, paid our admission fees, went through the door and that's when it hit us!

'The atmosphere inside was like nothing I ever experienced anywhere before (and since for that matter); it was so thick you could literally cut it with a pair of scissors. I remember thinking to myself "Wow, this is for me!" It was packed, dancers doing all sorts of acrobatics. I had never seen this before, for most of that first night I stood in amazement just soaking up the atmosphere.

'So started our regular weekend fix of Northern Soul. We very quickly became members of the Torch, and visited the club every week until its sad closure.'

Like many Torchies, Rod has great memories of the night Major Lance appeared live. But his are slightly different: 'I recall being at the *Major Lance Live at the Torch Night*, sitting up in the alcove at the side of the stage, when I felt my back become soaking wet. I spun round ready to give someone a piece of my mind when, lo and behold, it was him, Major Lance, standing there looking at me, smiling, saying sorry for spilling his drink all over me in the push. "Woa, no need to say sorry, Major, do it again anytime."

'I saw Sam & Dave there one time, and what a show they put on. Fantastic. Even the Drifters were there and I actually met them that night, and the week after they were at Batley Variety Club – where we met them again and they remembered us from the Torch and they could not believe the atmosphere at the Torch. They were asking us all sorts of questions about the place. That was the effect the Torch had on people.

'We used to start on a Friday night at the Central Club, Leeds. Saturday night first stop was the Intercon at Wakefield, then we'd drive down to the Torch, leave in the morning, go for a swim at the baths in Stoke, head up the motorway to Burnley, home for work on Monday morning. Then to the Blue Room (Sale Mecca) on a Monday evening – that was some regular weekend soul living. God knows now how we did it!

'When the Torch closed we eventually moved on to Wigan Casino, and in my humble opinion it was just not the same. Yes it was busy, yes the music was OK (a bit poppy at times), but something was missing. I'm still not sure what that was, maybe the originality of the Torch or what? But soon after that I dropped out of the scene to start DJing (unfortunately not Northern Soul).'

*Roderick Baker's top ten Torch sounds*

'You're Gonna Make Me Love You' Sandi Sheldon
'Free For All' Philip Mitchell
'Cause You're Mine' Vibrations
'Running For My Life' Roscoe Sheldon
'Just Like the Weather' Nolan Chance
'A Love You Can Depend On' Brenda & the Tabulations
'I'm Standing' Rufus Lumley
'A Little Togetherness' Younghearts
'That's Alright' Ed Crook
'Hold On To My Baby' Cavaliers
'Blowing My Mind To Pieces' Bob Relf

Eric 'Ezzie' Brown of Gloucester was given some magical memories in May 1998 when his brother returned his 'best box' of Torch sounds, all on original labels.

'Too Late', 'Standing in the Darkness', 'Quick Change Artist', 'You Just Don't Know', 'One in a Million' and so on, are some of the titles that jumped out at Ezzie and took him back to the great Tunstall venue.

He says: 'You ask for memories – just seeing Sam & Dave in full-length fur coats and big beards . . . Junior Walker lying on the stage playing his sax . . . the Drifters – wow – Edwin Starr . . . Major Lance . . . my brother fell asleep on the balcony and missed the whole two sets! Chubby Checker blaring as you go into the reception areas ready to pay – and then the incredible buzz. What about the flooded toilets? And the entire Staffordshire constabulary wandering around in massive raincoats trying to blend in, desperate to catch someone doing something, anything, illegal? It was all part of the magic.'

One Torch DJ immortalized on the famous *Major Lance Live at the Torch* LP is Martyn Ellis. When the band started to play and stopped suddenly owing to a technical hitch as Major waited in the wings, MC Martyn quickly ad-libbed to fill in the embarrassing pause. He decided to take the blame and quipped: 'Another typical Martyn Ellis cock-up!' So listeners to the LP

THE TORCH - TUNSTALL
Stoke-on-Trent
*"The All Night Event of 72"*
Saturday, October 14th 1972

**The**
**Drifters**

ON STAGE AT MIDNIGHT
OPEN 8-30 pm to 8-30 am

№    400

Advance Ticket £1        Guests £1-25

are still to this day treated to Martyn's immortal words before Major Lance thunders on to the stage to tumultuous applause.

Martyn, from Wythenshawe, Manchester, was another vital part of the Torch success story. Another graduate of the youth club DJing school, Martyn was appearing at the over-21s club, Mr Smith's, in Manchester while still at school. From there it was a short hop to the Twisted Wheel, where he refined his knowledge and love of rare soul music. Roscoe Robinson's 'That's Enough' and Chuck Jackson's 'Chains of Love' were just two of the Wheel sounds that convinced him of the direction in which he wanted to move.

Trips to Blackpool Mecca and DJing stints at the Pendulum in Manchester enhanced his reputation as a DJ with an in-your-face personality. 'I've never been a shrinking violet,' said Martyn. 'I have always thought that my job was to entertain. If people are entertained by someone putting on records and saying nothing, fair enough. A lot of people liked me because of my big mouth and others said it got on their nerves. I once announced the Invitations' "What's Wrong With Me Baby?" and a couple of minutes later a girl came up to me with a list of ten things that she said were wrong with me!'

Martyn landed himself a job at the Torch by sheer cheek. He was part of the travelling army of punters that made up the Torch regulars and became friendly with resident spinners Colin Curtis and Keith Minshull. After he regularly hung around the decks trying to see what records they were playing, they agreed to let him have a go. Martyn responded with his own brand of rare and current release items and became part of the team.

The highlight for him was working with legendary Chicago soulster Major Lance during the live appearance and album. 'I had been listening to his recordings like "Investigate" for years and to actually meet and work with the guy was amazing. He was such a professional. He walked from the back of the Torch all the way to the front through hundreds and hundreds of people and stood at the side of the stage sweating buckets. I introduced him and the band started to play and then suddenly they stopped.

'I said "Another typical Martyn Ellis cock-up" because I didn't want the crowd to get upset with the band. It was a technical problem with the recording. I decided to take the blame. The band started up again and they were brilliant.

'After the show we went out to the recording truck and Major was listening to the tapes. He couldn't believe that all these white English kids loved his music so much. He was a really nice guy – he sang "Gypsy Woman" to me a cappella. It was brilliant.'

Martyn readily admits that drugs were part of the culture of the Torch all-nighters and that he was no angel. 'I used to use amphetamines. It wasn't big. It wasn't clever. But I took them. The drugs problems at the Torch were no worse than at the Casino, but the drug squad were there practically every all-nighter. All we wanted to do was stay up all night and enjoy the music.'

After the Torch closed, Martyn started to attend Wigan Casino as a punter. After a few months he was added to the DJ roster, and began to play his trademark oldies during his 5 am spot. 'People were starting to flag by that time and I decided to give them something they would know. That got them back on their feet and got everybody dancing again. As long as the floor was full I knew I was doing something right.'

And if they didn't dance, Martyn would bully and cajole them back on to the floor with his infectious delivery. After a 20-year break from the scene, Martyn is now back DJing and enjoying every minute.

Guesting at a soul night in 1999, at Preston Grasshoppers

Club, Martyn found complete strangers shaking his hand and slapping him on the back. 'That's what gives me the biggest buzz. Call it ego if you want, but it's brilliant that you can make people feel like that,' he said.

*Martyn Ellis's Top Ten*

'Too Late' Williams and Watson
'Girl Across the Street' Moses Smith
'Love, Love, Love' Bobby Hebb
'Everything's Gonna Be Alright' P P Arnold
'Time's a-Wasting' The Fuller Brothers
'Take Your Love and Run' Barbara Lewis
'Magic Potion' Lou Johnson
'Share a Little Love With Me' The Monitors
'Soul Galore' Jackie Wilson
'Music To My Heart' Patti Austin

Keith Minshull himself, while agreeing that the Major Lance gig was awesome, says there were many top-class live acts, like Edwin Starr, Otis Leavell, and Junior Walker at the Torch. But the one that stands out in his mind as the greatest was the Stylistics.

By 1973, the attentions of the authorities were making life difficult for Mr Burton and the Torch clientele because of overcrowding and drugs problems. Keith and Colin decided 'it wasn't a very healthy place to be' and took up residence back at Blackpool Mecca.

The police were frequent visitors to the club, with an eye on both drugs and overcrowding. Chris Burton says he did his best to cooperate with the drug squad, and even approached them for help in November 1972, but he must have felt he was fighting a losing battle. On the roads to and from the Torch, police were mounting spot checks and even roadblocks to capture soul fans who they felt were giving their town a bad name.

Colin Curtis said: 'I don't think the drug taking was out of control in relation to what went on at Wigan Casino and today's Ecstasy scene. People were doing drugs because they cared about the music and wanted to stay awake. However, we didn't need all the negative stuff that was going down at the Torch. It was depressing and we decided to move on.'

The Stoke's *Evening Sentinel* reported in May 1973, two months after the club's closure, how two men, aged eighteen and twenty, were each sentenced to three months in a detention centre for going equipped for burglary. They had planned to raid a chemist's shop to steal drugs to sell at the Torch, magistrates were told. Mr J Farnon, representing both men, said the Torch was 'a den of iniquity'. He added: 'Boys and girls came from all over the country. Drugs were peddled right, left and centre. Unfortunately these two boys got involved in that club . . . and got under the influence of other people at the club.'

Another case reported by the same newspaper told how police stopped several vehicles on the A500. A Cheltenham man who was found with yellow tablets that he admitted he was going to sell at twelve for £1 at the Torch didn't know whether to laugh or cry when analysis revealed they only contained a harmless mixture of vitamins. Three other men in cars stopped by police on the A500 were fined for possessing amphetamines.

This was merely the tip of the iceberg as far as the pressure on the Torch was concerned. When Chris Burton went to court in March 1973 to renew the club's drinks and entertainment licence, he found massive opposition from the police. Under the headline TUNSTALL CLUB A DRUG CENTRE, the Stoke *Evening Sentinel* reported how senior police were appalled at the goings-on at the country's leading soul venue. The paper told how Mr David McEvoy, for the police, informed the city licensing justices that 'The Golden Torch has a national reputation as a place where drugs can be obtained, and for trafficking in drugs.'

The report went on:

Since July 1972, 40 people had been involved with drugs offences in connection with the Golden Torch. Many of these were cases where the individual had packets of tablets ready for distribution on the premises. The club's all-nighter on Saturdays had attracted people from a wide area – from the south coast to the north of England. Some came from

Scotland, Mr McEvoy said. Since the all-nighters started last March, the drug problem had grown and the police had become concerned. From October, the country drugs squad had had people on the premises, he said.

'The Justices were told that Mr Burton had visited the Burslem police station in November and admitted that a drugs problem existed in the club and said he wished to cooperate with the police. But police say this was a mere pretence on Burton's part. The police arrested a considerable number of people who were there, but this was not due to Burton's help,' said Mr McEvoy.

Mr McEvoy said the main police objections to the renewal of the licences were the drugs problems, young people being admitted under age, people with criminal records – some for violence – being there, poor hygiene at the club, and the practice of padlocking and chaining emergency exits.

Finally, he added, the club, which had a licence for 400 people, had been catering for well over that number. On one occasion there were over 1,000 people present.

Things did not get any better for the Torch as the hearing went on. The following day, readers were treated to the headline 70 PER CENT OF CLUB USERS 'INVOLVED WITH DRUGS'.

The report began:

The head of the county drug squad yesterday told city licensing justices that nearly three-quarters of the people visiting the Golden Torch, Tunstall, were involved in drugs. 'Using information from neighbouring drug squads as well as my own officers, I would say that 70 per cent of the people going to the club are involved in drug abuse,' said Detective-Sergeant Ernest Gardiner.

He explained that many youngsters visiting the club had to travel great distances. 'They leave home early on Saturday and return late Sunday – they need a stimulant. This is the most popular club of its type north of London – I do not know of a similar one in the country.'

The report told how Detective-Sergeant Gardiner said the problems at the Torch came to his attention in the early months of 1972. In September he detailed two officers to visit the all-nighter. After a meeting with Mr Burton it was arranged that he should point out to the police the people who pushed drugs in the club. The detectives would then take the dealers outside and arrest them.

But Mr Burton did not do that, claimed the officer. Detective-Sergeant Gardiner said: 'We set out to show there was a problem and not to deal with it. We realized we could not possibly deal with it because of the immensity of it. We are a force of seven and more than 400 people are involved,' the *Sentinel* reported.

Detective-Sergeant Gardiner denied under cross-examination that the drug squad had gone out to 'set the club up'. The justices heard that many of the Torch regulars were aged fifteen and sixteen. Detective-Constable Malcolm Cartwright said: 'When I was there, there were 1,500 present. Pills were being pushed openly in front of me and most of the conversations I heard were about drugs.'

The onslaught against the Torch continued with testimony from a resident living directly opposite the entrance. He told the court: 'The noise of people departing from the premises is very bad. I have had to get up at 2 am or 3 am on a Sunday morning to go downstairs. Once someone was strumming a guitar in the street.'

He admitted, however, that Mr Burton had helped to solve the problem by supplying No Parking signs in the street and had put someone on the entrance to the club to stop the disturbances.

Chris Burton finally got to put his side of the story when he went into the witness box, giving rise to the headline NO JUNKIES IN MY CLUB – MANAGER.

Chris told the court: 'We are very proud of the people we deal with in the club. They are a wonderful set who love their music. They are not junkies.' He challenged the 70 per cent figure that the police had put forward as the ratio of drug users in the club: 'I would say that probably five per cent is a possibility,' he said.

The *Evening Sentinel* report detailed how the owner first became aware of a drugs problem in September, when members alerted him to the situation.

'We decided this sort of situation was not in the interests of the club. We banned these people from the club, withdrew their memberships and took photographs of them,' Chris was reported as saying. 'We dealt with around ten to twelve people during that month. The photographs were kept in the pay box so that the cashier could identify them. I went to the police about the drug problem. I was genuinely assisting them to stamp out the problem at the Torch.

'I do not care about people taking drugs as long as it is not on my premises. As licensee I have an obligation to report the situation to the police.' He told the court that on one occasion he had pointed out a pusher to the police but was told not to take any action.

Chris revealed that since the Torch opened on 31 January 1965, more than half a million people had visited the venue. In 1972 there were 62,000 customers from a membership of 12,500. 'This is a specialized form of music that has its devotees and they are very passionately involved with their music. We have catered for a need – the demand has been there,' he told the court.

His defence concluded by denying police claims that emergency exits had been padlocked. He personally unlocked the doors each night. He said the club was well-known nationally. There were only two other all-night clubs in the country where the same facilities existed, and a club in Bolton (Va-Va's) that occasionally ran all-night sessions.

The then *Blues and Soul* editor John Abbey, and journalist Frank Elson were among the defence witnesses called to speak out for the Torch. Mr Abbey said the Torch was one of the best venues in the country. 'Drugs and soul music do not go hand in hand,' he said.

Mr Elson said: 'Occasionally I do see passing of drugs and talk about "gear", but you have this in every club you go to.' He added that 99 per cent of the people who went to the Torch went for the music only, and since the drug squad had moved in the problem had virtually died out.

Another regular, soul music promoter David Daniels, said some of the evidence given against the Torch had been exaggerated. 'The Torch is one of the establishments in the area that has tended to be well staffed . . . they do not have any trouble at the club,' he said.

The parting shot for the police case came from Mr David McEvoy, who said it was clear there was a substantial drug problem in the area. 'The only way to remove it is to close down the premises. This was not a bona fide club and there have been breaches of the regulations. They have been packing individuals in to maximize profits,' he claimed.

And that was that. The licensing magistrates retired to consider their decision and returned to utter the words that Chris Burton and all soul fans had been dreading: that the Golden Torch's liquor and entertainments licences were being revoked.

Under the headline TORCH CLUB REFUSED NEW LICENCES, the *Evening Sentinel* reported, on 16 March 1973, how licensing chairman Mr Gordon Dale had declared: 'Young people are attending this club and we have got to protect the young people in this city. The Licensing Committee feel they cannot allow these things to carry on where young people and drugs are involved.'

Technically, the club could still operate pending an appeal, but Chris abandoned that option, knowing that the odds were stacked against him. For sale signs went up outside the Torch and Chris declared he was making no appeal. 'Because of the bad publicity that was given to the club I don't think it could ever get back to the success it once enjoyed on the policy of soul music for teenagers. With the publicity – whether true or false – I think parents would be right in keeping their kids away. The club is labelled as a drugs centre. I don't think it will ever get rid of that image or stigma.'

Dave Evison remembers the last all-nighter with some sadness. He said: 'There was hardly anybody there and it just fizzled out. It wasn't a big celebration. There was no announcement that it was going to be the last all-nighter. It closed about 3 am and we all went off to Leeds or somewhere.'

The Torch left Dave and many other regulars with a host of great memories and a wealth of musical knowledge that in the coming years he would pass on to Wigan Casino patrons.

Dave smiles at amusing incidents like when a girl with heavily lacquered hair asked him for a light and he accidentally set fire to her hair. He solved the problem by pouring his pint over her head. On another occasion when he was sporting a shirt bearing the name 'Eddie Parker' – his all-time favourite singer – he was lambasted by a stranger for being so arrogant as to have his own name put on his clothes.

'For me,' said Dave, 'the Torch had more camaraderie and good old-fashioned atmosphere than anywhere I've ever experienced either before or since. It was destined to be a great venue and it certainly lived up to it.

'I have to say that had it not been for the quality soul music that the Torch DJs, especially Keith and Colin, introduced me to, I in turn would not have had the honour and pleasure of doing the same thing for thousands of soul fans at Wigan Casino and countless other venues years later.'

He does not attempt to deny that drugs problems existed at the Torch, but he thinks the situation was exaggerated. He said: 'The police didn't like what was going on at all. The problem did exist, but it wasn't as bad as it was later at Wigan. In fairness to soul fans, the reason they took drugs was to stay awake and enjoy the music. Many saw it as all right for the weekend, but on Monday it was back to work and that was it.'

Chief Superintendent Kenneth Gibson of Stoke police told the *Evening Sentinel* in 1973 that he was pleased to have rid the town of the problems associated with the Torch. 'In my view the closure of the premises was the only solution to the problem. The outcome has been most satisfactory.'

Satisfactory for him, maybe, but for thousands of Northern Soul fans it was devastating.

Chris Burton recalls: 'The drug problem was there and was used as the excuse to close the club. The real reason was the residents opposite, and who could blame them. I feel that the authorities were out to get me . . . success does create its problems with some.

'I have no regrets about the Torch, and I would do it all the same way again. I wish I had it now!'

\*

*20 selected Torch floorfillers*

'Sliced Tomatoes'  Just Brothers
'Surprise Party for Baby'  Vibrations
'Unsatisfied'  Lou Johnson
'Prove Yourself a Lady'  James Bounty
'I Still Love You'  The Superlatives
'I've Got Something Good'  Sam and Kitty
'Quick Change Artist'  The Soul Twins
'Compared to What'  Mr Flood's Party
'Just Like the Weather'  Nolan Chance
'A Little Togetherness'  The Younghearts
'Crackin' Up Over You'  Roy Hamilton
'Free For All'  Philip Mitchell
'Our Love is in the Pocket'  J J Barnes
'Time's A-Wasting'  The Fuller Brothers
'I Got the Fever'  The Prophets
'Just Ask Me'  Lenis Guess
'Angel Baby'  Darrell Banks
'Crying Over You'  Duke Browner
'I Love You Baby'  Cindy Scott
'Inky Winky Wang Dang Do'  Dramatics

*Dave Evison's Top Ten Torch tunes*

'Keep On Talking'  James Barnett
'You're the One'  Ronnie Walker
'Love You Baby'  Eddie Parker
'I'm So Glad'  Herb Johnson
'Potion of Love'  Ambers
'Have More Time'  Marvin Smith
'A Mighty Good Way'  Robert Banks
'I Can't Get Away'  Bobby Garrett
'What Would I Do'  Superiors
'I Feel Strange'  Wonderettes

# 4

# Turn the Beat Around

*'Here are 2,000 soul brothers and sisters grooving out to a
record that was never issued here, and which wasn't even
in the American Top 100.'*

Believe it or not, Ian Levine never wanted to be a DJ. That may
seem a bizarre statement, almost like saying that Alan Shearer
never had any intention of becoming a professional footballer,
but Ian insists it is true. He wanted to discover, own and let
others share his enjoyment of the best soul music he could lay his
hands on.

Thoughts of picking up a microphone and dropping the
needle on to the latest rarities in front of crowds open-mouthed
with admiration were far from his mind when he discovered his
taste for black American soul records.

The idea of going into a recording studio on the other side of
the Atlantic with his childhood soul idols and laying down
hundreds of tracks for his own record label was a mere fantasy.
The thought of moulding the early careers of boy bands like
Take That back in the UK never even entered his head.

No DJ before or since has ever inspired such high feelings
among the Northern Soul crowd. Ian Levine has experienced it
all – from the adulation of being hailed a messiah in the early 70s
and being an award-winning record producer, to the bitter
personal attacks several years later that led to him quitting the
scene in disgust.

He seems to attract controversy and admiration in equal
amounts, but one thing is certain: his place in Northern Soul

history is assured. The Blackpool-born son of wealthy club-owners Sidney and Ruth Levine, Ian started collecting Tamla Motown records while in his early teens. By 1968 he had started hanging around Gary Wilde's cigarette kiosk near the offices of the town's evening newspaper. It was there the local Mods and soul fans would gather to chat, smoke and talk about the music being played at this club called the Twisted Wheel in Manchester.

Gary, a soul fan and mobile DJ, would meanwhile sell them records he knew were big at the Wheel for up to £5 a time. ('He was the first rare soul dealer,' says Ian.) Ian and his friends were fascinated by the music and the lifestyle led by the older lads but the young Levine realized his parents would never allow him to go to the Wheel. This didn't stop him enjoying the Wheel's music, however, and through his mates Bob Stevens and Stuart Bremner he developed a lifetime's passion for non-mainstream soul music.

From commercial Tamla Motown to less well-known items he was hearing on Kenny Everett's Radio Caroline show, Ian's record collection grew weekly. His friend Bob was buying British releases that would form part of the future Northern Soul playlists as they came out – Rufus Lumley's 'I'm Standing', The Incredibles' 'There's Nothing Else to Say', the Sapphires' 'Gotta Have Your Love' among them.

Stuart put Ian on to sounds like the Impressions' 'You've Been Cheating', and his quest for rare records was on. Ian started to tour shops in Blackpool which stocked ex-juke box records. He would snap them up at bargain prices and then swap them for rare records. 'I was buying them for two shillings and getting five shillings each for them, so it was quite profitable,' he recalled. 'It was fairly commercial stuff. "Heaven Must Have Sent You" (the Elgins), "These Things Will Keep Me Loving You" (the Velvelettes) was the sound I was into at the time and it got me into proper Northern Soul.'

All this time Ian was watching his older pals setting off for the Wheel. All the talk was of records like the Dynatones' 'The Fife Piper' and the American Poets' 'She Blew a Good Thing'. 'I longed to go, but it wasn't until I was seventeen that my parents would let me go,' he said.

By now, Levine had built up a collection of several thousand records, courtesy of holidays in the States with his parents. They would enjoy the sunshine and the USA experience, and young Ian would spend his holiday scouring junk shops and record shops for bargain 45s.

It was on one trip to Miami in 1968 that he made a discovery that was to change his whole outlook on soul music. Through his friend Stewart and the odd imported 45s that turned up in England he was gaining a taste for what would become known as Northern Soul. But nothing prepared him for the moment when he bought J J Barnes' 'Please Let Me In', on the Ric Tic label, for 'next to nothing'. He took it back to his hotel thinking he was going to get a Memphis-style non-Motown-sounding soul record of no great significance. When he dropped the needle on to the disc on his battery-operated portable record player, his heart skipped a beat. '*That* was the moment,' he recalls. 'I didn't expect it to have the Marvin Gaye-type sound that I would love. I heard his voice and I just melted. I must have played it fifty times in a row. From then on, I started collecting for real.'

His expeditions also unveiled Rose Batiste's 'Hit and Run', on Revilot, and other gems by Pat Lewis, Sonny Stitt and the Fantastic Four. Ian was discovering the commercial flops of Detroit and finding he liked them as much as the million-selling recordings of the likes of the Four Tops, the Supremes.

By the time he made it to the Wheel, he had tucked away some exclusive rarities that no one had ever heard of in the UK. He entered into the cooperative spirit of the Wheel with gusto, handing records to DJs for a trial spin.

He watched with amusement as he handed DJ Les Cockell his copy of Rose Batiste. As the perfectly paced exciting soul stomper set the dance floor alight at the Wheel, with the fans clapping and spinning in unison, Les 'practically fell to the floor, clutching his head and shouting Oooooh.'

Ian brought another box the following week, and Les gave more records their first British airing to an appreciative crowd. The Levine legend had begun. Who was this kid from Blackpool? How had he got hold of all these rarities? How many more had he got?

The answer was – plenty. By 1972, Ian Levine had a staggering 20,000 records, which grew to a peak of 60,000. Many of these records would form the staple diet of the playlists at the Blackpool Mecca and become part of Northern Soul folklore.

By 1971, the Wheel had closed and suddenly there were hundreds and hundreds of soul-hungry teenagers in search of a spiritual home. Ian and many others found one very close to home – at the Blackpool Mecca Locarno ballroom in Central Drive.

The vast 4,000-capacity venue had a main ballroom downstairs that attracted holidaymakers and visitors on free coaches in massive numbers. Drinking, cavorting and copping off with the opposite sex to the latest chart sounds were the order of the day among the trendy clubbers in the downstairs domain.

Upstairs, however, housed a smaller, oblong-shaped room called the Highland Room. It was dominated by a polished rectangular dance floor and was presided over by local DJ Tony Jebb – 'the first superstar DJ', according to Ian.

Tony was playing Motown tunes like Smokey Robinson and the Miracles' 'Tears of a Clown' and the Elgins' 'Heaven Must Have Sent You' and touching on the edges of Northern Soul.

Fellow DJ Stuart Freeman was playing pop records, which led Ian to recommend Les Cockell from the Wheel. Stuart found himself out in the cold and Les (backed by Ian Levine's records) was ensconced behind the decks with Tony at the Highland Room.

By now, Ian had perfected the art of skipping college (he was supposed to travel to Manchester University each day) and spending his train fare, scouring record shops for bargains which he could later re-sell. He recalls how Tony Jebb also benefited from the rapidly growing record mountain he was amassing at home. His playlist varied from the mainstream soul sounds of Arthur Conley's 'Sweet Soul Music' and Wilson Pickett's 'Land of a Thousand Dances' to the more obscure Little Richard's 'I Don't Want To Discuss It', Bobby Garrett's 'My Little Girl', Mamie Galore's 'It Ain't Necessary' and Johnny Sayles' 'Can't Get Enough of Your Love'.

'He paid me for borrowing my records,' said Ian. 'He fed off me, but I still had no aspirations to become a DJ at that time.' By the time *Blues and Soul* journalist Dave Godin made his first visit to the Mecca, Ian Levine's influence was becoming obvious, yet he was still not part of the line-up. The *Blues and Soul* article includes pictures of the DJs and main characters involved with the Mecca. Levine is referred to only as 'Ian', a local soul fan, and can be seen on three of the four pictures of regulars at the venue.

Dave Godin's piece of course increased the reputation of the Mecca tenfold as it was so obvious that he enjoyed the music, the crowd and the vibes. He even drew comparisons with the by-now sadly missed Twisted Wheel.

Godin talked about the passion that DJs Tony Jebb and Stuart Freeman had for the music, and the friendliness and genuine warmth he felt when introduced to many of the Highland Room regulars.

> I think it shows how soul music has become the only true underground music in the country now. Here are 2,000 soul brothers and sisters grooving out to a record that was never issued here, and which wasn't even in the American Top 100. And the record companies continue to sneer at what we fans try to tell them, and if they issued it would take all the credit and the BBC DJs would consider themselves way-out super cool cats for playing it! They just don't know how to cut the mustard, and each and every one of the young, together, hip people having a good time in the Highland Room that night

could tell them just where it's at and put them to shame in the process.

The theme of British-based record companies' ignorance of what was going on around them is a theme that would recur with great regularity over the next few years. It was only with the advent of the Northern Soul boom in 1974/5 and Pye Disco Demand that companies felt compelled to act and reissue rare soul recordings.

Godin's Mecca piece concluded euphorically: 'Maybe there are some who read this in the southern part of Britain who find it hard to understand why I rave so much about the Northern Soul scene, and perhaps this is because they have never been there and seen it first-hand themselves. Believe me, there is no equivalent in the south.'

Blackpool-based financial adviser Steve Kozlowski remembers the air of expectancy when it became known that *Blues and Soul*'s Dave Godin was going to visit the club.

Steve was a teenager living in Clitheroe when he first began to visit the Highland Room. Like many others, he classed himself a suedehead – short hair, sideburns, made-to-measure suits and the coolest music. By 1971 he was a regular at the Saturday night soul events and was captivated by the unique music. He said: 'It was unbelievable the amount of people who turned up because they heard Dave Godin was coming. It was absolutely heaving. I was chuffed to bits to meet him.'

Steve became aware through friends of a Blackpool lad called Ian (Levine) who seemed to have the ears of the DJs, particularly Les Cockell. Steve became friends with Les, who would often give the Clitheroe lads a lift to the Mecca. Les would usually have a girlfriend in tow, but it later became apparent this was all a sham, for Les was gay.

The Mecca's reputation for great music was growing steadily, but it was not uncommon for punters to bring their own singles along to play, particularly early in the night. Steve remembers a soul fan called Andy Grimshaw, whose mother ran the Lodestar at Ribchester, lending him a copy of Earl Jackson's 'Soul Self Satisfaction'. It was utterly unknown, and Ian persuaded Tony

Jebb to give it a spin. The next Steve heard, Tony had bought the record off Andy and it went on to become a Northern Soul anthem.

Records like 'Angel Baby' (George Carrow), 'Cracking Up Over You' (Roy Hamilton), and 'Talk of the Grapevine' (Donald Height) typify the early Mecca playlist for Steve.

Steve, who can nowadays be found running SK Financial Services in Blackpool, said: 'It was wonderful music. It was rare soul, not Northern Soul. No one was using that term then. Everyone was very smart. You had to be smart to get in. The Mecca was my favourite venue. It could be cliquish just like any other place. There were the backstabbers and a lot of guys that would rip you off just for fun. I knew Ian Levine just as a face in the crowd. I never had any idea he would become the lynchpin of the whole Northern Soul scene.'

The drugs problems that had dogged the Wheel and the Torch were by no means absent from the Highland Room. Even though it was not an all-nighter, amphetamines were still used, particularly if dancers were 'warming up' for an all-nighter.

A former regular said: 'I reckon about 80 per cent of the people there were on gear. It was a big part of it. The drugs squad were always there, and we knew who they were. If there wasn't an all-nighter on, we would go back to people's houses afterwards.'

Ian's Stateside trips were becoming more of a pilgrimage, with him returning home from holidays with his parents with up to 4,000 singles a time. His wealthy background was undoubtedly a help, as in the early 1970s foreign holidays were the domain of the privileged. Going to the States, not the neatly-priced package deal that many families enjoy today, was considered a once-in-a-lifetime experience.

The Levines, however, were able to go regularly, which gave the young soul fan access to warehouses, stores and second-hand shops that other Northern Soul DJs could only dream of. And Ian was showing a good business brain which showed that he could be self-sufficient. He would collect £100 each from half a dozen record collectors and DJs from the Highland Room to finance his trip. He would come back laden with brilliant soul obscurities, which he would pass to the grateful collectors. The going rate for such rarities in England was far greater than in the USA, where they were junk-shop fodder, so Mr Levine made a profit and everyone was happy.

Ian insists that he would still have the success he enjoyed in his life without his wealthy background. 'I would have got there in the end. I had the desire and the passion for it. My trips to America were funded with cash from record collectors. I had no money of my own at that time. I was fortunate that I was going on family holidays, but I would have succeeded in the end through another route.'

So the 5 cent junk-shop finds became £1 and £2 records among the Northern Soul fraternity, and would often be re-sold at many times that sum if a record became a 'monster' at the Mecca or elsewhere.

Meanwhile, Ian was getting a little frustrated with the playlists of Les Cockell. He felt Les was playing softer sounds like the Nitelighters' 'Kay Gee', whereas Ian's tastes were for sounds 'with real bollocks'. Sounds like Jackie Lee's 'Do the Temptation Walk' and Richard Temple's 'That Beating Rhythm' were more to Ian's liking. The latter track, a vocal version of Jimmy Conwell's 'Cigarette Ashes', was a key record in the development of rarer and rarer items on the Mecca's playlists. 'We knew about it but we didn't believe it existed,' said Ian. 'Nobody had ever seen a copy. We went down to the Catacombs one night and I found out what it was. I thought to myself, "I think I know where to find that." The next time I was in Miami I found it and brought it back.' Reputations are made on such stuff, and it was only a matter of time before Ian Levine would emerge from the shadows to be a top-name DJ.

One week Les Cockell got the flu and Ian was persuaded by Tony to do a stint behind the decks. 'I was so nervous, and apparently my microphone technique was atrocious!' But the sounds were brilliant and the pressure on Ian to continue the following week was immense. Les was horrified at the news that he was being replaced, and in a compromise his friend agreed to do alternate weeks.

Another significant event was the opening of the Golden Torch all-nighters in Tunstall, Stoke-on-Trent in 1972. Tony Jebb was 'poached' by Torch promoter Chris Burton, and Ian and Les were left to hold the fort.

Ian eventually realized that the Mecca's Saturday night soul sessions could not compete with the massive Torch all-nighters. Championed by Tony Jebb, Ian began to fight tooth and nail for a spot at the Torch. Eventually Chris Burton agreed and Ian joined Tony, Alan Day, Colin Curtis, Keith Minshull, Martyn Ellis, and the gang down in Stoke.

Ian, whose first DJ stint coincided with the now legendary live appearance of Major Lance, found at the Torch all-nighter how much the Northern Soul scene had evolved from his days at the Wheel. The music had become more obscure, and more import-based. Records were changing hands for big money. Jackie Lee's 'Darkest Days' fetched £50. Duke Browner's 'Crying Over You' was sold for £60.

This was the time when the Torch's drugs and overcrowding problems were bringing them to the attention of the authorities, and DJs began to desert it. Stoke-based DJs Keith Minshull and Colin Curtis left the Torch to reopen the soul nights at Blackpool Mecca, while Blackpool-based Levine passed them on the motorway to play the Torch!

Martyn Ellis and Ian, with help from Andy Hanley, shared the DJing at the final Torch all-nighter. Looking back at the main changes in those days, Ian said, 'I think the Wheel pioneered the scene, and the Mecca raised it to another level. The Torch was unique. It was everything that Wigan Casino aspired to be, but it was real. People who went first to the Wheel loved the Torch, but lots of people who went to the Torch hated Wigan.'

With Keith and Colin attracting big crowds at Blackpool Mecca, Ian began regular stints at the Top Rank in Hanley. But he was frustrated at the success the Mecca was enjoying, pulling in more than 1,000 regulars, while he was playing to smaller crowds in Hanley.

Ian and Colin Curtis had enormous respect for each other's musical tastes and ability to unearth the best Northern Soul records, and when, in the summer of 1973, Keith Minshull left the Mecca, Ian found himself in partnership with Colin Curtis back in the Highland Room. 'We were the most unlikely team,' said Ian. 'It was like Laurel and Hardy. Colin was the tall, skinny one with long hair and I was the short, fat one!'

Appearances aside, they formed a formidable partnership. For many people, these were the halcyon days of Blackpool Mecca, and the beginning of a fierce rivalry with the soon-to-open Wigan Casino all-nighters.

Ian and Colin made a secret pledge – to find and play the greatest Northern Soul records ever heard. Said Ian: 'We were both finding fantastic new records. We decided we would get together and unearth the greatest records anyone had ever heard on the Northern scene. I would go to America and find the records and I knew that if I came back with the greatest amount of records ever there would be nobody to touch us. I think the summer of 1973 was the best period ever in Northern Soul history.'

One of Ian's legendary scouting missions took him to a record warehouse called the Good Will in Miami, where there were a mind-boggling 250,000 US singles. Ian spent from 9 am to 6 pm every day of his summer holiday sifting through mounds of records in the former Salvation Army building. The vast majority had no sleeves on and some were in poor condition. Some were known, some were unknown, and Ian snapped up 4,000 of them at between 5 and 25 cents each. Among his finds were 'The Larue', Lara Edmund Jnr; The Glories' 'I Worship You Baby'; The Sweet Things' 'I'm In a World of Trouble'; Lee David's 'Temptation's Calling My Name'; Sam and Kitty's 'I've Got Something Good' to name just a few – and 'virtually every RCA white demo'.

The chief problem was keeping sounds exclusive and thwarting the bootleggers. A Mecca monster sound could very easily after a few plays end up in the shops as a 90p pressing, often a poor-quality and unauthorized reissue. All you needed was the title, artist and label, and enterprising record vultures like Simon Soussan would be able to track down a copy. Or a copy would be 'borrowed' from a DJ and pressed up in double quick time. Suddenly then every teenager had a cheap copy of the latest in-demand dancer, robbing the DJ and the venue of their exclusivity.

That's when the practice of 'covering up' records came into full swing. The only way to protect the identity of a record was to literally cover the label and invent a fictitious title and artist. In that way the DJ could hope to keep the real identity of a record secret for weeks, if not months. But Northern Soul fans are nothing if not resourceful and determined, and the secret usually came out eventually.

In the meantime, the DJs could buy time by calling the Coasters' 'Crazy Baby' 'My Heart's Wide Open' by Freddie Jones; Edie Walker's 'Good Guys' became 'Patricia Valentine's "You Can't Tell the Good Guys from the Bad"'; Melvin Carter's 'Midnight Brew' became 'Shing-A-Ling' at the Go-Go'. 'Breakaway' by the Steve Karmen Band became 'The Black Ship of Hell'. Sometimes, if the bootleggers were really baffled, they would press the disc with the fictitious title.

Ian and Colin devised a numbering system – Secret Sounds 1, 2, 3, etc – to cover up all their one-offs. Using a piece of patterned wallpaper, they would cover front and back of the label. Then just to make sure there was no tell-tale information in the run-out groove, they would add small pieces of Sellotape.

'We didn't cover up records to prevent other DJs from finding out what they were, it was purely to stop the bootleggers,' said Ian. 'But there were a lot of knowledgeable people around and eventually someone would come up with the real title. We used to have grand "uncovering ceremonies" in the Highland Room when it became pointless trying to keep someone a secret any longer!'

Even today Ian is fiercely proud of the records that he played first at the Mecca which became anthems at the Casino. 'Afternoon of the Rhino' by the Mike Post Coalition is seen as synonymous with Wigan Casino. 'I played that first,' says Ian. R D Taylor's 'There's a Ghost in My House' was also aired at the Mecca. But Wigan Casino founder Russ Winstanley's argument, whatever the who-played-it-first, is 'There's a big difference between playing a record and breaking it.'

Ian was a guest DJ in the first few months of the Wigan Casino events, but found himself given an ultimatum by Mecca manager Bill Pye: 'Choose them or us.' Ian chose to stay at the Mecca, as he was less than impressed by the Casino's music policy. 'Wigan never added anything to the picture,' he said. 'It wasn't innovative enough. I like Russ very much now, but there became a heated rivalry between me and Russ. He banned all my records from being played at the Casino and there was a sort of war. People say it was war between the Mecca and Wigan crowd, but in reality it was between Levine and Winstanley.'

In essence, this feud could be traced back to one record by an utterly unknown group called the Carstairs. That one record was pivotal in the music policy of Blackpool Mecca and sparked a division from which the Northern Soul scene has never really recovered.

Ian heard the Carstairs' 1973 recording of 'It Really Hurts Me, Girl' on a Miami radio station while on holiday in the States. Recorded for the US-based Red Coach label, it was a ground-breaking sound in every way. Firstly, it was a brand-new recording. Secondly, it had a different tempo to that normally associated with Northern Soul. Far from a Motownesque on-the-fours stomping beat, the Carstairs opened with rhythm guitars and soft strings. It was soft shuffler as opposed to an acrobatic 100 mph dancer, but it was undoubtedly soul with a capital S. Twenty-five years later, writer and lead singer Cleveland Horne would be moved to tears at the Blackpool Mecca reunion when he saw the adulation and respect his song was given by Northern Soul fans. When he and (an admittedly new) Carstairs took to the stage, he explained he had written the song after breaking up with the love of his life. His anguished vocals, the pain of the lyrics, his yearning to turn back the clock and regain the love they shared, were all real.

Ian *had* to have this record the minute he heard it. The radio station told him the single had been released as a promotional copy only, but never released. He came home empty-handed, but kept trying back in the UK. It was Soul Bowl's much-respected boss John Anderson who found him a copy and shipped it to him, thinking Levine had finally gone off his rocker.

When Ian finally plucked up courage to play the Carstairs at the Mecca, he urged the dancers to give it a chance. From a lukewarm initial response, the demand grew and grew and the track became so huge that even today it features in many people's all-time top ten favourites.

Said Ian: 'The Carstairs was the record that changed the scene. Up to 1974 the Northern Soul scene was thriving on a diet of 60s recordings with the Motown stomping beat. The Carstairs was an early 70s record and it had a different beat, and it became the biggest floor-filler ever at Blackpool Mecca.

'The Carstairs record of course wasn't welcomed at Wigan at first, but then they had to play it because of the demand. There was no conscious decision on my part to change the Northern scene, it just crept in. I still liked the stompers, I just felt there was a better way at the time. The Carstairs pointed the way. From there we got one or two other records going like Don Thomas's "Come On, Train" and James Fountain's "Seven Day Lover", and there was a slightly different beat.'

From there it was just a short hop to current US releases with more of a disco beat. By 1975 the Mecca playlist was including dancers like Cameo's 'Find My Way', all hi-hats and a contemporary feel, and the Rimshots' 'Do What You Feel', probably the nearest to a pure disco record to date. But the modern feel was balanced by traditional Northern stompers like Jerry Fuller's 'Double Life' and Ronnie McNeir's 'Sitting In My Class'. Records were turned over very quickly – an antidote, Ian feels, to Wigan's mainly-oldies music policy.

Vicky Sue Robinson's 'Turn the Beat Around' became another massive record, a current release that Ian felt retained the spirit of Northern Soul. Levine was using his considerable influence to subtly change the complexion of the Northern Soul scene, and not everyone was happy. But it was his next move which would earn him many opponents.

Ian had become increasingly appalled by the Pye Disco Demand output issued in the UK on the strength of plays at Wigan Casino. Wayne Gibson's 'Under My Thumb', Nosmo King and Javell's 'Goodbye, Nothing to Say', and 'Footsee' had irritated him. The final straw was when his old adversary Simon

Soussan took the Sharonettes into the recording studio and had a UK hit with 'Pappa Ooh Mow Mow' on the Black Magic label. 'When I heard Simon Soussan's effort with the Sharonettes it went so against the grain that it pushed me over the edge into actually going to New York and working with proper session musicians,' said Ian.

So in February 1975 he took the Exciters into the recording studio for 20th Century records and put together 'Reaching for the Best' with the Exciters' Herb Reed. Despite never having written or produced anything, Ian found that his work came instinctively from years of playing and collecting rare soul records. 'Reaching for the Best' – even the title was a dig at Mr Soussan, based on a fictitious record title on one of his old record lists – became a Top Twenty hit, the first of forty he would have as a producer.

L J Johnson's 'Your Magic Put a Spell On Me', Evelyn Thomas's 'Weakspot', Barbara Pennington's '24 Hours a Day', James Wells' 'Baby, I'm Still the Same Man' were quickly added to the Levine hitlist. He was now working in New York and Chicago with black American artists and musicians and writing or co-writing everything. Often working with arranger Paul David Wilson, Ian varied between out-and-out Northern dancers and the more discofied productions he was being increasingly drawn towards.

Being the resident DJ at the Highland Room, it was natural enough that Ian would use that venue to 'break' his latest productions. In the course of a night you could hear each record several times, and for every person who loved them there was another who said: 'Hang on, I'm getting fed up of being brainwashed by Levine.' These records were seen by cynics as being 'tailormade' for the Northern Soul scene by a British Northern Soul DJ. Punters would keep track of the high number of Levine productions played at the Mecca, and disenchantment grew. Ian is even today unrepentant: 'Of course I played a lot of my own productions. Did anyone complain about the number of Van McCoy productions, or George Kerr productions we played during the night? Every record I made had a Northern Soul beat, they were recorded with black artists in Chicago or

New York, but because it was Ian Levine I got a lot of flak.'

The 'Levine Must Go' campaign started as something of a joke, a tongue-in-cheek dig at his growing manipulation of the scene. Soon there were petitions, badges and even an 11-foot-long banner which was carted around the Highland Room by stompers fans Peter King and Paul Shevington. Ian himself entered into the spirit of it, sporting a Levine Must Go badge himself. But there was a gradual shift and the campaign became more and more personal and ill-tempered.

Russ Winstanley banned Ian's productions from being played at Wigan Casino, and the Wigan/Mecca split was born. Said Ian: 'Up to late 1976 I went to Wigan almost every week after the Mecca. I would stay until about five or six in the morning, but I stopped going when it became clear I wasn't welcome. Russ and I were at each other's throats. I hated the music at Wigan – that was the reason I moved away from the stompers. I have this memory of Gary Lewis and Playboys being played, *Hawaii 5-0* and all that kind of stuff. I was never very into oldies anyway at the time, I never went into Mr M's.'

*Blues and Soul* journalist Dave Godin also wrote that Ian Levine was 'ruining the soul scene', and began championing the Cleethorpes all-nighters ahead of Blackpool Mecca and Wigan. It was the start of a sometimes bitter feud between the two men.

By now the Mecca's playlist was becoming more and more contemporary, moving away from the traditional stompers and focusing on 70s shufflers. It was still authentic black American music, and not, like in later years, cynically targeted at the booming disco market, but it had a softer sound and a different beat from what Wigan was playing.

One influence on Ian was Tony Cummings of the magazine *Black Music*, with whom he became friendly. Tony had a very contemporary outlook on soul music, and steered the Blackpool DJ towards 70s releases. 'He was the reason I started playing more modern records,' said Ian. 'He had a shop called Black Wax in London and we used to sleep on his floor. He turned me on to a lot of records like Johnny Baker's "Shy Guy".'

The Voices of East Harlem with 'Cashing In', The Anderson Brothers' 'I Can See Him Loving You', Marvin Holmes' 'You

Better Keep Her', Black Nasty's 'Cut Your Motor Off', Stanley Woodruff's 'What Took You So Long', Willi J & Co's 'Boogie With Your Baby', Hosana's 'Hipit', and Silvetti's 'Spring Rain' typified the 'new' Mecca sound. Some of them crossed over to the Casino when sheer audience demand made it irresistible.

Other classic Mecca tunes, although current releases, kept the Northern Soul spirit. Today's People with 'SOS (All We Need Is Time For Love)', and East Coast Connection's 'Summer In the Parks' were massively popular at all the top venues.

But a split was developing, one which Ian now regrets. 'We started going in different directions and we were pulling apart something that was very precious.'

Another key moment in Ian's outlook on the soul scene came when he visited New York's gay discos. Here was a vibrant, colourful dance scene with records being tailormade for the scene by enterprising DJs and producers. Ian was amazed to find that the New York clubs had a similar music policy to his, and he became the first British DJ to mix records after studying the master mixer Tom Moulton.

Soon Ian's Mecca playlist was moving away rapidly from Northern Soul – Dr Buzzard's Original Savannah Band, Crown Heights Affair, Brass Construction, and Sylvester were heard more often than the traditional 60s obscurities. Colin Curtis helped create a balance with the less discofied offerings of George Benson and Roy Ayers, but there was no turning back now.

In the space of just three years, the Highland Room had ceased to be the domain of the tattooed, vest-wearing, muscular Northern Soul dervishes dancing to pounding, aggressive beats. It was now the 'hip' place to be seen. Drainpipe pants, even bondage trousers, poser sunglasses and Roxy and Bowie-inspired fashions were the cool things to be seen in. Couples even jived to the jazzy beats of Dr Buzzard's. Some of the male clientele looked decidedly un-macho. Many of the women seemed to have stepped straight off the catwalk of the chicest fashion houses of the continent. Jazz-funk was coming on to the playlists more and more, with the 'beautiful people' of the Highland Room grooving in a decidedly funky style to 10-minute instrumentals.

It was still great fun for many regulars, but it was all a far cry from Northern Soul. 'With hindsight, we took it too far,' admits Ian Levine today, 'but I never lost my love of Northern Soul. We just thought that there weren't enough quality new discoveries coming through to keep the scene going.'

Meanwhile the Levine Must Go campaign was gathering momentum. Verbal abuse was becoming a regular occurrence for Ian. Levine Must Go T-shirts appeared, and in one ugly incident outside the Ritz in Manchester, Ian's friend Steve Naylor had his glasses broken. In Sheffield, Ian's car was surrounded by a mob banging on the windows and kicking the tyres. 'I was sickened by the whole scene,' said Ian. 'My turning away from Northern Soul was partially brought on by the abuse and hatred that I encountered in the 1970s.'

By the late 70s the Mecca had completely turned its back on Northern Soul. Disco and jazz-funk were the buzzwords. Southern-style soul funk records by chart acts like Parliament and Funkadelic and even reggae-style tunes like Dillinger's 'Cocaine in My Brain' were by now Mecca dance floor anthems. Said Ian: 'It all got out of hand. The funkier Colin got, the more disco I got, but I never lost my love of Northern Soul.'

In 1979 he left the Mecca and pioneered the high energy scene at Heaven in London. Although he turned his back on the Northern Soul scene, he insists it has always lived in his heart. And he has always promoted the soulful Philly-type sound rather than empty dance music. His success with his self-produced Evelyn Thomas's 'High Energy' – it sold seven million copies around the world – helped to fund his well-intentioned but ultimately ill-fated Motorcity project in the late 80s, when he got a host of ex-Motown stars back into the studios to record 800 tracks. The idea was simple – to relaunch the careers of dozens of ex-Motown singers and give back to them some of the pleasure they had given to him over the years. But sales were disappointing and massive debts and bills for studio time built up until it almost ruined him. Ian even sold all but 10,000 of his huge record collection to prop up his finances. The Motorcity output received lukewarm sales, the only ray of light being a Top Twenty hit in Britain for Frances Nero in early 1991.

The former 'Keep On Lovin' Me' singer was found by Ian running a Detroit minicab office. Ian wrote her comeback song with Steve Wagner and Ivy Jo Hunter, and co-produced it with Rick Gianatos. It was the only hit Ian had to show for all his months and months of work. 'It nearly broke me and I almost lost my house,' he said. 'I risked everything on Motorcity and it was a horrible time for me. In 1990 and 1991 I really hit rock bottom. I literally had the bailiffs at the door, and survived by the skin of my teeth.'

Things looked up for Ian when he was introduced to a man from Sony who was seeking a producer who could give the Motown/Philly sound to a new band called the Pasadenas. Ian worked with them, and together they had a hit with a version of New York City's 'I'm Doing Fine Now'. A successful album followed.

Another example of Levine's recovery powers came with the early career of Take That. Despite investing a million pounds in the boy band, the record company had seen their first four singles flop. Ian was brought in to produce them and three hits followed – 'A Million Love Songs', 'Could It be Magic' and 'I Found Heaven'. Then there was a reshuffle at the top of the record company and Ian found himself pushed out.

His revenge was to cultivate his own boy bands like Bad Boys Inc, Boyzone, and Upside Down. Which just goes to show that you can love him or hate him, but you can never ignore Ian Levine or his vast contribution to the Northern Soul scene.

Ian insists today that it is the artist and not the British DJ who should take the credit for the many years of pleasure Northern Soul fans have derived from rescued 60s obscurities. 'The music was there to be found, we just got there first. All we were doing was looking for records with the right beat. DJs can't take all the credit – if a record is great someone will turn it up. We didn't make the records – someone else did, and that's what's important.'

Ian Levine's input into the Northern Soul scene is hotly debated even today. Many soul fans accuse him of splitting the scene in two. Many others uncharitably found his wealthy background and Jewish faith reason enough to dislike him. One DJ said: 'Levine was born with a silver spoon in his mouth, and it is something he has had to live with all his life. He has this image problem, but people don't even know him.'

Another key Northern Soul personality remarked: 'I have the utmost respect for Ian as a DJ, but he has such an unfortunate manner about him. If only he would shut up and listen . . .'

Ex-Wigan Casino DJ Kev Roberts said: 'If you were serious about the music the Mecca was the greatest ever venue. I was a young DJ and a serious collector of music and I found out immediately that if you wanted to talk about rare soul music you went to Ian Levine. I have enormous respect for him and the records he discovered. The Mecca attracted a different crowd to Wigan. Some of those people were just so intense. Ian was the same – he had this talent for finding records and thought that everybody in the world wanted to know that. They should have done, but in reality people just wanted to hear the music. He took it all too seriously.'

Londoner Chris Lalor, now living in Belgium, befriended Ian Levine in the early days of the Mecca. He was among the first to leap to Ian's defence as the former Blackpool DJ came under fire from critics on an Internet site in 1999. 'He never stole anyone's records and he was honest. None of those DJs were Red Cross workers: they covered up 45s, told us bogus names, nicked records, etc. I was the good guy, the knobhead who lent his records out only to get them nicked. There was a small clique who had the market pretty much cornered. We all had our own secret source of US singles, and nobody told the others who it was.

'But Ian never was like that. He always was upfront in all his dealings with me. Ian's contribution to Northern Soul is unrivalled.'

*Ian Levine's all-time top ten Northern Soul sounds*

'The Key to My Happiness' The Charades
'Stick By Me Baby' The Salvadors
'It Really Hurts Me Girl' The Carstairs

'You're Gonna Make Me Love You'  Sandi Sheldon
'Blowin' My Mind to Pieces'  Bob Relf
'Let Our Love Grow Higher'  Eula Cooper
'I've Got the Vibes'  Jo Armstead
'Just Got to be Careful'  Carolyn Crawford
'Gonna Be a Big Thing'  Yum Yums
'Gotta Have Your Love'  Sapphires

The name of Colin Curtis is virtually inseparable from that of Ian Levine in Northern Soul folklore. Together the two innovative DJs took the soul scene along for a roller-coaster ride the likes of which had never been seen before or since. Determined to keep their playlists fresh, playing and discarding many fine sounds, together they set out to unearth a mountain of Northern Soul records which would delight a generation of dancers. And together they decided some years later that the number of quality Northern Soul records was drying up.

As Ian went more and more towards playing out-and-out disco records, Colin leaned towards 70s soul, funk and eventually jazz.

Even today, Colin's passion for the music remains undiminished as he recalls his partnership with Ian, first at the Torch, then in Blackpool, which won (and lost them) legions of fans all over the country.

Colin admits that while they often had musical differences of opinion, he and Ian got on well and formed a strong partnership. 'I can only work with people I have a rapport with and we had a good rapport. I liked him as a character. I liked the fact that sometimes he could be a bull in a china shop. I could believe in what he was believing.'

While Ian was off on his transatlantic record-hunting expeditions, Colin was left slightly frustrated because of his fear of flying. But his own sources in the UK were turning up a goldmine of US rarities. He would spend up to twelve hours a day in record shops and warehouses all over the country looking for soul gems. One such contact had a stall on Bradford market, and would lock Colin and Keith Minshull in for the day, surrounded by boxes each containing 50 to 100 copies of sought-after labels. All kinds of rarities turned up, including the Salvadors' 'Stick By Me Baby', and MGM gems like Dotty Cambridge's 'Cry Your Eyes Out', and April Stevens's 'Wanting You'.

Colin also found the Charades' 'Key to My Happiness', which Ian Levine cites as his all-time favourite record. 'I flogged that to him after a trip to Bradford,' says Colin.

On one such warehouse trip, a whole box of Verve releases spilled across the floor, and Colin spotted something on the Bell label among them. That record was Bernie Williams's ultra-rare 'Ever Again'.

The Mecca punters were also a great source of quality records. In time-honoured Twisted Wheel fashion, they would hand them to Curtis and Levine to play to the Highland Room faithful. Said Colin: 'There were lots of stalwart collectors from Nelson, Burnley, Bolton and places like that, who would bring stuff for us to play. If they had faith in a record they knew it would become big through me or Levine. That was how records like the Silhouettes' "Not Me Baby" and Freddie Chavez's "They'll Never Know Why" became big. I bought Earl Jackson's "Soul Self Satisfaction" for 50p off Keith. He had loads of them and no one was really interested in it until we started playing it at the Mecca.'

Meanwhile, Ian was sending over ten-page letters containing lists of unknown records he had found in the States. Back in England, they would sift through the records in Ian's house in Blackpool prior to the Mecca, evaluating and picking out the best sounds.

They also became big customers of record dealer John Anderson at Soul Bowl in King's Lynn. During their regular visits, John would sort out a pile of records awaiting their arrival. Colin would have £50 cash and a cheque which he would expect to bounce. Then Ian would produce £1,000 in cash (around £8,000 in today's terms) and the pair would be free to roam around the entire store.

'Ian just had this encyclopaedic knowledge of soul music,' said Colin. 'He would flick through piles of records and know instantly what was what. He would say "Yes", "No" and flick them around the place until John would decide we had got our money's worth. Of course, I was getting all the spare copies of things off Ian.'

Colin said he enjoyed the banter with his partner about the merits of certain records, and there was a certain satisfaction to be gained from making popular a record that the other hated. 'We didn't share the same tastes in music all the time. I used to love defying him and love making records big that I knew he hated. I detested some of the girlie things he played, like "Contact" (the Three Degrees). Why on earth play something like that when you had Linda Jones? It was disgusting. The Spiral Starecase's "More Today Than Yesterday" used to drive me mad. I would be going "For God's sakes get 'Job Opening' on or something with some bollocks."'

Colin also respected and was influenced by DJs like Graham Warr from Birmingham. It was he who recommended and sold Colin a copy for £3 of an utterly unknown record. That turned out to be the Epitome of Sound's 'You Don't Love Me', one of many people's all-time classics.

During one of his Stateside trips, Ian was frustrated not to be able to find a copy of the Carstairs' 'It Really Hurts Me Girl' after hearing it on a US radio station. Colin found three – in the 50p bin at Soul Bowl.

Colin agrees that that record shaped the future of the Mecca. 'It was like a breath of fresh air,' he said. 'The 60s stuff was drying up. We couldn't keep up the standard. We could have carried on playing second-division 60s stuff but what was the point? There was so much great new black music coming out.' He started to champion 70s releases like Larry Saunders' 'On the Real Side' and Gill Scott-Heron's 'The Bottle'. Black Nasty's 'Cut Your Motor Off', Cameo, the Rimshots, all found their way on to the Mecca playlists. During a visit to Wigan Casino, Colin had seen what for him was a frightening glimpse of the future. He was never impressed with the Casino's early playlists and hated Mr M's, the oldies room. 'I was sitting in Mr M's one night and I said to someone, "This is the beginning of the end." I felt sad. People were running away from new records. Once that started a pattern followed. We had a vision and as times changed our vision changed. If we had had no vision, we would have gone backwards like Mr M's.'

From there, the Mecca playlist rapidly developed a 70s feel until it was all new release material. George Benson, Crown Heights Affair, Brass Construction, and 10-minute album tracks and 12-inchers were a million miles away from the 60s rarities that Colin and Ian had played. The duo were also two of the first ever British DJs to mix records, a style which has been copied and refined by today's dance DJs.

Colin is unrepentant about the massive change in the Mecca's music policy. He said: 'We were still playing soul. If we had been doing something wrong, the place would have been empty. All the clubs we did were full. The Northern Soul scene was going nowhere. I was playing the most relevant black music at the time.'

Soon he was among the line-ups at all-dayers pulling in 3,000 capacity crowds at the Mecca, the Manchester Ritz, and jazz-funk venues like Cassinelli's in Standish, near Wigan, and Rafters in Manchester, into the 1980s.

He went to see legendary DJ Chris Hill and was impressed by his patter, wit and control of southern soul fans. Colin decided that the element of fun was missing from northern clubs. But he felt the north was musically more up to date. 'We were way ahead of what they were doing in London. We were closer to what was happening in New York. I had a fantastic time right the way through. I don't know why people insist on talking about us splitting the Northern Soul scene. I don't think we did take it all too far. Why put barriers where there are no barriers? It was just great music, take it or leave it.'

Colin, now a father of four living in Newcastle-under-Lyme, near Stoke, finally gave up a full-time career as a professional DJ in 1987. He now works for a local video and computer game company, but is still in great demand at revival events, soul nights and weekenders around the country. 'I still get a great buzz from the music,' he says. 'I get a buzz from the crowd, and if people come up to me at a venue and tell me they have admired me, it can be awesome. I've had a brilliant time all the way through.'

*20 selected Blackpool Mecca Northern Soul monsters*

'Hung Up on Your Love'  The Montclairs
'I Can See Him Loving You'  Anderson Brothers
'Find My Way'  Cameo
'Do What You Feel'  Rimshots
'Sitting in My Class'  Ronnie McNeir
'The Larue'  Lara Edmund Jr
'Talking 'Bout Poor Folks'  Lou Edwards
'SOS'  Today's People
'Cashing In'  Voices of East Harlem
'Love Factory'  Eloise Laws
'House for Sale'  Millie Jackson
'Soul Self Satisfaction'  Earl Jackson
'Ton of Dynamite'  Frankie Crocker
'On the Real Side'  Larry Saunders
'You're My Main Squeeze'  Crystal Motion
'Main String'  Oscar Perry
'I Got What You Need'  Oscar Perry
'It Really Hurts Me Girl'  Carstairs
'Key to My Happiness'  The Charades
'Seven Day Lover'  James Fountain

*20 selected 70s/funky Blackpool Mecca sounds*

'New York City'  Miroslav Vitous
'Boogie with Your Baby'  Willie J & Co
'Like Her'  Gentlemen and Their Lady
'Jaws'  Lalo Schifrin
'Open Sesame'  Kool and the Gang
'Do Ya Wanna Get Funky With Me'  Peter Brown
'Going Back to My Roots'  Lamont Dozier
'Ali Shuffle'  Alvin Cash
'You're the Cream of the Crop'  André Maurice
'The World is a Ghetto'  George Benson
'I'll Play the Fool'  Dr Buzzards
'Cherchez La Femme'  Dr Buzzards
'Car Wash'  Rose Royce

'Galaxy' War
'Running Away' Roy Ayers
'Movin' Brass Construction
'Dancin' Crown Heights Affair
'You Make Me Feel' Sylvester
'Shame' Evelyn Champagne King
'Cocaine in My Brain' Dillinger

**HEART OF ENGLAND SOUL CLUB**

JOIN 4,000 SOUL FREAKS AT BRITAIN'S BIGGEST EVER
SOUL ALL-DAYER ! !

**BLACKPOOL MECCA SOUL FESTIVAL**
**BANK HOLIDAY MONDAY MAY 29th**
**NOON TILL 11 p.m.**

Featuring Live on Stage — Direct from New York — The Disco Bosses...

# BRASS CONSTRUCTION
### plus Britain's very own "ROKOTTO"

PLUS DISCO-FUNK ALL-DAY FROM DJ's — IAN LEVINE * COLIN CURTIS
* NEIL RUSHTON * PAUL SCHOFIELD * IAN DEWHURST
FREE Records, T-Shirts, Badges etc. — Films — Lots of V.I.P. Guests

PLUS ALL-DAY IN THE HIGHLAND ROOM
**NORTHERN SOUL**
DJ's — RICHARD SEARLING * PAT BRADY * DAVE EVISON
* GINGER * BRIAN RAE * SOUL SAM

Licensed Bars — Food available All-Day — Record Stalls each Floor.
Advance Tickets available now. HESC & HIGHLAND CONNECTION MEMBERS — SEND £2.25 (+ SAE) —
to HESC (Festival), 37 Lichfield Street, Walsall, West Midlands.
NON-MEMBERS — Send £2.50 (+ SAE).

ADMISSION ON THE DAY £3.00 — SO SAVE MONEY AND SEND TODAY ! !

SPECIAL DISCOUNTS FOR COACH PARTIES—
RING WALSALL 31383 OR BURNTWOOD 3022 FOR DETAILS ! !

*BLACKPOOL MECCA*
The Highland Room · TIFFANYS · Central Dr. Blackpool
**WE'RE BACK**

THE DATE YOU'VE ALL BEEN WAITING TO HEAR
IS SATURDAY JANUARY 28th 1978
EVERY SATURDAY 7·30 pm. –2 am. ADM. £1·00

STARTING SAT. JAN 28th. WE WILL BE OPEN EVERY SAT.
APART FROM THE FOLLOWING FIVE DATES :–
18th – 25th. FEB. 8– 4th, 11th, 25th MARCH.
UNFORTUNATLY THESE FIVE DATES ARE BOOKED FOR PRIOR
ENGAGEMENTS – SO PLEASE MAKE A NOTE OF THE
DATES & REMEMBER WE WILL BE OPEN EVERY SATURDAY
FROM NOW ON APART FROM THESE DATES .

**D.J's IAN LEVINE and COLIN CURTIS**

BRINGING YOU THE FUNKIEST, NAASTIEST, BAAADEST
SELECTION OF DISCO FUNK YOU'LL HEAR ANYWHERE IN
THE WORLD.
PLEASE NOTE :– FROM NOW ON WE ARE OPEN FOR
MEMBERS ONLY, SO TO BE SURE YOU CAN GET IN ON
THE 28th. JAN. – SEND IN YOUR MEMBERSHIP FORM NOW
TO JOIN THE HIGHLAND ROOM CONECTION WITH £1·00

'THE HIGHLAND ROOM CONNECTION' (MEMBERSHIP FEE
£1·00 per year )
NAME _____
ADDRESS _____
_____ PHONE Nº __
I UNDERSTAND THIS WILL ENABLE ME TO BE ADMITTED TO
THE HIGHLAND ROOM EVERY SATURDAY. I WILL BE ALLOWED
TO BRING TWO GUESTS FOR AN EXTRA 50p EACH
PAYABLE ON THE DOOR. I ENCLOSE £1·00 MEMBERSHIP
FEE.     Signed....................

# VA-VA

### GREAT MOOR STREET

# BOLTON

## *Presents* EVERY FRIDAY

# THE MOST SENSATIONAL ALL NIGHT SOUL SESSION IN THE NORTH

### with D.J. RICHARD 'S'

Hear the Country's Top Soul Sounds between 1 a.m. and 7-30 a.m.
Sound like: "CAN IT BE"– Mel Williams, "I CAN'T HOLD ON"–
Lorraine Chadler, "WHAT SHALL I DO"– Frankie & The Classicals,
"I'VE GOT TO HAVE YOUR LOVE" – The Volcanoes, "YOU'RE A
PUZZLE"– Jive Five, "HEARTS DESIRE"– Billy Joe Royal, "ONCE
UPON A TIME"– Orlons.
Plus: Little Jimmy Scott, Sharon Soul, Johnny Howard, Adventurers,
Roy Thompson, Thrills, Carl Jackson, Jerry Cook, Vel-Vets, Linda
Jones, Debbie Dean, Amazers, Diplomats, Sapphires, Gladys Knight,
and various other obscurities

## ALL-NIGHTERS EVERY FRIDAY OF THE YEAR

### Admission
### £1.00

### Bars Open ★
### 'Til 2

★ WE ALSO CATER
FOR TRENDY
WEDDINGS

# Part III

**WIGAN CASINO SOUL CLUB**

SATURDAY, SEPTEMBER 19th, 1981

12 Midnight to 9.00 a.m.

0743

# END OF AN ERA - LAST NIGHTER

WITH THE COUNTRY'S No. 1 SOUL SPINNERS

## RUSS, RICHARD, KEITH, DAVE, BRIAN, PAT, GARY, KENNY, STUART & STE

*9 NON-STOP HOURS ON TWO FLOORS*

FREE DRAW AT 3.30 a.m.

FOR MUSIC CENTRE - T.V.'s, RADIOS, ETC.

**FINAL OF DANCE COMPETITION**

1st Prize - £100, 2nd Prize - £75, 3rd Prize - £25

EVERYONE WILL RECEIVE
A FREE BADGE AND
SOUVENIR POSTER

OLDIES ALL-NIGHT IN
Mr. M's WITH
KENNY, STUART, STE &
BRIAN

Tickets £5.00 each   Members Only

*Britain's Top D.J.'s, Management and Staff say goodbye to the Best Ever Venue and Most Loyal Supporters*

## THANKS FOR EIGHT INCREDIBLE YEARS

# 5

# I'm Coming Home in the Morning

*'The Casino was a carry on from the Torch. People thought it would only last for a short length of time.'*

The birth of the disco era saw dancing suddenly become fashionable. By the end of 1974, night clubs were springing up all over Britain in ever-increasing numbers. Existing clubs were having major revamps to cater for the masses wanting to dance, smooch and pose in their patterned shirts and wide flares to the 'hip' disco sounds.

Pop record producers were waking up once again to the fact that 45s with a dance beat had super-commercial prospects. George McRae with 'Rock Your Baby', the Hues Corporation's 'Rock the Boat', Gloria Gaynor's 'Never Can Say Goodbye' and a whole glut of Barry White records were getting the youngsters bopping under the glitter balls in cheesy venues.

These pop-soul outings and the success of Gamble and Huff's Philadelphia sound of the Three Degrees, TSOP, etc, led to much bandwagon-jumping. Suddenly there were tailormade disco offerings from Disc-O-Tex with 'Get Dancing', and Kenny with 'The Bump'. This cynical music-making would lead eventually to the ultimate of horrors, the Village People.

Northern Soul fans were having none of it. For at least the last five years they had moulded their own secret dance scene, their own music and their fashions. As usual they carried their scene on in their own way and ignored the masses.

By the time the Bee Gees had in 1979 scored the multimillion-selling soundtrack to *Saturday Night Fever*, disco fever was gripping the nation. An examination of the film's storyline has a familiar ring. A paint store worker, Tony Minero, is stuck in a dead-end job in a poor city neighbourhood. He is a classic under-achiever, with little relief from the drudgery of his every-day life. His one talent is for disco dancing. At the weekend he is a star, with girls queuing up to date him, and his fellow males looking on enviously as he captivates the club with his silky dance moves. When he walks into his local club he is treated like a king. The dance floor is *his* territory. This is where he becomes a *somebody*, and it's all down to music and dance.

Ignoring the slick settings, unsoulful dancing, the laughable white suit and mainly white pop-soul soundtrack, *Saturday Night Fever* could easily be seen as a cleaned-up and Americanized interpretation of the Northern Soul scene.

The medallion-wearing superstuds who started to frequent British discos finally discovered what soul fans had known since the mid-60s. That men could express themselves through music on the dance floor without being thought of as cissies. And they could have a great time.

Northern Soul fans, of course, wanted to distance themselves from such mainstream tosh. They kept the faith with rare black American recordings at their own, often downmarket, all-night venues.

One such venue, and the antithesis of the 70s pop disco, was Wigan Casino . . .

### David Nowell takes a personal look at Wigan Casino

Through the rain-lashed night a familiar sign appeared: SERVICES ½ MILE. Charnock Richard near Preston, Lancashire. A welcome break for thousands of M6 motorists and all-nighter-goers alike.

It was 11 pm on Saturday, 19 September 1981. The usual pit stop en route to the greatest dance club the world has ever seen: Wigan Casino. Except this was no ordinary night. This was the gut-wrenching, heart-tugging farewell Saturday all-nighter.

Eight years of the Casino's domination of so many lives and the whole of the Northern Soul scene were coming to an end.

Although its demise was inevitable, nobody wanted to miss the chance of another eight hours in Soul Heaven.

As we pulled into the Lancashire service station in my recently acquired metallic-brown, R-registered Ford Capri, a myriad of mixed emotions were battling inside me. Sadness, excitement, relief, pride, apprehension, just to name a few.

Sadness because eight years of the venue's reign were about to come to an end. And a chapter in my life was about to close. I had virtually grown up attending the Casino all-nighters and six years of enjoyment was a hell of a lot of memories. A hell of a lot of friends. A hell of a lot of great nights. A hell of a lot of records going around in your head. And, yes, even a few regrets.

Excitement. Well, that's easy, because the Casino seemed to bring a knot to the stomach that began with packing your holdall full of clothes earlier that evening. Sitting chatting with friends over a pint en route to Wigan heightened it. Arriving at Charnock Richard services, just a few miles down the road from Wigan, was the start of the final high.

Relief. Yes, to be honest, there was a comforting sense of relief. Nothing lasts forever, and at twenty-three I was secretly glad my life was about to move on. I was still mentally and physically in one piece (unlike some who over-indulged in the drug culture that has forever been associated with the Northern Soul scene), I had a good career as a journalist. And I wanted the Casino to bow out like the world champ it had become, not like a tired old boxer making one too many comebacks. Now was the right time.

Pride. How could you feel anything else, having been associated with a magical venue during a magical era? I could look back on some great friendships, great nights and, through an accident of birth, the good fortune to have grown up during the Casino's heyday. Still at primary school during the Twisted Wheel era, too young for the Torch, the Casino was my chance to live the Northern Soul experience at its peak, its most groundbreaking and its most frantic. Even now, younger club-goers than us battle-weary thirty- and forty-somethings want to know: 'What was it like at Wigan Casino?'

A similar question will be asked, no doubt, in twenty years' time of the London's Ministry of Sound, which is to the 90s dance scene what the Casino was to 70s youth culture. It was, and is, in spirit, such a large part of so many people's lives.

Apprehension. Not just amphetamine-induced, but a slight feeling of concern about the coming night and the years afterwards. Everyone wanted the farewell all-nighter to be *the* perfect night. The right people. The right atmosphere. The right emotion. What if it was poorly attended? No worry there, the event was a sell-out. What if the required 'faces' didn't turn up? No problem, the phone had been red hot all week with friends from Blackburn, Preston, Leyland, Chorley and Scotland all making arrangements: 'See you at the services.' – 'See you outside at about twelve.' – 'I'll pick you up at nine and we'll go for a pint on the way.'

What if the drug squad, everyone's worst nightmare, decided to ruin the night by coming along mob-handed? It had been known in the past for carloads of the sods to make life difficult for soul fans en route to the all-nighter. Standing in the car park being painstakingly searched at 1 am on a freezing morning was not the ideal way to start the night. Always very polite, but with a slightly sarcastic manner, the squad would be *very* thorough.

'Take your belt off, please.' – 'And now your shoes and socks.' – 'How have you got here? By car? Oh, good, we'll have a look at that afterwards.' – 'Have you got anything on you?' – 'Have you any criminal convictions?' – 'What, none at all?' – 'What have you had tonight, then?' – 'Right, give us your name and address and you can be on your way.' Well, if they wanted to pay their last respects to a venue which had given them so much sport and paperwork over the past eight years, so be it. *Nothing* was going to spoil the final night.

What was it about motorway service stations that was so appealing to soul fans? The food and drink was always mediocre and overpriced and anyone carrying a holdall adorned with Wigan Casino badges drew strange looks from the ordinary clientele. Particularly in the mornings when you all piled in hollow-eyed and knackered. You could see mums and dads eyeing you with suspicion and practically hiding their children behind them and whispering: 'Keep away from them, they've been to that Wigan Casino place.'

Anyway, for the two hundredth time in the last six years we pulled into the southbound services carpark to go in search of friends. An hour to go before the all-nighter, and many soul fans would be getting changed, having a brew or stretching their legs after the long journey from the north. As usual we weren't disappointed. A quick visit to the toilets found various characters in a state of undress. There were Tommy, Hank, Jiggy, Justin, and God knows how many other Scots madmen hogging the sinks and pulling on jeans and T-shirts . . . casual and cool attire.

Wigan Casino was no fashion parade. It was a dance venue and these seasoned veterans knew better than to waste their trendy clothes on it. Narrow-bottomed jeans and a T-shirt or short-sleeved shirt were comfortable and functional in the last years of the Casino. No more 32-inch-wide Spencers and vests with badges on them. They had become a bit of a cliché amid all the media hype in the mid-70s.

'Excuse me, please.' Passing travellers would warily edge their way by the gum-chewing soulies warming up with some soul moves on the slippy floor while spraying deodorant liberally under their armpits and on their bare torsoes.

A few handshakes and insults were exchanged among the Casino crowd before further inquiries revealed that the Scots lassies were either in the ladies', or in the café. Within minutes a coach pulled into the carpark and disgorged another hoard of soul fans. 'It's the Dundee coach,' somebody said, recognizing a familiar face. First off the coach – a guy in a kilt performing a nifty couple of moves in the darkness to the amusement of a passing motorist. Laughs all round.

Back in the toilets various pills and powders magically appeared and everybody was almost ready for the off.

A quick search of the café revealed Avron, Barbara, Jean, and the rest of the Scots lassies. A few kisses and hugs and the world seemed a happy place as we prepared for the final journey through those famous Station Road doors.

Much has been written and said about the Casino, some of it accurate, some of it distortion, misunderstanding and myth. The Casino Club venue ruled the Northern Soul scene from the night it opened its doors on 23 September 1973, to the day it shut in 1981.

Certain facts are indisputable:

How its DJs unearthed a mini-mountain of rare records that scored hits not only with soul fans but also with the pop-buying public: R Dean Taylor's 'Ghost in My House', Casualeers' 'Dance Dance Dance', Wayne Gibson's 'Under My Thumb', Frankie Valli's 'The Night', and so on.

How the Casino put Northern Soul in fashion and propelled what had been a fairly close-knit underground music scene into the minds and ears of the entire country.

How TV and radio crews, magazine and newspaper journalists and coachloads of drug squad officers made sure the venue stayed regularly in the news.

How it attracted more than 100,000 members, many of them so fanatical that a three- or four-hour journey each way to Wigan was no big deal.

How it helped relaunch the careers of many 60s soul artists, from Edwin Starr and Tommy Hunt to Junior Walker and Martha Reeves.

How the Casino's commercially minded management team alienated many Northern Soul purists by helping to launch such embarrassments as 'Footsee' (Wigan's Chosen Few) and 'Skiing in the Snow' (Wigan's Ovations) on to the unsuspecting pop public.

These are the indisputable facts; there are also many disputable stories – spread by the disgruntled and by the press – which I hope this book and an earlier book, *Soul Survivors*, will dispel.

Like many Northern Soul fans, my devotion to the music, and to the Casino in particular, bordered on the obsessive. Like many Casino devotees, I felt gutted when I realized the end was nigh in 1981. Not because I felt as if life wasn't worth living without the Casino, but because I realized it marked a crossroads in my life.

The night that no one wanted to arrive was rain-sodden, blustery and miserable. Quite appropriate, really, as it heralded the death knell of such a great club.

It literally was the end of an era for many people, who took the Casino's demise as the cue to marry, stop going to all-nighters, or concentrate on their sadly neglected career.

All 2,000 tickets had been sold in advance for the nine-hour music marathon at the Casino club on Saturday, 19 September 1981. Hundreds were disappointed and had their cheques returned. It seemed like virtually every one of the Casino's legion of fans wanted to turn up to say thank you for so many happy nights and some great memories.

As we battled through the torrential rain in my beloved Capri, the stereo cassette belted out the stompers and the heater belted out the warm air while the windscreen wipers to-and-fro-ed on double speed. It was a damned sight more comfortable and luxurious than previous cars I'd had during my Casino career dating back to 1975. An Austin A40, a Morris Minor traveller with wooden back doors that were so fragile that I dared not even park it in the Casino carpark for fear of having it nicked; a Vauxhall Marina that would barely start; and a battered Ford Cortina that got rained in so much that in winter the carpets froze and made a crunching sound when you stood on them. It was amazing, however, what having a car meant in those days. Nodding acquaintances would start offering you drinks during the week. The phone started ringing more frequently at home from guys casually enquiring: 'Are you going to Wigan tonight?' (Translation: 'Can you give me a lift?') And once inside the cauldron that was the Casino, virtual strangers would sidle up at 7.30 am and act like your long-lost brother, working up to asking for a lift home.

I once was harangued and ridiculed by two guys whom I dropped off at Wigan Hospital in the morning (don't ask), because I refused to hang around for a couple of hours and run them over to Burnley for an all-dayer starting at noon.

Pulling into the Casino carpark, it was obvious that it would be a sardine-like existence inside the venue. We drove for seemingly ages before finding a space in the vast bumpy public carpark opposite the imposing Casino Club building. Having settled for a spot at the rear of the carpark just about as far away from the club as you could get without tumbling down the grass verge behind you, we slammed in a cassette and settled down for a smoke and a chat.

The red Casino Club sign beckoned in the distance, and there was a constant flow of soul fans flocking towards the entrance, but I wanted to savour this one last look at the building before entering. We talked, and smoked and smoked and talked, and suddenly 'BLOODY HELL! It's 1.30 am!'

We grabbed our holdalls out of the boot (mine was a badge-free Speedo one which contained a cassette recorder to record some of the last night for posterity), and legged it swiftly the 100 yards or so to the entrance. Handing over our tickets at the cash desk, we turned right up the steps and kept climbing and climbing until we reached the double doors at the top, all the time squeezing past both moving and immobile bodies on the stairs.

I pushed open the top doors and the heat hit me like an electric fire. First the temperature, then the condensation and finally the smell of nearly 2,000 bodies (and Brut) working hard. The Casino was always a cauldron, but the farewell all-nighter was exceptional. I stood there, wrestling with the cassette recorder on the balcony and looking down the full length of the teeming dance floor below, and took a deep breath and savoured the Casino experience.

The image lives with me today just like a photographic negative. It will hopefully stay locked in my brain until the day I die. Mere words cannot convey the atmosphere, the emotion, the sounds, and the smells. Nor can they adequately explain the passion for the Casino and zest for life that emanated from that dance floor. It was as if everyone was completely locked into having the greatest night ever with an old friend they knew – but daren't admit to themselves – they would never see again.

The particular Casino atmosphere and the special acoustics that set it apart from other venues seemed doubly heightened that night. As did the camaraderie and poignancy with which every DJ signed off his spot: 'Thanks for being a great crowd . . . I'm sure we'll meet again.' – 'It's been eight great years.'

The dance floor in both the main room and Mr M's was so full all night you could barely move. There was hardly any thinning-out in the final hours. No one was going anywhere. But in the end it was over all too quickly.

My mind wandered back to the first time I ever walked through those doors in Station Road. The date was 26 April 1975, and Betty Wright was appearing live. Those who were there will tell you it was the greatest live performance they ever saw at the Casino, and it is hard to argue with that.

For me, it had been a strange journey to finally discovering the Casino. Growing up to the sounds of the Beatles and moving into heavy rock in my early teens, I was convinced that I hated soul music. I loved alternative music. Music with balls. Music with bite and a driving beat. Music with meaning. Sod the pop charts. It seems comical looking back, but my impression of soul music was only through hit records like 'Baby Love' by the Supremes, 'Betcha By Golly Wow' by the Stylistics. I found it all a bit twee and lightweight.

Then when I was about fifteen a curious thing happened. I attended a disco at my school, Parklands High in Chorley, Lancs. It was the usual affair, boys and girls dressed in their finest, trying to look cool and risking the odd dance in between nipping outside for a crafty fag or a sly snog. Soul and funk was the popular dance sound, with the odd bit of reggae and the obligatory 'Al Capone' by Prince Buster thrown in. The lads were doing a cross between the skinhead moon stomp and a soul shuffle while trying desperately not to get a crease in their two-tone parallels, a twist in their braces or a scuff on their blood-red Doc Martens.

As usual I was a bit of a spectator. With my heavy rock background I hadn't a clue how to put one foot in front of another without looking a complete moron. Then a record came on that lifted me off my backside and started my massive love affair with soul music.

> See how I'm walking,
> See how I'm talking,
> Notice everything in me,
> Feel the need,
> Oh, feel it,
> Feel the need in me.

The Detroit Emeralds' 'Feel the Need in Me'. I had heard this record on the radio and liked it in spite of myself. It had a feel-good factor and a smoothness that appealed to me, and the minute it came on I knew I had to dance, tentatively at first, and then with less self-consciousness. The combination of those silky vocals and chugging rhythm made you want to move your feet. It felt right, it felt good. And all the time I'm thinking, 'Hang on, I don't like soul music.'

Little did I know then that it would be a pivotal moment in my social life. 'Feel the Need in Me' was basically a pop soul record, but it struck a chord within me that equated soul with feeling good, movement, and emotion. The second pivotal moment came some time later when I went to see the blaxploitation movie *Superfly* at the pictures. The soundtrack by Curtis Mayfield was awesome, and deeper soul than I had ever heard. Again the devilish voice kept whispering in my ear: 'You don't like soul music.' From there it wasn't too far to more Curtis Mayfield material, Isaac Hayes, Barry White, and so on.

By the time I went to Blackpool for a day out on the beer with the lads in 1974, I thought I knew what soul music was. How wrong I was. It was a boiling hot summer's day and having drank our way from the resort centre up to the Pleasure Beach, we found ourselves in a basement bar.

It was dark, cool and almost deserted inside. Beer was expensive, awful, and served in plastic glasses. The DJ was playing to an almost empty venue. Empty, that is, apart from a shirtless skinhead wearing a pair of white baggy jeans and a pair of Doc Martens. We watched with mouths open as this hard-looking character posed, slid, and span around the otherwise deserted dance floor to the strains of a frantic, almost-jazz-sounding record with a screaming vocal. That record I now know is 'Manifesto' by James Lewis, which was massive at the Torch, Wigan Casino and just about everywhere else.

The lads were torn between chuckling at this bizarre display (and risking a smack in the face from the handy-looking gentleman), and harbouring a sneaking admiration for his guts in an era when almost no man would ever be seen dancing alone. I was hypnotized. What was this music? It was obviously soul, but it was so much harder and rougher than anything I had ever heard. Where could I hear more? How did he learn to dance like that?

Back at school, my mates explained it was Northern Soul. Soon the conversations all around the school corridors was of 'Sliced Tomatoes', 'Bok to Bach', 'Cigarette Ashes' and other strange-sounding records of which I had never heard. And of a place called Wigan Casino, although at the time none of us were old enough at fifteen or sixteen to dare to try to go.

Still I wasn't totally convinced that it was for me. Then a mate took me to one side. 'Look, Dave, forget this rock crap. Soul music is what all the birds like,' he said, with a twinkle in his eye. That did it. I saw it as the solution to my singular lack of success with girls. Soul music, cool dancing, the best-looking girls and an underground scene all of our own. Lead me to it.

'Entry level' venues followed. Working Men's Clubs that played half an hour of Northern Soul each Friday night. The odd visit to the Rose Room in Burnley. An all-dayer at the Circulation Club in the same town. Still I hadn't made it to Wigan Casino. But all that changed with my seventeenth birthday, when my parents finally gave in to my incessant demands to visit the all-night venue that everyone was saying was a massive den of iniquity. My dad told me years later: 'I reckoned that if you really wanted to take drugs, you could get them without having to go to the Casino, so there didn't seem to be much point in stopping you going.'

That first visit to the Casino was exciting and intimidating in equal measure. Myself and best mate Dave Lancaster caught the 11.30 pm last bus from Chorley with a couple of dozen like-minded youngsters. Portable cassette recorders squawked out the latest Northern Soul favourites. Vests or bowling shirts, 36-inch wide baggy pants, brogues and trench coats or bomber jackets were the norm for the lads. Long, loose strappy dresses or a flared skirt and T-shirt for the girls. Holdalls and clothes were adorned with badges: 'Wigan Casino – Heart of Soul', 'Night Owl', 'The Torch Lives On', 'Soul Lancashire', etc. By now the badges had become such a fashion accessory that most youngsters had one (even though many had never been anywhere near the Casino).

Arriving at Wigan bus station at around 12.15 am, there was still an hour and a quarter before the Casino's doors opened. It didn't matter, the night had already begun and time would fly. Turning into Station Road, we became aware of huge crowds milling around. Literally hundreds and hundreds of soul fans wandered backwards and forward oblivious to the occasional car that tried to negotiate the one-way street outside the Casino. Eventually the police arrived and tried to usher people on to the pavements on either side of Station Road, but to little avail. There were probably 2,000 or more soul fans all wanting to get as near to the front of the queue as they could. A young male soul fan taunted a uniformed copper singing 'My pills are in my pocket' to the tune of Darrell Banks's 'Our Love is in the Pocket'.

Queue is probably the wrong word to describe the way soul fans waited to get into the Casino. Scrum would be more accurate. A fairly orderly queue would form along the pavement, but then others would join it until it was ten deep. Then others would join from the west, and north until there was just a mass of people trying to get through the narrow double doors from three different directions.

In the queue half an hour before the doors opened I became aware that I could not move at all. My holdall and arms were pinned by my side and nervous laughter broke out as others realized they were powerless. Pity the poor souls near the wall. The doors opened to the familiar shouts from the bouncers: 'Stop pushing!' (which would have made us laugh if we had any breath). I became more than a little apprehensive as I realized Dave Lancaster had vanished. My feet were now a good few inches off the ground and I had no choice but to sway with the crowd of hundreds of bodies crushed tightly together. Just when you thought you were making progress towards the sanctuary of the brightly lit reception area, the crowd would sway and you would be ten yards further away.

After an interminable and extremely uncomfortable wait, (was it thirty minutes or an hour?) I found myself in front of the doors, still unable to move. The bouncer removed his beefy arm blocking the doorway and with a mighty squeeze from the crowd, I was propelled, gasping, into the Casino, minus holdall. It would be another few minutes before my bag would follow me in with more pale-looking soul fans. My mate Dave was, as usual, in hysterics. He always saw the funny side of any frightening or unnerving experience.

Offering our blue membership cards and hard-earned money to the no-nonsense Hilda Woods (Mrs Woods to you) at the cash desk, we started the long climb up the stairs to the top of the Casino. No venue before or since has had the same aura as the Casino. Known locally as the Emp (Empress Hall), the three-storey building was built by the Atherton Brothers around the time of the First World War.

It had been variously a garage, a billiard hall, and later, under owner Eddie Farrimond, a venue to jive the night away to the best dance bands. A second club called the Palais (later Mr M's) was added and in the 1960s a brewery bought the building and changed its name to the Casino Club.

By the early 70s the team that would propel the Casino into world fame consisted of owner Gerry Marshall, a local business-man, and management team Mike Walker and Harry Green.

The Casino could have been custom-built for the Northern Soul scene. It was basic, atmospheric, and had the biggest and best-kept dance floor anyone had seen to that point. From the concrete floors of the Twisted Wheel to the more modern but moderately-sized Torch, the Northern Soul scene had moved up a notch. The Casino was the first true mass dance event, with more than 2,000 music fans immersing themselves in eight hours of soul in two rooms.

The main room, with its ornate balcony and dome-shaped ceiling, was always at the heart of the action. Around the upper and lower floors was a scattering of wooden tables and chairs which always seemed permanently occupied. The only lighting was provided by two fluorescent lights over the oblong-shaped sprung maplewood dance floor, ensuring that anyone with bright colours glowed brilliantly as they danced.

On the raised stage in front of dancing masses the DJs held court, feeding the soul-hungry crowd an endless stream of rare records, interspersed by minimum chat. No one was here to listen to the DJ's inane patter or play silly party games – the music said it all.

Walking into the venue on that first night, we initially felt like gatecrashers at someone else's party. So this was the great Wigan Casino. The home of the rarest music, the best dancers, the most knowledgeable soul connoisseurs in the country. How would we fit in? Would the handstands and somersaults brigade laugh at our meagre efforts on the dance floor?

We needn't have worried. It was so packed there was barely any room to stand, let alone dance. And once you were inside you seemed to be instantly accepted as part of the crowd. The heat was at times unbearable, with a humidity level of about 98 per cent. The sweat poured off us as we simply stood there soaking up the sights and sounds. The dancers moved and clapped without missing a beat to some of the most awe-inspiring and utterly obscure records I had ever heard. I knew there and then that I had found what I had been looking for in my teenage life. A 'club' and a lifestyle which I wanted to adopt for myself. So this was real Northern Soul and Wigan Casino. What a combination!

Betty Wright came on stage at around 3.30 am with so many backing musicians and singers that they were practically falling off the stage. Right from the opening song, the Afro-haired performer had the crowd in raptures. The sound, her energy and the professionalism of the show converted all the doubters who thought she might only do 'Where Is the Love' and then peter out. The roar from the audience reminded me of a first division football match – this wasn't a show, this was an experience for both Betty and ourselves. It all added to the magic of that first all-nighter, which was followed by many more that year.

In the coming months I would meet Dave Allen from Leyland and Colin Roughley from Chorley and become firm friends, travelling together to soul nights in Colin's cranky old Austin A35. I would also soon get to know and love a whole stream of Northern Soul anthems: Lou Pride's 'I'm Coming Home in the Morning', the Jades' 'I'm Where It's At', Eddie Parker's 'Love You Baby', Lorraine Chandler's 'I Can't Change', Lara Edmund Jr's 'The Larue', Yvonne Baker and 'You Didn't Say a Word',

Don Thomas's 'Come On Train', Danny Monday's 'Baby, Without You', Earl Jackson's 'Soul Self Satisfaction', Ramsey Lewis's 'Wade in the Water' . . . the list goes on.

For the next six years the Casino became the focal point of my social life, much to the chagrin of my parents. Like many long-suffering parents of Northern Soul fans down the years they wanted their son to be like 'normal' people. 'Why do you have to stay out all night?' – 'Why do you have to dress like that?' – 'So-and-so doesn't come home at ten in the morning from a night out', etc. Such were the remonstrations repeated in a thousand homes around the country at that time. Eventually, they accepted their only son had a strange affliction that set him apart from others, and the nagging stopped.

More difficult was keeping a steady girlfriend, especially if she was not into the Northern Soul scene. The oft-used line 'Can we just go for a drink tonight, because I'm off to Wigan later' was not usually well received when she stood there in her finery ready to go clubbing. Many a time I would get home from a 'normal' night out at midnight or later and get an irresistible urge to go to the Casino. One hour later I would be walking through the door of the all-nighter, all arrangements for the following day suddenly cancelled. It was utterly selfish, hedonistic and exhausting, but what the hell. You're only young once. (By the way, none of my relationships survived the Casino years!)

In the following years I would come to appreciate many of the funkier and smoother Blackpool Mecca sounds both at that venue and at the Casino, such as the Anderson Brothers' 'I Can See Him Loving You', Cameo's 'Find My Way', the Rimshots' 'Do What You Feel', Oscar Perry with 'I Got What You Need' and Main String.

My circle of friends from Chorley, Leyland, Blackburn, Horwich and surrounding areas seemed to keep growing – Dave Ward, Nick Varela, Noel Smith, Roger Wormald, Carole Thornley, Ste Livesey, Kev Birchall, Mick Stevenson, Mick Roberts, Andrew and Fiona Nevin, etc. Then we got to know the Scots crowd and the list kept growing – Tommy Cockburn, Jackie Pritchard, Hank (God rest his soul), Una, Avron, Barbara, Ailsa, Jiggy, Justin, et al.

The live acts were always a draw and varied between brilliant and mediocre – among those I remember are Tommy Hunt, Edwin Starr, Jackie Wilson, the Marvelettes, Junior Walker, Archie Bell and the Drells, Gloria Jones, Billy Butler, and the Chi-Lites.

Yes, there was some rubbish played too (a certain *Joe 90* theme tune, Muriel Day and some of the tailormade instrumentals spring to mind), but the quality of oldies and newer stuff was generally tremendous. Mr M's had an identity and atmosphere all of its own, and was a great learning ground for us young uns to learn the old Wheel, Torch and Mecca sounds. Dave Evison in particular, with his policy of reviving little-played oldies, enriched every all-nighter he appeared at.

Richard Searling was for my money by the late 70s well ahead of the pack on new discoveries. His Saturday night spots alone, following Russ in the early hours, made the trip to the all-nighter worth the effort. I can picture him now announcing Bobby Hutton's 'Lend a Hand', Betty Boo's 'Say It Isn't So', Larry Clinton's 'She's Wanted in Three States', Seventh Wonder's 'Captain of My Ship', the Del Capris' (alias Construction) 'Hey Little Way Out Girl', Little Ann's 'When He's Not Around', J C Messina's 'Time Won't Let Me', John and the Weirdest's 'Can't Get Over These Memories', Adam Apple's 'Don't Take It Out on This World', Court Davis and 'Try To Think', and a hundred others. These and many other records would run around your head for hours after the all-nighter, at the motorway services, at a friend's house, at a Sunday all-dayer, or at home trying to unwind after the night's exertions. It was all part of the Casino experience, and none of us wanted it to end.

It's impossible to describe the emptiness that I felt as I emerged, blinking, into the harsh daylight of a cold autumn morning after that final all-nighter.

Trench coat buttoned up, holdall slung over my shoulder, feet aching from almost nine hours of dancing and sweating, I took one last look at the famous Station Road building. Hundreds of weary-looking soul fans from all over Britain trudged out shaking hands and hugging each other for possibly the last time.

It was 9.30 am – a good hour and a half after the normal finishing time of the best-known soul night in the world. The DJs had tried in vain to clear the venue, but the dance floor remained full and the crowd chanted, whistled and stomped until the music re-started. Again. And again. And again.

And then finally the lights went up and we had to file slowly (because it was still so packed) outside and try to face the rest of our lives without Wigan Casino. It seemed a terrible prospect – the Casino was more than just a club to its regulars, just as Northern Soul has always been more than just music to its devotees. To say that the Casino was just a club is like saying that football is just a game. Or the Beatles were just a pop group. We all have our obsessions and loves and the Casino was ours.

The Casino wasn't perfect, and neither were its clientele. The venue was a shrine to the good, the bad and the downright criminal. And musically – maybe the Casino did live too much in the past. Certainly the monthly oldies' all-nighters became a focal point for many regulars who would normally have gone to the Saturday events. Maybe the Casino had had its day – Saturday attendances were disappointing in the final months. Maybe we took it all too seriously – after all, it was only a night out, wasn't it?

No it wasn't. The Casino was a piece of social and musical history and certainly set the benchmark for every dance club (Northern Soul or otherwise) that has existed since. I'm damned glad I was part of it.

No other club in the Northern Soul history has even come close to equalling the achievements of Wigan Casino. The sheer size of the events, the Casino's international reputation, and its longevity (remember its all-nighters ran every single week for eight years) are the stuff of legends.

The Station Road venue built on the foundations laid by clubs both small and large, and took Northern Soul to a different level. Initially borrowing heavily from the musical gems aired at clubs like the Twisted Wheel, the Torch and Blackpool Mecca, it soon formed its own identity. And the Wigan era is still seen as the golden age of Northern Soul and provides the definitive images in many people's minds of what the scene was all about.

When Wigan DJ Russ Winstanley suggested holding an all-nighter at the Casino in the autumn of 1973, he could not have foreseen the phenomenal success that lay ahead.

Russ recalls of those early days: 'We were all very nervous. It was a big adventure. We ran it not knowing what would happen from one week to another. After about a year it was like a monster running along with us hanging on to the back of it. Everybody wanted to come.'

By the time the venue was forced to close in 1981 to make way for a council civic centre that was never built, it had an incredible 100,000 members. It had been voted the best disco in the world by the American music magazine *Billboard*, ahead of the rich playboy's paradise Studio 54 in New York.

Record companies were trekking up the M1 in droves to ask the Casino DJs' advice on what rarities from their own vaults they should re-release. Millions of viewers watched a Granada TV documentary on the Casino in 1977. The almost-constant media attention created a hype and mystique around a club that had never previously been seen.

But it wasn't all plain sailing. The success story of the Casino was also peppered, in time-honoured Northern Soul fashion, with controversy, tragedy, musical differences and petty rivalries.

Russ Winstanley dropped the stylus on to the Sherries' 'Put Your Loving Arms Around Me' and kicked off the Casino legend at 2 am on 23 September 1973. As 652 soul fans poured into the venue to see what it was like, Russ provided the sounds almost single-handedly for eight hours. His friend Ian Fishwick provided the cover when Russ took a break, but it was basically Russ's show right through until 8 am.

The night was a success and was to be repeated the following week. Crowds grew and grew and it was soon clear that Russ would need some more help behind the decks. His first recruit was young Midlander Kev Roberts, who was virtually pushed up on to the stage by his pals who were impressed with his record collection.

Soon the Casino was pulling in 1,000-plus punters every Saturday and its reputation was spreading far and wide. The pressure was on the DJs to deliver the goods. Kev Roberts recalled: 'In the early days Russ was no record collector. You couldn't chew the fat with him about records all night. He made sure the dance floor was full, whatever kind of record it was. He had a different scene going there to the Mecca. The Casino was much more working-class than the Mecca, which was becoming more of a fashionable place. People would just jump into cars on a Saturday night and go there because it was the place to go, and if you asked some of them on a Sunday morning what had been played the night before they wouldn't be able to tell you.'

Kev said because of the Mecca's more elitist music policy, some DJs found it hard initially to take the Casino seriously. 'We were disrespectful of Russ. We were our own worst enemy. I can see where he was coming from now, but then we had no respect because we all wanted to be doing what Ian Levine was doing.'

However, the records kept turning up, the music got better and the Casino started to forge its own identity. A lot of the credit in many people's eyes has to go to the entrepreneur and record collector Simon Soussan.

Los Angeles-based Simon bought the rights to Mirwood, landing himself some classic songs by the likes of Jackie Lee, the Olympics, and the Belles. Simon also had a keen eye for discovering previously unknown Northern Soul gems on his travels around the USA, and would use a number of British DJs to build up a demand for them. Once his acetates, often carrying false names of both the artists and song, were firm dance-floor favourites, Simon would issue them on his own Soul Galore and Soul Fox labels. Up to 1973, Kev Roberts was one of the DJs used by Simon to 'break' his discoveries. Then in 1974, as the Casino's attendances were rising rapidly, Soussan decided to ditch him in favour of Russ Winstanley.

Kev said: 'Soussan was finding loads of records. He was shipping them over to the UK DJs all the time. When Russ came along, Simon realized there were bigger fish to fry. Russ had 2,000 people in every Saturday and Simon saw how Russ could break records for him.'

Early examples, like the Checkerboard Squares' 'Double Cookin' (covered up as 'Strings A Go Go' by the Bob Wilson Sounds), proved to Simon how he had an eager audience. Then he got even more ambitious and decided that instead of cruising the USA discovering records, he would make them.

So he went into the recording studios and manufactured 'tailormade' instrumentals like the Soul Fox Orchestra's version of Earl Wright's 'Thumb a Ride'. From there it was a short hop to a deal with Nottingham-based Select-a-Disc and the formation of the Black Magic label. This saw Bob Relf's 'Blowing My Mind to Pieces' being reworked. (Ian Levine would later say that Bob Relf told him whoever sang on that version wasn't him), and the Sharonettes' 'Pappa Ooh Mow Mow', which made the British pop charts.

Veteran Northern Soul DJ Soul Sam agrees that Simon had enormous influence on the early days of the Casino and the Northern Soul scene in general. 'Simon Soussan more or less provided Russ with his early playlist.'

Another key moment came when Russ recruited his third DJ – Bolton's Richard Searling. It was a partnership that would in turn bring them both fame, national recognition, friendship, and, regrettably, even animosity.

Richard Searling's enthusiasm for Northern Soul was fuelled by visits to clubs like the Pendulum in Manchester. 'Deep soul with a dance beat' is how Richard describes Northern Soul. During those Sunday nights at the Pendulum in 1971 he heard records like the Prophets' 'I Got the Fever'. 'I was intrigued by that,' he recalls. 'I just had to hear more.'

It was around this time that he was approached by Barry Tasker of Global Records in Manchester, who specialized in importing soul music from the States. They were looking for a warehouseman, and was Richard interested? You bet he was, because part of the job involved trips to America on record hunts.

Shrewd British businessmen had discovered American warehouses which kept tens of thousands of 'reject' USA releases and were only too happy to offload these flops to insane foreigners. It's easy to forget that in the 70s, transatlantic travel was mainly for the extremely wealthy or business people. The ordinary person would not consider or could not even afford the air fare, let alone a Florida holiday, which many people now would consider *de rigueur*.

So the American record warehouses were slow to twig that the English soul fans were making vast profits from their trips across the water. A record which the warehouse would release for 10 cents could fetch £5 among Northern Soul devotees back in England. Global Records would buy in bulk and then sell their 'finds' on record lists.

On one trip to the States, the young Searling found literally pallets full of virtually every Northern Soul in-demand release on the Philips, Chess and Musicor labels. One hundred copies of Duke Browner's 'Crying Over You' were among the finds that changed hands in the USA for comparative peanuts.

Richard recalls: 'I would be left alone in a warehouse the size of an aircraft hangar with just a tuna sandwich or something, for hours on end. There would be no one else around and pallets and pallets of records.'

On one trip, he was just about to leave with rich pickings when he stepped on to a record near the lift. That record, minus sleeve, was Gloria Jones's 'Tainted Love' on the USA Champion label. Richard dusted it off, thought he would give it a go and played it to great success at the Va-Va's all-nighter in Bolton. 'Tainted Love' went on to become a Northern Soul anthem and was immortalized when Soft Cell had a number one pop hit with their cover version in 1981.

Richard discovered he had a knack for DJing and drew a strong following in the Greater Manchester area. A couple of spots at the Pendulum led to Va-Va's in Bolton and a chance to air more and more of his 'discoveries'.

'The money I earned as a DJ was very useful to us in those days. I was earning something like £17 a week at Global Records but I could earn £8 a spot DJing for just a couple of hours so I kept doing it. Nobody knew how long it was going to last.'

During those trips to the States, Richard would come back armed with mouth-watering piles of records that were becoming more and more sought-after by the Northern clubs. Not just American issues, either, but demo copies by the hundred, which were even more valuable to collectors. 'We got some great stuff, but God knows what I must have missed,' said Richard. 'I wouldn't go back without bringing away three or four thousand pieces. There were Sandi Sheldon demos, Jimmy Conwell demos, a snapped DJ copy of Johnny Moore's "Walk Like a Man" which I mended and it played OK.

'At the House of Sounds in Philadelphia there were linen baskets full of records. Virtually every rare record must have been there. "Countdown Here I Come" – the Tempos'; 100 copies of "I'm On My Way", and loads of Tobi Legend's "Time Will Pass You By", which was a huge record at the Pendulum.

'I would go over there with wants lists from Simon Soussan. It was a great time. When I was going over there not many people had been there. John Anderson (of Soul Bowl in King's Lynn) had just been over. I remember when I first went, "Walk on the Wild Side" (Lou Reed) was playing on the radio. All these superb records were in that warehouse, and all for a few cents each.'

The seeds of his love of the rarer side of soul music had been sown by his teenage girlfriend (now wife) Judith, who had been to the Twisted Wheel. ('I could have gone to the last night at the Wheel, but I didn't because I was too young and I was afraid of the consequences,' Richard recalls.)

Now Richard was in a strong position to take advantage of his imported 'discoveries' by airing them to his growing army of fans at Va-Va's and other clubs around the north-west. When Va-Va's went the way of most Northern Soul all-nighters of the time and was closed down by the authorities, Richard lost his major stage. But his reputation had by then brought him to the attention of Russ Winstanley.

Richard was 'breaking' a host of Northern Soul sounds like 'Tainted Love' (Gloria Jones), 'My Dear Heart' (Shaun Robinson), and 'What Shall I Do' (Frankie and the Classicals) to the crowd at the atmospheric but short-lived venue. The young Searling guested at the Casino several times and consolidated his reputation as a top-class soul DJ. Within a couple of years, Russ opened a record shop in Wigan and chose Richard as manager. By then Richard was sharing top billing with Russ as the Casino's name DJ, and went on to become one of the most respected and forward-thinking soul music DJs in Britain.

Kev Roberts goes further: 'Richard has stayed the course and is undoubtedly the most innovative rare soul DJ of the past twenty-five years,' he says today. The relatively shy Bolton soul spinner was hired on a monthly cycle for the first three months, and then did a weekly job from March 1974. He said: 'Initially, the Casino was just another all-nighter. I went there as a punter on the very first night. I remember one of the big records was Tony Clarke's "Landslide". I remember thinking "I think I know where this one is . . . in a warehouse in Philadelphia." Next time I was over there I found five copies.

'People thought the Casino would only last for a short length of time. But it seemed quite quickly to get plenty of new faces in addition to holding on to the hard-core.' The size of the Casino was unprecedented in a Northern Soul all-nighter and as its reputation grew, Richard admits it made the early stages of his DJing career somewhat nerve-racking. 'I used to get incredibly nervous before my spot. I didn't play exactly what I wanted to play for fear of clearing the dance floor. It was only in later years I had the confidence to play my best records. I didn't really consider Wigan to be at the cutting edge at the time. You went to the Highland Room at Blackpool Mecca expecting to hear the newest and rarest stuff but that wasn't always the case at Wigan.'

'Simon Soussan,' Richard reflected, 'possibly made Wigan Casino what it was in the first couple of years. His ability to pick up these records was remarkable, you can't deny him that.' Soussan knew that Russ had the biggest platform in the country for promoting 'his' Northern Soul sounds, and soon bundles of future dance floor favourites were winging their way to Wigan from across the Atlantic.

Said Richard: 'Russ stuck with records that I used to shudder about. Certain records, like "Jerk, Baby, Jerk", I would never have continued with. But Russ had a more open-minded attitude to what was a dance record and so he was the perfect partner for Simon Soussan. That isn't meant as a criticism of Russ.

'When you look back on certain records like "Footsee" and others it's easy to demean them because we appreciate them now as pure pop records. Back then, it was a bit different. I wouldn't knock anything that got people through the doors of the club. People might have got into the music through the more "poppy" stuff but then they would go on to discover the real thing.'

The pulling power of the Casino and its sheer reputation meant that a few airings of a record, whatever its origins, could guarantee it cult status, a re-release or certainly the inevitable bootlegging. Soul Sam recalls playing Joe Cook's 'I'm Falling in Love with You, Baby' and Gwen Owens' 'Just Say You're Wanted and Needed', at the Cleethorpes all-nighter. Both went on to become Wigan anthems, and there aren't many people who would argue that they were 'Cleethorpes sounds'. Sam himself isn't bothered: 'I don't worry about who discovers a record, or plays it first, as long as it gets played. The music is more important.'

Richard comments: 'You could hear a record at the Mecca or Cleethorpes, but once you got it going at Wigan, the Casino would take the credit. The people in the know would know the real story, of course, but once you got Wigan behind a record it became huge.'

The halcyon years for Northern Soul discoveries, Richard feels, was between 1972 and 1975, when there were so many quality records unearthed it was sometimes impossible to keep track of them. And the Casino was always at the forefront. 'The Casino maximized that surge of interest. It was the right size, it held the right amount of people and there was such a fantastic atmosphere. The geography was fine too.'

One of Russ Winstanley's early successes was with the anthemic 'You Didn't Say a Word' by Yvonne Baker. Nowadays the classic Cameo Parkway recording is sure to feature in almost every soul fan's all-time top ten. But Richard recalls how when Russ started to spin the then unknown record, which had been sent over to him by Simon Soussan, it took a while to take off. 'It was a slow starter,' said Richard. 'The reaction was OK in the early days, but the demand built up through the dance floor and took it on its way.

'The crowd made that club, not the DJs. The crowd made those records and encouraged Russ to go after records that we thought maybe weren't all that great.'

The discoveries that Richard unearthed and continued to play right up to the club's closure in 1981 enhanced his reputation as one of Britain's most up-front and contemporary Northern Soul DJs.

He counters modestly: 'Who discovers a record? The guy who finds it, the guy who hands it to a DJ or the DJ who breaks it to the crowd. I can't claim credit for very much at Wigan.

'From 1977 to 1981 I was in the privileged position of being involved with John Anderson of Soul Bowl in King's Lynn. He used to give me acetates of the stuff that he brought back from America. When the final analysis is written on the most influential people in Northern Soul history, John Anderson will be right up there with Ian Levine and Simon Soussan. He's very reluctant to take any credit for it, but there's no doubt about it. His Grapevine label was going at the time and Wigan was the cutting edge of the soul music scene. I would cover up the tunes to keep them exclusive. I drove down to King's Lynn every month to see what he had, and he had just about everything. I shudder to think what he left behind on his trips to America!'

As far as the Casino is concerned, Richard is in no doubt as to its place in Northern Soul history. 'It was the best venue ever. It was great. The Wheel and the Torch were great but the Casino was in a different class. It was the right place at the right time. We were very lucky to be involved. It would be very petty of me to say that I could have done what I have done without Wigan Casino. It gave me the break I needed. But getting the breaks is one thing, it's making the most of them that counts.'

If Russ was often seen as the 'poppier' end of the Northern scene, Richard was more of a purist, although he did have his moments. He freely admits playing Gary Lewis and the Playboys' 'My Heart's Symphony', a dreadful piece of blue-eyed pop soul that sounds so teenyboppish today that it's laughable. And he remembers once having to flee from a hate mob after a gig in Blackburn because he had played it.

'There were certain records that were played at Wigan and became big and stayed big purely because people were asking for them. "Jerk, Baby, Jerk" was another one. We played it because of the demand from the dancers – it wasn't the DJs, it was the punters that liked records like that.' In general, however, Richard says he played what he wanted. And apart from some pressure from Mike Walker, the Casino's manager, to play some of the latest Spark releases (Gene Latter's 'Sign On the Dotted Line', etc), Searling was left alone to choose the material for his own spot.

One famous occasion when the opposite happened was at the fourth anniversary, when a group of Pye representatives attended the all-nighter. Flushed with the success of the Disco Demand series, they brought some acetates of unreleased material with them. Richard examined suspiciously a white label that read 'Layla'. Thinking of the Derek and the Dominoes song, he quizzed the Pye man and was assured it was a different song.

Richard popped it on to the decks after one beer too many and, sure enough, it *was* the same 'Layla'. 'It sounded exactly the same. That lasted about twenty seconds before I whipped it off and put something else on,' said Richard.

Russ also was chairing weekly DJ meetings to present a current playlist and ensure that chosen sounds were 'broken' to the Casino crowd at the Saturday all-nighters. The main DJs would play four chosen tunes twice during each spot to test audience reaction. In this way, new discoveries quickly became sought-after items or were unceremoniously dumped as soul turkeys. Differing opinions and tastes, particularly with regard to Blackpool Mecca's more 'modern' playlist (which Russ all but banned at the Casino), often led to heated exchanges.

'Wigan had its detractors,' Richard said, 'but I think it doesn't get the credit it deserves for the amount of records it broke in the last two or three years. We played a lot of mid-tempo stuff, and Stafford continued where we left off. Stuff like Mr Soul ("What Happened to Yesterday"), John and the Weirdest ("Can't Get Over These Memories"), Phyllis Hyman, weren't traditional dancers and were all massive at Wigan.'

For every youngster who was attracted to the Casino by a newspaper article, a TV clip or a record on the radio, there was a veteran Northern Soul follower who thought it was all going too far. Their 'exclusive' scene was no longer exclusive. New faces appeared every week and journalists and record company staff were falling over themselves to project the Casino into the big wide world.

When Pye began its Disco Demand series, it had top twenty hits with tried and tested Casino favourites. Wayne Gibson's 'Under My Thumb', The Chosen Few's 'Footsee' (released as 'Wigan's Chosen Few'), and Nosmo King's 'Goodbye, Nothing to Say', were commercial successes and put the Casino on the lips of every youngster in the country. But they were not true soul records, just good dance records, and gave the public a false impression of Northern Soul. Testimony to the truth of that statement is in the fact that no self-respecting DJ would play any of the above three records today.

Neither would anyone dream of playing Wigan's Ovations version of 'Skiing in the Snow' or 'Superlove'. The commerciality of the Casino created a storm of interest, and unrest within the Northern Soul community.

In 1974, ex-Twisted Wheel DJ Brian Rae was added to the DJ lineup by Russ, and he remained there until the end. After the cellars and underground scene created by the Wheel, Brian found himself in a 2,500 capacity-venue that was rarely out of the media. The veteran DJ had no qualms about the public attention being paid to the Casino: 'My ambition is to convert everybody in the world into a soul fan,' he said. 'There's no other form of music that is as good to dance to as soul music. The more commercial things got, the better if it meant more people were discovering our music.'

Dave Rimmer, editor of the soul fanzine *Soulful Kinda Music*, was among those disenchanted with the more 'poppy' music policy adopted at the Casino in some periods. That was one of the reasons he stopped going to the venue in the late 1970s. He explained: 'Basically I am a soul music fan, it doesn't have to be Northern Soul for me to appreciate the music, just Black American music (although I'm not excluding some singers who sing with soul but happen to have been born white). Think about some of the crap that was played at Wigan . . . Themes from *Joe 90*, *Hawaii 5-0*, Muriel Day, etc. etc. I could go on and on.

'That's why I stopped going to Wigan. I'd rather stay at home and listen to a Bobby Bland LP than subject myself to that rubbish. There were other reasons as well, but they all boil down to the fact I didn't enjoy the records that were being played, so I didn't go. Then I moved to North Wales to work, and had to be at work by six o'clock on a Sunday morning. So that stopped me going out to nighters completely for several years.'

Steve Russell, who was co-founder of the West Midlands Soul Club, said: 'When it all got very commercial and stuff got in the charts, it was a bit of a downer. Northern Soul was always an underground dance scene where people knew each other, dressed differently and met up at certain venues. People wanted to try to keep it as it was, it was special to them.'

Pye Records' representative Dave McAleer was among the first southern visitors to see what the Casino had to offer. He was astonished at what he found on his first trip in 1974. 'Nobody danced like they did at the Casino. I had never seen anyone with such agility. I don't know how they did the spins like that so many times, and came out of it without any effect, and the things later that break dancers did but not as well. The kids down south thought they were hip and had it all, but it was nothing compared to what was happening past Birmingham.'

The music, which Dave was delighted to find included many releases on Pye-owned labels, was also mind-boggling. He said: 'These weren't just American records that were obscure. These weren't American hits of six years ago. These were the B sides of big, big flops; local releases on minor labels where there might have been only 1,000 copies pressed; and the kids in Wigan knew every beat.'

DJ John Vincent recalled how even eventual Wigan anthems like 'I'm Coming Home in the Morning' by Lou Pride took some time to become popular. 'I gave it a few spins (as James Lewis) although contrary to opinion it took nearly six months to take off. I cleared the dance floor completely for at least the first three or four plays, but that was something I was always good at anyway.

'The amount of pressure a DJ was under was immense – there was always plenty of backstabbing, covering records, racing down to John Anderson's to get first pick, and so on. It was just non-stop. I could certainly not have financed my collection without selling hundreds of emi discs each week!'

He added: 'As far as awful records are concerned, it is easy with hindsight to condemn some of the sounds that were played, some things I played make me cringe now, but they were right at the time. Lorraine Silver was a massive record for me, but I would not dream of playing it today. "Black Power" was massive for Richard but I can't imagine it's still in his box, but at the time it was an integral part of the play list, as was "The Trip". Although I can still remember crossing the road one morning and seeing a broken copy of this lying in the middle of the road!'

A major player in the Casino success story was undoubtedly manager Mike Walker, who tragically died in 1980 after helping to put the club on the international map.

Carlisle-born Mike got his love for soul music by visiting the Twisted Wheel in Manchester. After a spell as an assistant cinema manager in Wigan and later working on a local news-paper, he found himself attending a function at the Casino Club. He and then manager Gerry Marshall got chatting, and Mike was offered a job as a DJ at the club. Within a few months he was working five nights a week at the clubs, and when Gerry bought the business he installed Mike as manager. When Mike and Russ Winstanley became friends, together at Russ's suggestion, they persuaded Gerry to let them stage an all-nighter.

Walker and Winstanley made a formidable team – both naturally eloquent, born salesmen and very shrewd marketing experts. They managed the affairs of the Casino with con-summate skill, raising its profile, creating a mystique around the venue and marketing the music and the lifestyle in an ambitious way.

The constant media attention in the early years, the launch of the club's own record label (Casino Classics), the 'creation' of Wigan's Chosen Few and Wigan's Ovation, and the club's own magazine were all vital factors in putting the Casino on the map. It was all ground-breaking stuff, and paved the way for today's superclubs like the Ministry of Sound, which two decades later has its own merchandise, magazine and website.

Mike was the manager of the most successful and talked-about club in Europe, if not the world. Yet something was preying heavily on his mind. When he took his own life, his family, friends and colleagues were devastated.

Richard Searling recalled how Mike became very distant in the period leading up to his death. Nobody had seen him for months and Harry Green was running the club. Then Mike turned up one night somewhat the worse for drink and right in the middle of Richard's spot at 3 am demanded that he be allowed to play the 'Three Before Eight'. Richard agreed, and that was the last time he saw him.

'I felt awful when he died,' said Richard. 'There's no doubt that Mike was a major factor in the success of the Casino. On the face of it he had everything, but something was clearly troubling him.'

One of the top Wigan Casino DJs was the champion of the 'unsung oldies', Dave Evison. The ex-Torch-goer's regular spots playing little-heard and often-overlooked soul records from years gone by brought him a strong following.

But Dave's quest to 'educate' the younger soul fans also unwittingly led to the massive oldies-only all-nighters at the Casino, which many feel ultimately harmed the venue. The monthly Friday oldies' all-nighters detracted crowds from the regular Saturday night events, and led at times to something of a backward-looking music policy at the Casino.

Dave's career as an oldies DJ began by accident. After much persuasion he managed to get several Friday night spots DJing at the Torch, and after its closure found himself at the Top Of The World in Stafford with fellow DJ Kev Roberts. Kev went off to the toilet without leaving a record cued up, so Dave, who was standing in for him, quickly pulled out a 45 from his own 'sales box'. He put on Curtis Mayfield's 'Move On Up', which was hardly the rarest or least known piece of vinyl around at that time. Dave said: 'Everyone looked at me in horror for a moment, then they started dancing.'

That's when he realized that a record didn't have to be rare or unknown for it to please the crowd. He also realized that many soul fans might not have heard hundreds of records from clubs like the Wheel and the Torch. He set about specializing in oldies, and after an audition with Russ Winstanley at Burnley's Rose Room, he joined the Wigan Casino line-up in 1974 sharing a spot with Martyn Ellis.

Dave admits that he was at first a little intimidated by the Casino's reputation, but got through it thanks to his friends. 'I was one of the few DJs that could dance, and still can. I was a dancer first and foremost, then a record collector, and then a DJ. Because I was one of the regulars I was accepted. My friends didn't think I was showing off. I was a dancer who DJ'd.'

When Martyn left, Dave was on his own in the oldies limelight, and had great fun discovering and resurrecting relatively cheap records that he felt hadn't been properly appreciated in the past. Spyder Turner's 'I Can't Make It Any More', Millie Jackson's 'House for Sale', J J Barnes's 'How Long', and Silvetti's 'Spring Rain' were just some of the fairly common records that would suddenly quadruple in price as they became in-demand items after Dave's spots at the Casino. Dave recalled: 'I was always finding things that there were thousands of copies of and creating a new demand. I could turn the 50p Soul Bowl "ashtray" into a £5 monster. Spyder Turner was so common that no one would dare play it. I turned it into one of the biggest records ever. I couldn't afford the really rare stuff, and there was no need for me to pay silly prices. It was just great soul music that deserved to be heard.'

The famous strained relationship between Russ and Richard in the Casino's latter years is the stuff of legends. A clash of egos and musical tastes is one explanation; a natural drifting apart another. Both men were ambitious and wanted to be seen as the number one Casino jock. Both men wanted to work in the record industry and land regular radio work.

When Richard stopped working for Russ at his shop in 1978 and became employed by RCA as a record plugger, it heralded the start of a 'cold war' between them. Sources suggest the two men hardly spoke for the last two years of the Casino's lifetime. There were no big rows, just a distance that developed between them which has never been bridged.

In *Soul Survivors*, Russ spoke of the 'heated debates' between himself and Richard over the music policy. 'Both of us believed passionately in what we were doing and neither of us could be blamed for sometimes being stubborn or dogmatic,' he wrote. 'Although we may have trodden different paths we had the same goal . . . to make and keep the Casino at number one.'

Richard believes that the late Casino manager Mike Walker summed up the rift between him and Russ when he told him: 'Richard, it was your ambition that soured the relationship.' Richard admits today: 'Russ helped me a lot but I wanted to move on.' Both DJs wanted to be number one in their field and as Russ's popularity waned Richard's star was in the ascendancy. Richard points out that part of the essence of being a successful DJ is to try to create a better playlist than any other. 'Of course there's rivalry in the music. You want to play the best records you can. If there isn't the rivalry there, you might as well pack it in. That's one of the reasons why I'm not purporting to be at the cutting edge of the Northern Soul scene any more because I can't keep up with the collections of the top DJs.'

The end of the Casino left Richard with a bitter taste in his mouth, owing to the strained relationship between him and Russ and the fact that the Bolton-based DJ had booked Wigan Tiffanys for an all-nighter in early October 1981.

When the Casino announced it was holding another farewell all-nighter two weeks after the official final event, there was an unfortunate clash of dates. Four hundred yards down the road, Richard and partner Bernie Golding were running their Wigan Tiffanys event.

Richard said he came back from holiday to be told he had been banned from the Casino. He and Bernie agreed to continue with their event, but the Casino of course won hands down as the Tiffany's event had only pulled in about 150 people. There then followed a period when Tiffany's venue staged successful all-nighters, with the promotion of the venue alternating between Richard and Russ.

An argument between the two over whether Richard had agreed to DJ at one of Russ's events – as Russ had advertised – was the final straw. 'It was the beginning of the end for me and Russ,' said Richard. But he does not let the slightly sour taste of the Casino's final days colour his opinion of the venue's importance. 'The sheer size of the event got people talking about it. The scale of it was part of the attraction. Wigan built up a lot of small clubs as well. Because we had so many people in, people went away and wanted to hear the music in other venues.'

Russ is at a loss to explain why this apparent rift between him and Richard began – and continues even today. He accepts there was a falling-out over the clash of dates at the end of the Casino's life but believes professional rivalry is the real key. 'It's very sad. We were the best of mates. He has got himself into that situation and he himself can't really say why. I have written to him and spoken to him but I am still none the wiser.

'I would meet him tomorrow and shake his hand and say let's forget this cold war, if that's what it is. I would love to work for him at the Ritz or Blackburn.'

Russ also gets heartily fed up with the sniping at the small number of 'pop' records played at the Casino. 'I normally ask people to name me some and they start to struggle after ten. What about the 10,000 black soul records that we played? Why don't people go on about the great records? Let's see someone put on a night where they aren't allowed to play any Wigan sounds and see what's left.'

He stands by the Casino's music policy 100 per cent, and says he is glad that Ian Levine thinks it wasn't as innovative as Blackpool Mecca. 'The Mecca was very innovative and it disappeared up its own backside. The Mecca moved forward so much it became just like any other club around the corner and people stopped going.

'We thought that people came from all around the country to hear rare records they couldn't hear anywhere else. Ian changed things for the worse, which was a shame because I loved the Mecca.'

When the end came for the Casino, it was tinged with a hint of bitterness for Russ too. He still feels cheated that Wigan council demanded the Casino site for a civic centre extension that was never built. 'It was the most important soul venue ever,' he says. 'We never really thought that the day would ever come when it would finish.'

Sinclair Hogg, of Bathgate, Scotland, was one of the many Scots visitors who made the regular trip down to the Casino.

His treasured memories include: 'buying a pair of Spencers and splitting the arse out of them within an hour, Vernon from Bradford trying my kilt on at the 6th Anniversary, having my photo taken arms round each other with Edwin Starr, falling in love with Martha Reeves, and Tommy Hunt signing one of his records for me. Great times! Goose bumps just writing this. Best mates in the world – everyone at Okeh Soul Club, Jiggy, Avron, Carol, Jenny, Big Joe, Stuart, Tommy, Stew and Gary. John Neilson (you should have won the dancing competition). Vernon, Ralph (Stoke), Danny Spiers, the Southport crew – Tony and Carole and others far too many to mention.'

*Sinclair Hogg's Top Ten*

'I Walked Away'  Bobby Paris
'I Only Get This Feeling'  Chuck Jackson
'I Can See Him Making Love to You Baby'  Anderson Bros
'Nothing Can Compare to You'  The Velvet Satins
'I'm Gonna Find Me Somebody'  The Velvets
'Cause You're Mine'  the Vibrations
'If You Ever Walked Out of My Life'  Dena Barnes
'If You Ask Me'  Jerry Williams
'Born a Loser'  Don Ray
'When I'm Gone'  Brenda Holloway

Neil Austin of Chipping Norton, Oxfordshire, pays tribute to the sister club of the Casino, Mr M's. Formerly of the Lancaster soul crowd, he was a regular Casino soul boy in the late 70s, and was among the many fans of the smaller club-within-a-club which specialized in oldies only. He recalls:

'On Saturday nights at Lancaster station when the train to

London, stopping at Wigan was announced, 'we knew we were on our way! About thirty or so dedicated fans from Morecambe, Barrow and Lancaster were ready to jump on the train for the one-hour ride to Wigan'.

'The train would arrive at Wigan and we would run for last orders at the Station Arms and then go up and over the hill, down Station Road and sit on the steps by the ABC.

'You would hear three or four radio cassettes playing, some people would start dancing and as the crowd swelled you would have butterflies in your stomach. The doors would open and through the rush, the crush, our group would run up the steps to the main hall.

'Russ would be playing, the hall filling up and people would be dancing. This was the start of the evening, around 12.30–1.00 am. In the back of our minds was "M's will be opening" and "I wonder what they will be playing in there tonight?" 3 am would come, my friends and I would say goodbye to the main hall and burn through the doors to Mr M's, vying for a table, as M's filled up in a matter of fifteen minutes.

'Mr M's to us was a place for great dancers. Some black guys would do amazing acrobatics to the O Jays' "Looky Looky". The dance floor would be packed solid with the sounds of High Voltage's "Country Roads" and "My Hang Up is You" by the Skullsnaps.

'Mr M's had a soul fan following and a creative culture all of its own. If a sound was big in Mr M's, five or six weeks later it would be big again in the main hall. The only time we would be tempted out of Mr M's would be when the excellent Brian Rae was on the turntables, a DJ with his finger on the pulse of the Wigan crowd, really in touch with the music, comfortable in both Mr M's and the main hall.

'Mr M's closed at 7 am, and we would again pour back into the main hall to the sounds of Dave Evison, Burning Spear and the Majestics and finish with the "Three before Eight".'

*Neil Austin's Top Ten Mr M's spins*

'Everything's Gonna be Alright' P P Arnold

'Looky Looky'  O Jays
'Sister Lee'  Sam Ward
'Coming to Your Rescue'  Triumphs
'Country Roads'  High Voltage
'Blowing Up My Mind'  Exciters
'My Hang Up is You'  Skullsnaps
'Help Me to Find Myself'  Outsiders
'Love Music'  O Jays
'Seven Day Lover'  James Fountain

*Neil Austin's Main Hall Top Ten*

'Tough Girl'  Billy Arnell
'Not My Girl'  John Hampton
'I Walked Away'  Bobby Paris
'Don't Pity Me'  Sue Lynne
'Stop and You Will Become Aware'  Helen Shapiro
'You Got Your Mind on Other Things'  Beverly Ann
'Love, Love, Love'  Bobby Hebb
'How Can I Ever Find a Way'  Carol and Jerri
'That's Not Love'  Holly St James
'I Go to Pieces'  Gerri Grainger

She was known to tens of thousands of former Casino-goers simply as 'Mrs Woods'. Not many knew her first name was Hilda, even fewer would have dared to use that to her face.

No, she was Mrs Woods to everyone who ever went through the Station Road doors. The formidable-looking grey-haired lady on the cash desk suffered no fools. Woe betide anyone without a membership card or a valid ticket or anyone who tried to sneak in without paying.

She kept the hoards at bay – and they loved her for it, even sending holiday postcards to her and the other ladies who staffed the upstairs snack bar. Wigan woman Mrs Woods worked the reception desk from midnight to 8 am at every all-nighter after the first couple of events. She naturally enough felt tired, and couldn't even hear the music properly from her work station, but used to push back fatigue by stretching her legs and passing

*Above: Mary Wells – one of the early hit-makers with Tamla Motown.*
*Right: The Supremes, Motown's most successful recording artists.*

*Left:* Motown stars The Four Tops.

*Right, top:* A scooter rally on Blackpool seafront in 1965. Mods would create the demand for the music and lifestyle that became Northern Soul.
(Picture: Blackpool Evening Gazette)

*Right, bottom:* Mod culture has always been closely linked with the Northern Soul scene.
(Picture: Blackpool Evening Gazette)

*Below:* Motown artist Edwin Starr.

*Above, top left:* Ex-Twisted Wheel DJ Dave Scutt.

*Above:* The old Twisted Wheel building in Whitworth Street, Manchester, as it looks today.

*Right:* Ex-Twisted Wheel DJ Brian Rae.

*Left:* Regulars at the Up The Junction in Crewe in 1972: (from left) Mitch Moore from Market Harborough, Brian Taylor and Betty Peters from Corby.

*Left:* En route to the Up The Junction in Crewe, Margaret Smart and Betty Peters. Notice the necklace. Can you guess what it is made of?

*Below left:* A scale model of the Golden Torch.

*Below right:* Martyn Ellis and Terry Thomas at the Torch.

*Above, top left:* Major Lance on stage at the Torch as his famous live album was being recorded.
*Above, top right:* Junior Walker on stage at the Torch.
*Above, left:* DJ Martyn Ellis and singer Jimmy Thomas at the Torch in 1972.
*Above, right:* Singer Otis Leavill at the Torch.
*Right:* The site of the famous Torch all-nighters in Hose Street, Tunstall, as it is today.

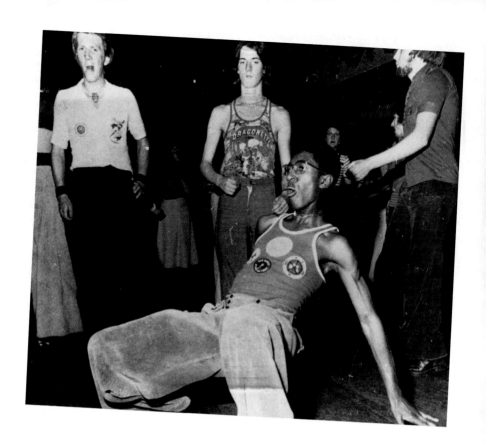

*Above: Time for a 'backdrop' at Wigan Casino.*
(Picture: Wigan Observer)
*Left: A teenage Richard Searling, soon to become a top Wigan Casino DJ, with his then girlfriend and now wife Judith.*
*Right: Wigan Casino in 1977.*
*Below: Wigan Casino.*

*Left:* The 1975 Spark album 'Tommy Hunt Live At The Wigan Casino'.
*Top, right:* The Casino on fire after its closure in 1981. *(Picture: Wigan Observer)*
*Bottom, right:* The Casino in the middle of demolition. Note the springs that once supported the dance floor. *(Picture: Wigan Observer)*

*Left:* Did we really used to wear those things?
*Below:* Scots soul fans John Neilson and Sinclair Hogg, with author Dave Nowell and Vernon from Bradford pictured at Wigan Casino.

*Above:* Blackpool Mecca (o.
Tiffanys), home of the
famous Highland Room.

*Above:* Crown Heights Affair at the Blackpool
Mecca all-dayer.
*Right:* Colin Curtis (left) and Ian Levine at
Blackpool Mecca.

*Right: The crowd at Morecambe Pier all-nighter.*
*Below: Gene Chandler with Morecambe Pier all-nighter promoter Shaun Gibbons.*

*Below: Gene Chandler on stage at Morecambe Pier in 1983.*

*Above:* Major Lance among the crowd at Wigan Tiffanys in 1981.
*Below:* Major Lance with soul fan Carole Thornley at the Hinckley all-nighter in 1982.

*bove: DJ Terry Jones (third from left) and
iends at the Southport weekender.*

*Above: A dancer enjoys the music at the 1998
Blackpool Mecca reunion event.*

*ove: Johnny Pearson and Káren Seddon
o promote monthly soul nights at the Preston
asshoppers Club.
ght: Dave Evison today.*

*Above:* The Tony's Empress Ballroom all-nighter in Blackburn. (Picture: Manifesto)

*Above:* Richard Searling at Jazz FM.
*Left:* DJ Kenny Burrell, with his £15,000 Motown single.

*Right:* Maxine Brown live on stage at the Cleethorpes weekender.

*Left:* DJ Ginger Taylor.
*Right:* DJ Soul Sam.

**Above:** The Keele all-nighter. *(Picture: Manifesto)*
**Right:** DJ Kev Roberts, part of the Togetherness team.
**Below:** The Kings Hall in Stoke, scene of the current biggest all-nighters in the UK.

*Above:* The 100 Club all-nighter
in London. *(Picture: Manifesto)*
*Right:* Ian Levine, former Blackpool
Mecca DJ and film maker.
*Below:* Author David Nowell,
former Motown singer
Brenda Holloway and soul fan
Mark Isles at the *Togetherness*
soul weekender.

the long hours of darkness with the young soul fans.

Said Mrs Woods: 'I got tired but I kept pushing it back until it was time to go home. They were a good set of kids. They were good fun. They used to come to the desk and ask for a pass-out and I used to stamp their hand. When they came back we used to have a little chat.'

She soon discovered, however, that her passout system was not foolproof. She was using a simple date stamp – easily obtained from many shops. Cunning soulies would stamp their own hands and sneak in without paying with the rest of the genuine pass-out crowd. Mrs Woods got the upper hand by having a new couple of stamps made – one saying Night Shift, the other Mastercard.

'All the regulars called me Mrs Woods,' she reflected. 'One or two called me "Ma". They were just out to enjoy themselves. The dancing was lovely. All that twisting and turning. I don't know how they did it. I wish I could have done it. I never tried it myself because I had arthritis in my leg even then.'

Mick Fitzpatrick, formerly of Nelson, Lancashire, and now living in Germany, remembers his indoctrination into Northern Soul: 'I cannot remember the day I became a "Soulie". What I do remember is being at a youth club when I was a kid and seeing a guy dance like I had never seen before. The 70s was a time when most people just shuffled around on the dance floor, and there was this guy jumping several feet into the air landing in the splits then spinning and moving his feet at a blistering speed.

'From that day on I was hooked. I was lucky, not only did I love the music, we belonged to an exclusive club. We turned our backs on the fashion of the day. No weird-looking seventies fashions for us. My first suit was made at Burton's the gentleman's tailors. Can you imagine it? The rest of the youth at the time looked like some Davie Bowie/Marc Bolan clones and there was us. Immaculately dressed and cool. When we moved into a club (we never called it a disco) we always took our music. Several 45s in a case. The DJs would always try and play some commercial soul to keep us happy. They soon played our special stuff. Why not – when you had a dozen people on the floor that could give Fred Astaire or Michael Jackson a run for their money it is free entertainment for the rest of the punters.

'The main clubs for us were the Casino and Blackpool Mecca. However, there were plenty of very good clubs that never quite got to the Casino rankings. You could do all-nighters and all-dayers from Friday night to early Monday morning and go nowhere near Wigan or Blackpool. Then it became fashionable. A couple of the records made it into the charts, everyone talked about Wigan, the clothes that we had to have tailormade could be bought in the shops. Every club you went to played our music, or they would have a Northern Soul hour. "Footsee" was played at every disco in the north. My claim to infamy was dancing to "Footsee" at my niece's birthday party. She was three, I was drunk.

'It was great, fantastic, and marvellous. We could dance, dance and dance. Then all of a sudden we realized that the commercialism that we stayed away from in the first instance was becoming part of our scene. My younger brother could dance like the devil but could never "keep the faith". To this day he relates our music to a "youth thing", a passing fad. On the contrary, our music is forever.'

The Casino, however, did not last forever and the Northern Soul scene struggled to fill the void it left behind in the 1980s.

*Richard Searling's Top Ten Wigan Casino sounds*

'Can't Get Over These Memories' John and Weirdest
'Just Ask Me' Bobby Thurston
'Where I'm Not Wanted' Eddie Holman
'The Duck' Willie Hutch
'You Didn't Say a Word' Yvonne Baker
'I Am Nothing' Al Williams
'My World is on Fire' Jimmy Mack
'I Don't Like to Lose' The Group
'Country Girl' Vickie Baines
'What Happened to Yesterday' Mr Soul

*Richard Searling's all-time Top Ten Northern Soul sounds*

'You Hit Me'  Alice Clark
'If That's What You Wanted'  Frankie Beverley
'Lend a Hand'  Bobby Hutton
'Stick by Me, Baby'  Salvadors
'Landslide'  Tony Clarke
'I Just Can't Live My Life'  Linda Jones
'You Just Don't Know'  Chubby Checker
'On the Real Side'  Larry Saunders
'Cheatin' Kind'  Don Gardner
'Key to My Happiness'  The Charades

*The full playlist of Richard Searling's last ever spot at The Casino in September 1981*

'Heartaches and Pain'  Pages
'Your Love Keeps Me Dancing'  Ike Strong
'Playing the Part of a Fool'  Embers
'Try to Think'  Court Davis
'Can't Get Over These Memories'  John & Weirdest
'What Should I Do'  Little Ann
'Where I'm Not Wanted'  Eddie Holman
'The Thought of Loving You'  Pierre Hunt
'Oh Yeah Yeah Yeah'  Vivian Carrol
'I Don't Like to Lose'  Cecil Washington
'What'cha Gonna Do'  Combinations
'That's the Way'  James Lewis
'Heartache Souvenirs'  William Powell
'Makes Me Feel That Way'  Rock Candy
'Mighty Body'  Leon Bryant
'How Can I Tell Her'  Curtis
'No Second Chance'  Deadbeats
'Love Slipped Thru My Fingers'  Herman Hitson
'What Happened to Yesterday'  Mr Soul
'All of My Life'  Nurons
'I Need Love'  Daybreak
'Let's Spend Some Time Together'  Larry Houston

'I'm Coming On Over'  Johnny Hunnicut
'Hurt'  Eddie Holman
'Packin' Up'  Damon Fox
'You Know What I Like'  Emmanual Laskey
'Giving It All to You'  Cheryl Berdell
'Sho Nuff No Funny Stuff'  Charles Mann
'Gonna Give You My Love'  Gary Glenn
'That's the Kind of Man I Am'  Bobby Adams
'Let's Talk It Over'  Dee Dee Gartrell
'Getting Ready for the Get Down'  ZZ and Co
'I'll Never Say Goodbye'  Vontastics
'Let Somebody Love You'  Kenni Burke
'Someone Special'  Rideout

*Twenty selected early Wigan Casino monster sounds*

'If You Ask Me'  Jerry Williams
'Dance, Dance, Dance'  Casualeers
'I'm Where It's At'  Jades
'I'm Coming Home in the Morning'  Lou Pride
'The Night'  Frankie Valli
'I've Got the Need'  Moments/Chuck Jackson
'Baby Without You'  Danny Monday
'You Didn't Say a Word'  Yvonne Baker
'Don't It Make You Feel Funky'  Joe Hicks
'The Trip'  Dave Mitchell
'I've Got to Find Me Somebody'  The Vel-Vets
'You Don't Love Me Any More'  Johnny Caswell
'I Belong to You'  Milton Wright
'Tears'  Lee Roye
'Can't Help Loving You'  Paul Anka
'Get Out (And Let Me Cry)'  Harold Melvin
'You Got Me Where You Want Me'  Larry Santos
'You Got Your Mind on Other Things'  Beverly Ann
'Come on, Train'  Don Thomas
'Love Don't You Go Through No Changes on Me'  Sister Sledge

*Twenty selected Mr M's floorfillers*

'Do the Temptation Walk' Jackie Lee
'What Kind of Lady' Dee Dee Sharp
'Girl Across the Street' Moses Smith
'Get on Your Knees' Los Canarios
'The Champion' Willie Mitchell
'Oh My Darlin' Jackie Lee
'My Little Girl' Bob and Earl
'Move On Up' Curtis Mayfield
'I Can't Make It Any More' Spyder Turner
'I Surrender' Eddie Holman
'If That's What You Wanted' Frankie Beverley
'Shake Me, Wake Me' Four Tops
'Lonely, Lonely Girl am I' The Velvelettes
'Someday We're Gonna Love Again' Barbara Lewis
'I'm Not Strong Enough' Four Perfections
'Time' Edwin Starr
'We Were Made for Each Other' Terrible Tom
'They'll Never Know Why' Freddie Chavez
'A Little Bit Hurt' Julian Covay
'You're Gonna Make Me Love You' Sandi Sheldon

*Twenty selected mid to late Wigan Casino/alternative tracks*

'You've Been Away' Rubin
'Captain of My Ship' Seventh Wonder
'She's Wanted in Three States' Larry Clinton
'Summer in the Parks' East Coast Connection
'Do What You Wanna Do' T Connection
'Lovin' is Really My Game' Brainstorm
'Who Said Honky's Ain't Got Soul' Bang Gang
'Spring Rain' Silvetti
'You Know How to Love Me' Phyllis Hyman
'Janice (Don't Be So Blind To Love)' Skip Mahoney
'What Should I Do' Little Ann
'I Don't Like to Lose' Cecil Washington
'No Second Chance' The Deadbeats

'Love Slipped Through my Fingers'  Sam Williams
'I Go to Pieces'  Gerri Grainger
'Up and Over'  Jay Traynor
'Ready for the Get Down'  ZZ and Co
'I Walked Away'  Bobby Paris
'The Only Way is Up'  Otis Clay

*For a more in-depth look at Wigan Casino, read* Soul Survivors:
The Wigan Casino Story *(Robson Books) by Russ Winstanley
and David Nowell.*

# 6

# Turning My Heartbeat Up

*'You are never sure what it's going to do to your body until sometimes it's too late.'*

This was the part Steve liked best. The rush as the speed kicked in, making his mouth dry and his scalp tingle. He felt as if he had been imperceptibly lifted off the floor by a couple of inches. He felt light, bright, talkative and bouncy. *Damn*, he felt GOOD.

Steve was a Northern Soul stalwart, spending most weekends attending one soul night or another. He had gradually been weaned off the 'ordinary' soul nights by the older lads who were visiting the real thing – the Wigan Casino all-nighters.

Now in his late teens, Steve had learned a lot from the older guys, the ex-Torch and early Wigan regulars. He learned a lot about the music, how to spin without falling over, how to spot a 'pressing' in a record box of so-called originals, and, most importantly, what drugs to take.

Steve had a regular job, a girlfriend, and lived at home with his parents. He was not an addict. But he took illegal substances on a far too regular basis to be good for his health. He was lean and reasonably fit through sport, but often looked gaunt and tired. And sometimes when he stripped off after a particularly gruelling weekend of soul, speed, no sleep and next to no food, he could count his ribs through his skin.

No, Steve had no drugs problems, he thought. The frequent colds, the exhaustion on a Monday morning, the complete apathy he felt for days after 'coming down' from the all-nighter was just one of those things, he told himself. His was a recreational habit and he had it under control.

Tonight he had followed his usual pre-all-nighter ritual. A good meal at teatime (God knows when he would be able to face food again), a nice hot bath and a bit of a nap on the settee. For the tenth time he checked the contents of his holdall – two clean shirts, a spare pair of trousers, a plastic bag for discarded sweaty clothes, Brut deodorant and talc, a pack of twenty Benson and Hedges and a packet of chewing gum (essential to alleviate the inevitable dry mouth).

He then made his peace with his kinfolk. First, the girlfriend ('can't see you tonight, Wigan's on'). Then the parents ('Oh no, you're not off to Wigan again, are you? What time will you be back?' 'Don't know. See you').

Nine o'clock came and it was time for a couple of pints with the other soul boys in a local pub. By last orders the moment had come and they all piled into Steve's Ford Cortina for the drive to Wigan Casino.

In today's langauge, they were all sorted. Black bombers, green and clears, chalkies and amphetamine powder were amongst the varieties of speed contained in Steve's car as it hurtled along the M6. The chatter became more and more excited and the car's cassette player grew louder as they cruised nearer and nearer to Wigan. After exiting at the Wigan turn-off, Steve pulled over to the side of the road in a darkened street for a 'gear stop'. It was time for the night to really begin. Everyone knew there was a chance of being stopped and searched by the drug squad or uniformed police near the Casino, so it was better to take your gear before you got there.

As Sandi Sheldon's 'You're Gonna Make Me Love You' blasted out from the car stereo, a bottle of fizzy drink was passed to Steve from the guys in the back seat. He removed a small plastic bag from inside his coat and produced two black bombers and a wrap of amphetamine powder. The bombers had cost £2 each and the powder £5. Nine quid for one hell of a night, he thought. (Remember this is the late 70s.)

He popped the pills and licked the powder out of the silver foil and took a big swig of the drink to rid his mouth of the bitter aftertaste. Others in the car did the same, they grinned at each other, and Steve gunned up the engine as they set off on the final leg of their journey.

Pulling into the Casino carpark 15 minutes later, Steve and his soul mates quickly grabbed their various bags and record boxes from the boot and made their way across Station Road. It was 12.30 am and the massive queue was starting to disappear. Steve locked his car and checked he had everything – coat, holdall, car keys. A familiar knot developed in his stomach as he approached the famous Casino building.

Gone was any tiredness or lethargy. As he handed over his £2 at the cash desk and made his way up the stairs, he could feel his heart starting to pound. With excitement. Or speed. Or probably both.

He popped a piece of chewing gum into his mouth as he walked up, and it tasted clean, minty and good. And then he was inside the main dance hall. The darkness and crashing music hit him like a sledgehammer and almost took his breath away. He recognized the tune being played by DJ Russ Winstanley instantly – 'Slipping Around' by Art Freeman. Yea, pretty good. He smiled to himself and felt somehow lighter as he pushed his way through the seething mass of people to find his favourite table.

All the usual crowd were there. Handshakes from the blokes, pecks on the cheek and hugs from the girls. Some of them looked as if they were further into the experience than he was – eyes bright, pupils dilated, conversations animated.

Steve's mouth suddenly felt very dry and he felt like laughing out loud as the gradual rush of the speed gripped him. What the hell was the DJ playing now? August and Deneen's 'We Go Together'. I normally hate this, but it sounds brilliant tonight, he thought.

Everywhere he looked, people appeared to be wide-eyed, sweating and frantically chewing gum. Steve's rush continued. His hair started to tingle, he couldn't feel his feet, he felt restless, and he wanted to dance. *God*, did he want to *dance*. In mid-conversation he suddenly walked away from a mate and headed for the dance floor. He felt fluid, weightless and hit every beat. Feet moving faster and faster, spin, clap, backdrop. He didn't miss a step. The atmosphere was electric. Steve felt really 'in the groove'. He wasn't even out of breath, but the sweat was starting to pour out of him in the sauna-like atmosphere. He felt superb. This was heaven. Every movement felt like poetry in motion.

Thirsty? Scrounge a drink from a complete stranger. Fancy a fag? ('I've left them in my holdall,' Steve remembered). Scrounge one from another stranger. There's no shortage of mates here, and the sense of camaraderie is awesome. Friends are everywhere. The conversation is always upbeat, girlfriends, drunken nights out and latest record acquisitions are discussed. There are plenty of laughs, and the inevitable question is exchanged between Steve and whoever he meets: 'Have you had anything tonight?'

'A couple of bombers and some powder.'

'Bombers! Haven't had them for years. How the hell did you get hold of them?'

Next stop the record bar. Some time later Steve realized he had been standing talking to a record dealer for nearly an hour. The only sound he had bought was a copy of Williams and Watson's 'A Quitter Never Wins' on Okeh for £5. Time after time his gaze reverted to his new acquisition – the famous deep purple label with white writing on it looked like a work of art to Steve. He gazed with wonder at the label. Just holding it in his hand felt beautiful. Steve was happy to stay there and talk and smoke, and chew gum and drink Coke for the rest of the night if necessary. His whole body was flooded with warmth and energy and good will. Steve glanced at his watch. It was 2 am. Where was the night going? He wanted it never to end.

*Much later* . . . Steve looked at his watch for the tenth time in as many minutes. Surely it must be later than 7.30 am? It was bloody 7.28 am last time he looked. He felt like shit. His mouth was dry and furry and tasted of too many cigarettes. He took another swig of Coke but it couldn't quench his thirst. His shirt was drenched with sweat and it felt clammy. His heart was thumping ten to the dozen, and when he went on the dance floor his legs felt like lead and he was breathless within seconds.

He could no longer think of anything witty or interesting to say as the all-nighter entered its final half-hour. He desperately wanted some fresh air but it was cold, dark and raining outside. The music was relentless, crashing over him and giving him a pounding headache. He felt alert but his nerves were on edge. A group of shaven-headed scooter boys in the corner appeared to be looking at him. He looked across again. Are they talking about me? he thought. Christ, they look hard cases. There's six of them and only four of us.

Someone appeared with a hot cup of tea and handed it to him. Steve noticed that his hand shook as he held the steaming cup. It tasted good but his stomach felt like he had been kicked by a mule.

Then someone bumped into him from behind and hot tea spilled on to his hand. It sent shock waves through him and for no accountable reason Steve was suddenly afraid. He felt lonely, nervous and empty. The speed was wearing off. He was coming down.

The caffeine kicked in and made Steve feel even hotter. He was still buzzing, but the 'good' high had been replaced by an edgy restlessness that he hated. He glanced across to the scooter boys once more. They definitely seemed to be looking at him. He thought about going to the toilet, but then realized that he might be cornered in there. Or the drug squad might pull him. He couldn't handle that. He certainly couldn't handle having his car turned inside out by the squad and being strip-searched down the local nick, like some friends had suffered the other week.

He wished to God he hadn't taken as much speed. Maybe one bomber and the powder would have been enough. On the other hand, he had had two bombers on their own the other week and wasn't then half as smashed as he liked to be. It seemed like he had to keep taking more and more to get the same high. He was certainly high last night, but now he was starting to feel paranoid and slightly unwell.

Steve looked across at Dave, who everyone knew never took drugs, and he seemed as happy as Larry on the dance floor. He could go home to his bed and sleep – not like Steve, who knew that hour after hour lying staring at the ceiling was in store for him. Waiting for the speed to wear off and natural tiredness to creep in.

How he hated creeping home and trying to smile at his parents as he stumbled in at 10 am. Was today the day, he thought? Would they finally take a close look at him and demand 'What on *earth* have you been taking?' He hated going back to his mate's flat for an hour or so, playing records very quietly and finding even a whispered conversation difficult. Trying to get his brain together to go home.

God, I feel like shit, thought Steve. Never again. Never.

A mate he hadn't seen for a few hours appeared next to him. 'All right, Steve?' he said.

'Not bad.'

'You look like you're well smashed,' his mate countered.

God, this guy was getting on his nerves. Steve considered telling him to fuck off but he couldn't get the thought out of his mind. Did he look so smashed?

He went to a nearby mirrored pillar and pretended to comb his hair. A maniac stared back at him. His eyes were wild and dark-ringed, his mouth clenched, cheeks sunken. He looked like he had just had an electric shock. His hair was matted and his shirt was stained with sweat.

Someone offered him a barbiturate to help reduce the effects of the speed, but Steve declined. He preferred to ride out the storm. He had seen what barbs did to some guys at all-nighters – one minute hyper, the next staggering around like a drunk. They were usually chucked out fairly promptly by the bouncers.

Eight am came and the lights came on. The remaining crowd were a mixture of happy-looking speed freaks, tired but content-looking punters who hadn't dabbled in anything other than the brilliant atmosphere, and blank-faced youths who were 'coming down' with a bump.

Steve was definitely in the latter category. His hands and feet felt cold and his dick felt like it had disappeared completely. Food was out of the question. He knew it would taste like cardboard for the next 24 hours or so.

His anxiety increased every minute and he felt burning hot. He hoped to God the scooter boys wouldn't corner him somewhere, or the police pull him over as he drove home.

He just *knew* he would lie in bed at home for hour after hour, sweating and tossing and turning with some soul tune or other playing inside his head over and over again. He just knew he would feel utterly blank and despondent for the next few hours until the effects eased.

God, he felt like shit. Never again. Never . . . Until next week . . .

'Steve' does not exist, but he is very real. He is a composite of many of the characters that have frequented the Northern Soul scene in the past twenty-odd years. He could have been me. Or you. Or your brother, son, or even your dad.

Steve is typical of the kind of person who has experimented with drugs on the northern scene. He is what would nowadays be called a recreational drugs user. That is not to minimize the illegality of speed or to play down the health risks associated with it, but merely to point out that not everyone who uses drugs is an addict, a loser, or destined for an early grave. Many people were shocked when Oasis frontman Noel Gallagher said relatively recently that many young people took drugs 'just like having a cup of tea'. Noel was probably being mischievous, but he said what most young people already know – that for thousands upon thousands of people, drugs are something that you use to enhance your night out.

Nowadays Ecstasy is the drug of choice for young clubbers. The Northern Soul fan's drug has always been speed. For many all-nighter-goers, speed was a tool for staying awake and enjoying the music and dancing more than could be achieved on any legal drug like alcohol. (Don't forget that all-nighters, if they have a bar at all, are not licensed even today beyond normal hours.)

Alcohol is basically a depressant drug. It may make you feel good initially, give you a rush of well-being and happiness, and relieve your inhibitions, but it is a relatively short-lived 'high'. In most cases alcohol consumption combined with tiredness merely exaggerates the loss of energy – just about the last thing you need at an all-nighter, when the objective is to keep going until daybreak.

The solution? A couple of pints on the way to the all-nighter, and then stay sober, fit, and active and let the body's natural adrenalin keep you going. Or, take the artificial option and opt for some stimulants.

It is a choice that has faced Northern Soul fans for the best part of thirty years. What proportion of all-nighter goers have plumped for the speed option over the years is open to debate. Suffice to say that police have, certainly in the 70s, taken the view that soul all-nighters are havens for drug taking, and have done all in their power to close them down.

A drug squad officer reckoned that 70 per cent of regulars at the Torch used drugs. By the time the Casino was hitting the headlines, another officer claimed that 90 per cent of that club's clientele were on speed.

Soul fans interviewed for this book have confirmed the view that most devotees have at one time or another tried speed at all-nighters. Some enjoyed the experience, others didn't. Yet others say they were never tempted or wanted to try stimulants. Some think speed users are 'idiots', others say they respect the individual's right to make up his or her own mind about using drugs.

Since speed rarely makes people behave in an anti-social manner, unlike drugs such as alcohol, its use on the northern scene has been more or less tolerated by patrons for nearly three decades. Whilst some speed users would happily admit, or even boast about, their enjoyment of amphetamines, others are more guarded. Even today, when simple possession of a class B drug like amphetamines is likely to result in a caution from the police rather than a court appearance, soul fans are not happy for their drug use in the past or present to become public knowledge. For this reason some names in this chapter have been changed to protect the guilty.

Dave, a Casino regular for more than five years, is now in his late thirties, a father of two and a respectable professional man. Like many Casino-goers he was introduced gradually to the club's drugs culture. His experiences are probably fairly typical of drugs users at the Casino: he was not an addict, he used what nowadays would be called 'recreational drugs'. But he found there was a darker side to the club and some of its regulars. This is his story:

I was about sixteen or seventeen when I started to go to the all-nighters. The energy and the atmosphere and the dancing at the Casino was unbelievable. Of course I knew about drugs. My parents assumed that *everyone* who went was on something or other and the papers were always full of scare stories about drug pushers and problems at the Casino, but that was no big deal to me. It didn't put me off, it probably added to the appeal. Drugs were something that other people did, not me. I had never touched a thing until I went to the Casino, not even a joint at a party.

I liked a drink and loved to go out and get ratted with the lads, and sometimes it went too far and I'd end up being sick or acted stupid or something, but that's just part of growing up. I was quite proud of the fact that I was pretty fit and didn't need drugs to stay awake or dance all night.

The Casino was superb. When you got there you could feel quite knackered yet by 4 am or 5 am the last thing you wanted to do was sleep. We were literally high on the atmosphere, the music and the comradeship.

It could get a bit difficult about 6 am or 7 am, when fatigue really started to set in and your legs were like lead, but once you got over that it was almost 8 am and time to go home. You could see all these guys and girls around you with huge eyes looking hyper and drawn and on edge and you would know they'd had some gear.

If someone asked me what I'd had that night and I said 'Nothing', they just shrugged and that was that. I felt quite smug and thought, I'll feel a damn sight better than you this afternoon. We would all pile on to the bus to go home and you would be sort of dozing on the way back. When you got in, you could have a good breakfast, chat to your mum and dad like a rational human being, and go to bed for a few hours, getting up about two or three in the afternoon. You were tired, but you were naturally tired, there were no artificial chemicals or stimulants involved. On Monday at work I would feel knackered but by Tuesday I was OK and fit for anything.

All this time, though, many of my mates were taking speed and saying how brilliant it was. All the talk was of gear, and things like chalkies, powder, blueys, bombers and all that kind of thing. I suppose it was inevitable that I would try some one day. When you saw guys on the dance floor for hours on end, barely out of breath, chatting away, wide-eyed and raving about every record, dance movement and passing girl, you began to wonder what it felt like.

One of the lads I knew was one of the best dancers. Tall, lean and with huge, staring eyes like car headlamps, he would just float around the Casino all night. Dancing, chatting and looking like he'd just found the secret of life or something. I asked him what it *actually* felt like on speed. He looked at me and said, astonishingly, 'Dave, if you take gear, soul music will never sound the same again.'

By that he meant that the music would never sound the same without gear, and I wasn't sure that I wanted to go down that road. Anyway, a few weeks later, there I was outside the Casino watching some of the lads going off in search of the pushers who usually sold the stuff. One of the lads came back with some chalkies – slimming tablets which were solid and white and tasted awful. I think they were about three for a pound at the time. He had four in his pocket and suddenly changed his mind about needing them. He said, 'Do you want them?' and I suddenly felt nervous as hell. I thought about it for a bit and said OK. So he gave them to me and I shoved them into my pocket and carried them around feeling like I had a flashing light on my head saying 'Druggie'.

It must have taken me about half an hour to get the courage up to swallow them. By the time I did, we were inside and I sat there waiting for something incredible to happen. I don't know what I expected, maybe to see little crabs running around on the floor or for everyone to turn green, but nothing seemed to happen.

I just got on with my normal night and after a couple of hours I thought, This is crap, I don't feel any different. This went on until about 6 am when I decided it was time to have a really good dance. It was on the main floor and the buzz was amazing. I was really enjoying the music and before I realized it, I was staying on the floor and dancing to every record and although I was sweating, I wasn't out of breath. It was the strangest feeling.

The night ended and we waited for the bus to go home and I felt really good, bright and chatty. We all had a good laugh on the way home and I remember rambling on about all kinds of rubbish as we waited for the first bus home. Everything felt so good. I went home, chatted to my mum and dad and had breakfast as normal. It was only when I got into bed I felt odd. My heart was pumping ten to the dozen and I couldn't get to sleep for ages. It was then I realized that the speed *had* worked and I was actually 'coming down'.

A couple of weeks later back at the Casino, my mates were full of advice. 'Try taking eight chalkies this time', 'Try some powder', 'I take about ten of those', and so on. So four chalkies became eight, and eight became ten and ten became fifteen. The frightening thing about speed is that you have to keep taking more and more to get the same effect as your body gets used to it.

Everyone knew who the pushers were, or knew someone who could point you in the right direction. Once I started to take speed, it seemed that almost everyone else did as well.

It was part of the Northern Soul experience, just like Ecstasy is today on the dance scene. I used to look at some of the characters there, who had quite bad drugs problems and would take stuff even during the week, and I would think myself lucky that I wasn't in the same boat as them. I thought I could control it. I never took any speed apart from at the all-nighters, but I was probably kidding myself that it was no big deal.

There was always something going round at the Casino, and most of the business would be done in the carpark before the all-nighter started. More often than not one of the lads from around our way would lay his hands on some gear before we even set off, so we were sorted without having to bother searching for stuff when we got there. One bloke's girlfriend used to work in a chemist's and used to nick stuff from there. I suppose there wasn't a lot the Casino management could do about it – the doormen used to keep an eye on the toilets and throw out anyone staggering around, but most people bought and had their gear before they even got to the Casino.

I had one or two bad experiences on speed, because the come-downs could be awful. When the speed kicked in, your mouth went dry, your scalp started tingling and you got this wonderful rush of well-being and friendliness and warmth and excitement. Everyone was your friend, and complete strangers became close friends. In some cases they really did, but in others it was just the drugs working on your brain. A few hours later someone whom you thought was brilliant company could suddenly be a right pain.

'When the gear started to wear off, it could be awful. Paranoia and restlessness were the worst – you couldn't stand still or relax and as you looked around, you wondered if the bloke walking towards you was the drugs squad or someone coming to kick your head in. You went on to dance and your heart was beating so fast and you were sweating so much you felt a bit ill. Once or twice the paranoia got so bad I was literally rooted to the spot, or rooted to my chair and wouldn't even go to the bar for a drink or to the toilets in case the drugs squad were waiting.

In those days the squad were known to grab people and take them off for a urine sample at the nearby nick. They would do you for possession if the sample was positive. Sometimes when the speed made you hyper and uneasy, you would think to yourself then, Hang on, this speed is supposed to make the night better, not worse. I've known guys close to tears, refusing to leave the Casino in the morning because they were absolutely convinced they were being followed for arrest, or maybe a beating. One guy I was giving a lift home to once made me go out to the car ten minutes before him and instead of walking straight across the carpark he made a massive detour around the streets and appeared, wearing dark glasses, from behind my car and got in. He was paranoid that the drug squad had been watching him all night.

Looking back, it's quite laughable but the terror was real at the time. I used to get home and lie there, sweating like hell, trying to get to sleep, with my heart pounding, for hours on end. Eventually I would give up and get up and put some music on. It had to be soul music. The music gave you a buzz and you were back at the all-nighter.

When the speed wore off, up to twelve hours later depending on how much you took, you would feel OK for a while but the next few days could be a real struggle.

Your mouth would taste awful, your legs felt heavy and you could feel physically and mentally exhausted. The depression was the worst – when you came down, you hit rock bottom and it could last for days.

Some of the lads took 'downers' after the all-nighter to bring them down – sleeping pills or barbiturates. They worked, and took the edge off the speed, but it was a dangerous game. I was terrified of going to sleep and not waking up, so I gave it a miss after a few times. Once I had a Tuinal at the end of an all-nighter and by the time I got to the car thirty minutes later I felt slightly drunk. It was terrifying. How the hell I drove home I don't know. I just went into the house and crashed out and slept for ages.

I realized then that it was getting a bit silly. Uppers to get you up, downers to bring you down, alcohol to make you mellow. It was a foolish way to carry on. I managed to keep my job going and kept myself reasonably fit with sport in between those binges at the Casino, but I realized that what I was doing wasn't particularly clever. I went to a few all-nighters 'straight' just to prove I didn't need drugs to enjoy them.

After that I went to the Casino about once a month and kept the speed down to a reasonable level. I never saw myself as a druggie, just someone who used drugs occasionally to enhance a night out. Lots of people did the same, with no apparent ill effects, but looking back I know there were deaths and problems caused by people I knew using drugs. Thank God I came through it unscathed. Some weren't so lucky.

The problem now is, what do I tell my kids? I've seen thousands of people use so-called soft drugs without any real physical problems, although mentally it's hard to tell. I've also seen and heard of people screwing up their lives because of drug habits they thought they could handle. The safest way is not to start in the first place. I'm not proud of what we used to get up to, but I'm not ashamed either. It was part of growing up. You live and learn.

Speed took many forms. The crème de la crème for soul fans seems to have been black bombers (Durophet). So-called because they were literally black capsules with the manufacturer's name, Riker, stamped on them. Originally prescribed as a slimming pill, they were very strong and very pure stimulants. Soul fans would steal or buy them from friends and relatives, break into chemist's shops to take them, or get them from your friendly neighbourhood drug pusher. White bombers existed as well, but soul fans naturally enough thought black was best. Dexy's Midnight Runners would immortalize them in their number one hit 'Geno' (about club performer Geno Washington): 'This man was my bombers, my dexies, my high . . .'

Ah yes, Dexy's. Dexedrine – small, usually yellow, tablets. Backstreet (i.e. homemade) versions of these also existed when plentiful supplies started to dry up in the mid to late 70s. As did 'backstreet blueys', a homemade version of the Smith Klein and French 'blueys' that Mods and all-nighter-goers loved.

It was not unknown for cynical youths to have 'Riker' or 'SKF' tattooes or badges made to show their liking for illegal substances. Whether this was done to wind up the ever-present drug squad or was an act of bravado to impress their mates is open to debate.

Filon ('Better than bombers – no come down', according to some soul fans), Duramin, ephedrine, 'chalkies' (Tenuate dospan), green and clears. These were all names familiar to soul fans in the 60s and 70s. Because they were all legally manufactured, but controlled, tablets and pills, soul fans took the view that there was little risk involved with these kinds of drugs. Of course, these drugs were not meant to be taken in the kind of doses that all-nighter goers indulged in.

A woman with weight problems, for instance, might be prescribed an amphetamine-based slimming pill to be taken perhaps twice or three times daily. A soul fan would think nothing of downing three, four or five times that amount in a single dose, risking possible drugs poisoning.

Less predictable, however, was the contents of a street wrap of amphetamine sulphate powder. This did not exist in any legal form for public consumption, so again illegal drug-making operations were set up to manufacture this highly marketable type of speed.

A senior drug squad officer said the 70s saw an upturn in the number of people prepared to manufacture amphetamine sulphate in do-it-yourself laboratories. Many GPs were becoming aware of the dangers of over-prescribing slimming pills and anti-depressants to patients, who could easily become hooked in the same way as drug abusers. Through cutting down on prescriptions, the number of speed-type pills in circulation was reducing and soul fans were finding it harder to lay their hands on illicitly-obtained pills and capsules.

Amphetamine sulphate was an alternative. Taking the powder form, which could be eaten, snorted or injected, this type of speed was relatively easily made by dubious individuals with a good knowledge of chemistry, the right equipment and criminal intent to make a fast profit.

The pure amphetamine sulphate would be cut down to as little as 5 per cent purity by mixing with glucose, aspirin, or heaven knows what else, before it reached street level. Therefore the profits to be made on a £5 or £10 wrap sold in clubs and pubs were immense.

# All-Nighter drugs probe

## Coroner's pledge after girl (20) dies

Meanwhile, the users were finding out the highs did not last for ever, and there was a price to pay for using speed. Soul fans would take massive amounts of speed to keep them going all night, and would often still be 'up' almost 24 hours later. Taking time-release capsules like Duramin meant that just when you thought you were coming down, the drug would kick in again. So it was possible to go 48 hours or more without sleep and find your nerves becoming increasingly frazzled.

Taking speed has been likened to taking out a bank loan. You 'borrow' the extra energy for a few hours, and the mental and physical energy your body exerts has to be paid back days later. Thus depression, apathy and exhaustion can live with you for days after coming down.

One former speed user said: 'Some people literally had fried their brains by the end of the speed years. They just frazzled themselves so much by being so hyper and so high. When it ends it's just one big crash.'

John, another former Casino-goer, said: 'I sometimes suffered pretty badly after taking gear, but it never stopped me taking it. You went to an all-nighter, you took gear, it was as simple as that. Almost everyone did it, it just affected some more than others. I remember one guy coming back to my house in the morning after Wigan and he just curled up on the settee and lay there shivering while I went outside and washed, hoovered and polished my car. I was still buzzing and I never noticed the time.

'I ran him home later and in the middle of the afternoon he rang me up and said he felt absolutely awful. He said his heart felt like it was coming through his chest. He said he was going to hospital. Suddenly he sort of screamed and dropped the phone. His brother came on the line and said: "He's fallen on the floor. I'll have to go. The ambulance is here." It was a bit scary. He went to hospital and they kept him in for a few hours for observation and then let him go home. It scared him so much he never touched speed again.'

As far as anyone knows, there has never been an in-depth study into the long-term effects of amphetamine abuse. The emergence of Ecstasy (MDMA) on the 90s dance scene has led to detailed studies of this designer drug, and recent findings should sound alarm bells for those who indulged, or still indulge, in regular large doses of speed.

Ecstasy is a hybrid drug of the hallucinogen mescalin and amphetamine. Users report a heightened sense of closeness with others, increased awareness of emotion and a greater ability to communicate. Up to two million youngsters in Britain are thought to use the drug regularly.

New findings from America suggest that many of these users could be risking serious and permanent brain damage. Brain scans carried out on fourteen former heavy users revealed changes indicating damage to specific nerves that produce the chemical messenger serotonin.

Serotonin, which carries messages between nerves, is thought to have wide-ranging roles in regulating mood, memory, pain perception, sleep, appetite and sexual activity. People with psychiatric disorders such as depression and anxiety often lack serotonin. Drugs like Prozac can boost levels of the chemical, relieving the symptoms.

Tests on Ecstasy users have shown they have far fewer serotonin transporters than non-users. Neurologists Dr George Ricaurte and researchers from Johns Hopkins Medical Institute in Baltimore revealed in the medical journal *The Lancet* in October 1998 that Ecstasy could cause 'depression, anxiety, memory disturbance, and other neuro-psychiatric disorders'. The researchers' findings confirmed the view that even recreational doses of Ecstasy could cause damage in users – even long after they have stopped taking the drug. The greater the use of Ecstasy, the greater the damage.

So what does this mean for Northern Soul fans who have, in some cases, taken amphetamines for many years? Apart from the short-term dangers of overdose, overheating, irregular heartbeat, or even strokes, are former heavy users now paying the price in their thirties, forties and fifties?

Soul fan Mick, now in his early forties, has been taking speed at all-nighters on and off now for more than twenty years. He thinks the dangers of drugs are exaggerated. 'What makes me laugh is that if I went out to the pub and had fifteen pints, got falling-down drunk, made a nuisance of myself and puked in the gutter on the way home, that would be a big laugh to most people because alcohol is legal. If I say I've had a good blast of speed, stayed perfectly in control of my actions, and had a good night dancing and doing nobody any harm, then I'm a druggie. I don't see that it's any worse than alcohol, except that it's illegal. I don't come home and beat up the wife or kids or anything like that.'

And how's this from a married woman in her thirties, whose husband also enjoys speed at all-nighters with her even today? 'I don't think it does you any harm in moderation. We can handle it. I think it takes a certain type of person to become an addict. You have to know when to say no. From our point of view, speed has done wonders for our marriage. We are both on the same wavelength and if we come home early from an all-nighter we stay up and have a good talk because the kids are still in bed. It's our quality time together. It's great because there's no point in going to bed when we get in, unless it's for something other than sleep! People just don't understand there can be a positive side to drugs.'

On the other hand, another woman told how she divorced her husband because she could not stand his drug taking. He started off by taking speed at soul events, and then it became so regular that it became part of his daily routine. The marriage collapsed as his drug-taking spiralled out of control. 'He was just a different man when he was on speed. It changed him completely. I couldn't stand it any more,' she said.

The two different scenarios illustrate how speed can affect people in different ways. The drug experts warn that the effects can be unpredictable. What one person can handle easily, another can find devastating. What leaves one person feeling pretty mellow and happy with life can make another aggressive, irritable or violent.

Amphetamines were first synthesized at the end of the last century and used as a stimulant. (Remember, heroin and cocaine were perfectly legal and widely used by Victorian society.) Speed works on the central nervous system to produce effects similar to those produced by the body's own natural stimulants, adrenalin and noradrenalin. The heart rate speeds up, the blood pressures rises and the body basically goes into overdrive.

They came into general use in the late 1920s, first as a powder, and then in tablet form. They were given to soldiers to keep them awake, used by students revising for exams, and even by athletes wanting extra energy. In the 1950s and 1960s, doctors freely prescribed amphetamines to overweight people – the pills usually suppressed appetite and speeded up the body's metabolism.

But there were disturbing side-effects. Many users innocently taking pills happily dished out by their GPs became psychologically dependent on them. And researchers found that when users stopped taking the pills, the weight just went back on in a 'rebound' action.

For that reason, amphetamines are no longer prescribed for obesity. And there was another reason for the phasing out of amphetamines – the widespread abuse by young people who were easily able to get their hands on them on the black market. Speed was outlawed under the Misuse of Drugs Act 1970, categorized as a class B drug. The Mods' and soul fans' favourite, Durophet ('black bombers'), is now no longer produced. Drugs like it are now legally prescribed only sparingly, hence the amount reaching the streets has dropped dramatically. The amphetamine sulphate now used by clubbers is made illegally and sold by villains.

Experts say that although it is difficult to overdose in the accepted way on speed, a dose could prove fatal. It can be a struggle for the liver to handle large doses of amphetamines. Mixing large amounts of amphetamines and alcohol together puts even more of a strain on the liver.

Dr Mohammad Musa, director of the drug dependency unit in Blackpool, said: 'First of all, people who use speed never know what they are buying. It isn't a pure drug, it is mixed with other stimulants or powders or even poisons like strychnine.

'Secondly, you are never sure what it is going to do to your body, until sometimes it is too late. You are never sure whether your body itself can take the drug or not. You might have a respiratory illness or a heart illness and you can end up doing damage to yourself. The extreme situation is loss of life.

'The immediate side effects are stimulation. The drug

increases blood pressure and increases your heart rate. You are physically hyperactive and the drug at the same time is putting strain on your vital organs. If a vital organ can't take all that pressure, it will stop.

'The long-term effects are mental, psychological and psychiatric. It can cause depression, anxiety, obsession and amphetamine psychosis. You could end up suffering from a schizophrenic-like illness.'

Dr Musa admitted that not all current and former speed users would end up with serious side effects from using the drug. But he warned: 'You always come across a drug which can suit X but not Y. What one person accepts another may not. You can use a drug for many years without any harm and then suddenly end up with the side effects. Some drugs have long-term effects that are very slow building up in the system. It's all about quality of life later in life. Somebody misusing amphetamines today may suffer the consequences a few years down the road.'

Dr Musa also had this to say to those who use, or used, barbiturates to help them 'come down' off the speed:

'There's a saying amongst amphetamine users that barbiturates release aggression. Amphetamines give you the energy to use that aggression. Mixing the two can have serious consequences. You may have been using a drug for some time without any side effects, and then suddenly you will end up doing something that you would never normally have done. Your actions could end up destroying your career, your future or your life.'

But surely speed can't be that dangerous if many Northern Soul fans who claim to have used it regularly for many years are still fit and well?

Dr Musa: 'That's just what smokers used to say. There are always exceptions. If my grandmother smokes and lives to be 110, that doesn't mean to say that everyone will be so fortunate.'

Cynics on the Northern scene – and there are many of them – suggest that instead of waging war on class B drug users, the government would be better focusing on alcohol abuse – currently claiming 33,000 lives a year. But Dr Musa said that although it is difficult to assess the number of deaths directly caused by amphetamines, there was no doubt about the dangers. 'The problem is that there can be quite a number of cases where death is attributed to other reasons, but the underlying cause will be drugs. The official cause of death might be heart attack, and it will be documented as such, but drugs misuse will often be behind it.'

Police policy towards class B and C drugs possession varies from force to force, but many forces now caution for simple possession where there are no aggravating factors. But anyone caught with a sizeable amount of speed, whether for them and their mates or not, risks being charged with possession with intent to supply. A prison sentence often results.

Dr Musa said the trend towards decriminalizing so-called soft drugs must not go too far. 'These drugs are illegal,' he said, 'and people who are using illegal drugs often reach a point where their social status forces them to stop, purely because of the illegality of that substance. Also, if drugs were made legal the number of people experimenting with them would increase by ten times. Society would suffer a lot more. The consequences on the world would be unbelievable.'

A mass raid which illustrates the enthusiasm the police had for wiping out all-night soul venues with drugs problems took place at the Metro Bistro in Wakefield in 1971. This short-lived venue was raided on its second week of opening, in the months after the closure of the Wheel.

Dancers were stunned when police burst in mob-handed at 2 am and began rounding up the 260-odd punters. By now it was illegal to have 'internal possession' of drugs, and police began closely inspecting the demeanour of the customers. A torch was shone into each customer's eyes and, based on the officer's judgement, soul fans were put into groups. A different coloured spot was placed on each soul fan as they were herded up – a black spot denoted 'smashed out of his/her head', a red spot 'possibly smashed out of his/her head', and a white spot 'doesn't look like he/she has had anything'.

The first two groups were full. The white queue held only *two* people. Everyone, apart from the lucky twosome and a handful of DJs, was carted off to Leeds central police station to give a urine sample, and that was the end of the Bistro Metro.

One of the biggest pushers at Wigan Casino used to live near a pharmaceutical company. The company made all kinds of drugs, including amphetamines, and used to dump all the substandard or damaged capsules literally by the barrowload. The pusher found it easy to persuade workers to accidentally lose the odd barrowload, which somehow found their way to Wigan Casino.

Bob, a former Casino-goer and now a father of two, told how the same pusher would sometimes hand him a wad of cash – sometimes up to £500 – at the Casino to look after in case the drug squad had their eye on him. His reward would be a £20 note when he returned it in the morning. But Bob also found himself on the receiving end of the law when he and a friend were pulled over in their car on the way to the Casino. He said: 'We used to know a few lads who would break into chemist's for methadone. So we would say to then, "While you're there, if you find any big canisters of pills, bring them to us." Sure enough, they did, and we had black bombers, green and clears and all kinds of things.

'One night we were going to Wigan and the police pulled us over. I had a big bag of gear which we were going to sell. There was no way I could say it was just for us, there was too much of it. I got two months for possession with intent to supply.'

A young soul fan was brought before Wigan magistrates accused of possessing drugs. When asked if he had anything to say for himself, he replied, 'The chippy on Wallgate does good chips but the gravy is a bit lumpy.' He received an extra £5 fine for his contemptuous effort at humour.

John, another former Casino-goer, was 'busted' twice in four months, much to the chagrin of his parents. On the first occasion he was caught red-handed with friends carrying black bombers and green and clears near the high-rise flats opposite the Casino.

Said John, 'They put us in the cells for the night and we were off our heads so all we did was sing songs. Obviously we couldn't sleep. I got fined £20 for possession and got a right slap off my old man. He really laid into me.'

Just a few months later he was caught again, this time in

Ormskirk with black bombers on him after a chemist's had been raided. A £75 fine followed.

Contrast these experiences with the case of Janet, a mother in her forties who still regularly uses speed at all-nighters and has never been in trouble with the law. She said: 'All this stuff about speed making you aggressive is rubbish. It lifts my mood and keeps me awake and helps you get into the music more. Speed doesn't make you want to fight or cause trouble, not like booze. When I'm coming down I just go quiet. I go home and I'm all right with everyone and that's it. I don't see a big problem with speed.'

One sad tale in the sorry history of drug abuse concerns a Lancashire teenager who hung out with the soul crowd in the mid-70s. Blackpool Mecca and Wigan Casino were a major part of the youngster's life. Slowly he was dragged towards the drugs fraternity.

His occasional use of speed led to a regular habit, then he began injecting. Addiction and a criminal record followed. From then, it was borstal and prison, and an untimely death caused by drugs in a bedsit at the age of twenty-two.

His anguished parents recounted in 1981 how their son changed from a normal, if timid, 13-year-old, into a secretive youth who stayed out late and went to all-nighters with an older crowd.

The lad's father said: 'He tried to give up several times but each time the drugs – and his drug-taking pals – were too strong for him. When he came out of prison the last time he rang us and said he'd found a flat. But he didn't want us to tell anyone where it was. He was determined to stay away from drugs.'

On the fateful night, the couple's son told his girlfriend he was injecting himself one last time. The inquest was told that the level of drugs he took was not enough to kill a healthy man. But his heart had been weakened by drug abuse and could not cope with the 'last fix'.

His parents were devastated. His mother said: 'People think it can never happen to them. All I can say is, keep watching all the time, even if it does mean invading a child's privacy.'

The above merely illustrates the fact that you are venturing into the unknown when experimenting with drugs, whether considered 'acceptable' on the dance scene or not. You may or may not regret it. You may or may not destroy your life. It's all a lottery. Feeling lucky?

# 70p.c. of club users 'involved with drugs'

The head of the County Drug Squad yesterday told City Licensing Justices that nearly threequarters of the people visiting the Golden Torch, Tunstall, were involved with drugs.

"Using information from neighbouring drug squads as well as my own officers I would say that 70 per cent. of the people going to the club are involved in drug abuses." said Detective - sergeant Ernest Gardiner.

He explained that many youngsters visiting the club had to travel great distances. "They leave home early Saturday and return late Sunday—they need a stimulant," he added.

# 7

# Don't Take Away the Music

*'There were thousands of people that would expect the soul
scene to move forward, and that's what it did.'*

The late 70s were a confusing time for Northern Soul fans. The
mental anguish was enormous – do you stick with the same old
Northern Soul sound; move towards the more discofied and
funkier offerings served up at Blackpool Mecca; or try to
combine the two.

The Ritz ballroom in Manchester provided the perfect
compromise by combining both cultures in (usually) perfect
harmony. The Ritz all-dayers are still talked about today with
the sort of reverence normally reserved for the major all-
nighters. In a time of change they provided traditionalists and
modernists with a winning blend of the old and the new.

Who could forget the famous raised bouncy dance floor?
(Hours of fun could be derived from watching your pint wobble
in time to the music if you were sitting at a ground-floor table.)
Who could forget the sight of funky fashions mixing with the
jeans and vests of the Wigan crowd? Or the way the two armies
of fans ebbed and flowed from the dance floor depending on
whether 'their' music was being played?

The man behind the success of the Ritz all-dayers was
Midlander Neil Rushton. The soul fan, journalist, entrepreneur
and, later, record label boss was a major force in the ever-
changing soul scene. He was gripped by soul in his early teens
and after graduating from youth clubs started to frequent clubs
like the Top Of The Stairs at Walsall. His tastes grew more and

more esoteric after listening to the offerings of major Northern Soul DJs like Carl Dean. By the age of sixteen Neil was DJing and going to top West Midlands clubs like the Catacombs in Wolverhampton.

The ambitious Rushton decided to try his hand at promoting his own event, and so with pal Bill Baker he started to run Tuesday night events at Dudley Zoo. When the pair promoted a packed-out all-dayer at the zoo and hundreds turned up, trainee journalist Neil made the equivalent of three months' wages in a single day.

He realized where the smart money lay and so in 1974 he formed the Heart of England Soul Club (cunningly adapting the name from the Heart of England Building Society). Neil put an advert for the HESC's inaugural event at Coalville Tiffany's in *Blues and Soul* and waited for the membership applications to roll in.

A sackful of 800 applications turned up, and come the day 900 had packed into the venue for the all-day feast of soul. Neil followed a music policy that he would adopt throughout his pro-moting career – he kept out of the Wigan Casino versus Blackpool Mecca debate by hiring DJs reflecting both venues' styles.

The Coalville success story grew and then a friend recom-mended that Neil have a look at the Ritz in Whitworth Street West, Manchester. The Mecca ballroom had a massive raised dance floor and stage, balcony, and a capacity of around 1,500.

Neil hired it for an all-dayer in 1976 which unfortunately clashed with a similar event run by Chris Burton's International Soul Club. 'We only got 180 people in, but it was a brilliant event,' said Neil. 'We knew it was the right place. A guy came up to me on the day and said "This is going to be it." The manage-ment weren't so sure but we were confident. By the time we had done four all-dayers we were doing 1,200 people a time.'

At the age of twenty-two, Neil was running the biggest all-dayer in the country as well as by now writing for *Black Echoes*. He stuck to his original across-the-board music policy by hiring Wigan Casino DJs like Richard Searling and Dave Evison alongside the Mecca duo of Ian Levine and Colin Curtis. 'I was friendly with all of them and I liked both kinds of music,' said

Neil. 'The first record played was "Cashing In" (the Voices of East Harlem). We were playing stuff like the Brothers' "Are You Ready for This", "Lady Marmalade" and all that. It was like Blackpool Mecca part two. At the same time we were finding lots of great records to please the oldies fans. No one was fighting each other. The music we were playing built up a lot of interest in the venue. At the time I wasn't bothered if I made £100 or £1,000, but we never lost money for four years.'

The Ritz kept pace with the latest releases championed chiefly by Ian Levine and Colin Curtis – Vicky Sue Robinson's 'Turn the Beat Around', Diana Ross's 'Love Hangover', Crown Heights Affair and 'Dancing'. Meanwhile the latest Wigan discoveries balanced the playlist for the traditionalists.

'Ian was and is one of my best friends,' said Neil. 'If I had to side with anything I would have to side with modern music. I was never just a Northern Soul stalwart. People look back now and say the scene was split, but when Northern Soul kicked off it was very revolutionary – the coolest guys, the sexiest girls and the music was anti-establishment.

'As the Northern scene evolved, people discovered disco and jazz-funk. Northern Soul was always about playing the newest things around and that just kept happening. Ian couldn't stop being a revolutionary. Some of the Casino crowd were a bit conservative.

'All these new sounds were coming in. The antennae that made me listen in the early days to Barbara Randolf and stuff like that instead of pop crap was working on the new stuff as well. It was as natural as breathing.'

Neil vividly remembers Soul Sam finishing his Northern Soul spot at one Ritz all-dayer with Jimmy Rae's Wigan stomper 'Philly Dog Around the World'. Those on the dance floor were left breathless after his storming 60s set. Then came Ian Levine – who kicked off with Rose Royce and 'Car Wash', which weeks later would become a Top Twenty hit.

'There was a stunned silence for a moment, and then the place went wild,' said Neil. 'People were really into it.' The old versus new debate appeared to be tolerated at the Ritz better than other clubs.

In October 1976, Neil ambitiously booked Tavares to appear live at the Ritz. The group's recent material like 'Heaven Must Be Missing an Angel' and 'Don't Take Away the Music' had been heavily played, and another capacity crowd ensured. Other live acts like Archie Bell and the Drells and the Moments and Rimshots were equally successful at the Ritz.

In 1977 the Heart of England Soul Club moved up another gear, with a massive two-roomed event at the Blackpool Mecca. Neil booked the 3,500 capacity venue and hired a whole host of DJs playing jazz-funk and soul in the large downstairs ballroom and Northern Soul in the legendary Highland Room. The main attraction live on stage was USA funk band Brass Construction, whose tracks 'Movin' and 'Changing' were just about the hottest tracks on the jazz-funk scene.

Neil again proved the doubters wrong when 3,100 people from all over the country turned up to the Sunday all-dayer. Followers of both styles of music danced the day away and wandered between the two rooms enjoying the blend.

Neil was delighted but astonished at what he had achieved, and at the profits involved. 'I walked out of the Mecca with a year's salary,' he said. Investing the profits into paying even more attention to the promotion, advertising and the quality of the events, Neil repeated the event at intervals over the next three years. Crown Heights Affair were another major attraction he flew in from the States to play for a capacity crowd. Meanwhile more people were either leaving behind the Northern Soul scene and enjoying the jazz-funk scene, or combining the two.

Said Neil: 'The modern stuff was the best black music that was around. The whole jazz-funk thing was great. There were thousands of people that would expect the soul scene to move forward, and that's what it did. Whenever a top band came over we would put them on.'

The customer profile was changing, too. The simple and stylish fashions of the Northern Soul scene were giving way to Hawaiian shirts, tight narrow trousers, plastic sandals and whistles. From being a predominantly white scene, more and more black customers were coming into soul clubs, attracted by the jazz-funk scene.

Far from being the domain of lovers of only the rarest 60s soul music, the late 1970s soul scene was becoming a haven for fashion-conscious lovers of pre-release and album track current recordings. Dan Hartmann's 'Instant Replay', Peter Brown's 'Do You Wanna Get Funky with Me', the Real Thing's 'Can You Feel the Force', and the Sugar Hill Gang's 'Rapper's Delight' were all played at the Mecca, Ritz and other leading jazz-funk venues.

Gone was the exclusivity of the north-west soul scene. The north's playlist were being mirrored in the south, the USA and, later, in the smarter pop clubs.

Still the atmosphere at the Mecca all-dayers was one of friendly rivalry, and a tug-of-war was even arranged between the Northern Soulies and the jazz-funk fans in the downstairs main ballroom. But by 1980 warring factions on the jazz-funk scene were at each other's throats and violence reared its ugly head. The lowest point was when the Moss Side and Bradford gangs decided to try to eliminate each other at the Mecca and a girl was stabbed in the ensuing brawl.

That was the end of the Mecca all-dayers for a sickened Neil Rushton. And when he looked around, he felt that the Northern Soul scene was petering out. 'The Northern records were still brilliant but they weren't cool any more. We were almost part of the mainstream club scene then,' he said.

This was reflected in sales of singles on Neil's own Inferno record label. Set up in 1978, Inferno released 26 singles and one compilation album. All releases were properly licensed from the original owners and gave Northern Soul fans the chance to own previously rare items for the price of a normal 45 rpm disc.

It was a competitive market in the UK, with Black Magic, Casino Classics, Grapevine and Inferno all issuing chiefly re-releases for the Northern Soul fraternity. Inferno's best sellers included Gloria Jones's 'Tainted Love' and Freda Payne's 'Band of Gold', which each sold around 45,000 copies. Neil said: 'We licensed them all properly but by the time the stuff came out the Northern Soul scene was dying out. Suddenly it all stopped. Nobody seemed to give a fuck about Frankie Beverley and whatever else we were putting out. I had 80,000 Northern Soul records and I couldn't sell any of them. My salary wasn't even covering the interest I had to pay and I went back to being a reporter.'

Inferno ground to a halt in 1980 but Neil would later re-emerge to make another tidy profit out of the house and dance scene, again running his own label. Like other Northern Soul fans, he never lost his love of the music and is now firmly back on the scene with stakes in two specialist Northern Soul labels, All-4-U and Joe Boy. He also co-promotes all-nighters at Trentham Gardens in Stoke-on-Trent with Chris Burton.

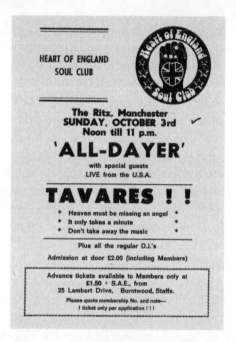

Neil says the promoting game in the 1990s is vastly different from what it was in the 70s heyday.

'It's interesting, but it's nothing like it was. We have a much more limited market now. The scene is basically a revival scene now, and there's nothing wrong with that.

'It doesn't look like we are going to get kids in their twenties coming in doing backdrops to Northern Soul.'

For thirteen months the all-nighters at Cleethorpes, Lincolnshire, shone brightly as a credible challenger to Wigan Casino. Some still insist today that the music was often better and more adventurous than at the Casino. Whether Cleethorpes would have proved a long-term contender we will never know, because after little more than a year the authorities called a halt to the fortnightly events.

Mary Chapman – dubbed the Queen of Northern Soul – was the driving force behind the Cleethorpes events. At 11 pm on 7 February 1975, resident DJs Chris Dalton and Dave Appleyard kicked off the Cleethorpes Pier all-nighters with Frankie Valli's 'You're Ready Now'.

Boasting a massive 700-capacity wooden dance floor and a 300-seater café, the Pier was big enough to prove a realistic challenge to the Casino. From a diet of mainly 60s soul, the music at the pier all-nighters developed a more contemporary feel, mirroring the playlist at Blackpool Mecca. Regular DJ appearances from the likes of Soul Sam, Ginger Taylor and Eddie Antemes, and John Vincent, kept the music moving forward.

Six months after its opening, Mary had to hire the nearby Winter Gardens to run in tandem with the pier to cater for the masses turning up at the fortnightly events. Live acts, including Major Lance, Trammps, and Tamiko Jones, enhanced the venue's reputation further.

Mary recalled in the sleevenotes to Goldmine's *The Cleethorpes Story* CD: 'Our DJs' musical policy was not only the envy of every other club in its day but the most varied ever attempted on the Northern scene up to that time. It led the way with a reputation for activating more unknown rarities as well as countless currently in-demand releases.

'The DJs were brave in the face of criticism and the dancers, often oblivious to the price tag on any given record, the most adventurous and skilful.'

Dancers of the 70s, like Black Nasty's 'Cut Your Motor Off', Troy Keyes' 'If I Had My Way', East Coast Connection's 'Summer in the Parks', Raw Soul's 'The Gig', The Crows' 'Your Autumn of Tomorrow', and Liberty's 'Girl, You Better Wake Up' all featured alongside the traditional oldies.

Denny Johnson, formerly of Widnes and now living in Johannesburg, South Africa, enjoyed travelling to the Cleethorpes all-nighters in between trips to the more local Wigan Casino. 'One of the things about travelling to Cleethorpes (or St Ives for that matter, which was our gang's other "regular" besides Wigan), was that the distance turned it into a bit of an adventure,' he said. 'I'm a "traditional" Northern Soul fan, i.e., the sounds that are associated with the Torch and the Wigan stompers. At the time I never really took to the introduction of the modern, funkier, psychedelic jazz sounds that the Mecca moved to.

'I used to get annoyed at Cleethorpes when they'd play something magic like "Lend A Hand", then immediately followed it with stuff like "Summer in the Parks" or "Cut Your Motor Off" – for me this was real "ugly" music, and didn't belong at a Northern Soul all-nighter. Too many of the sounds played there did not meet the generally accepted definition of Northern Soul. I think they tried to fill the divide that had been created between the Wigan sound and the Mecca sound, when it was just not necessary. There were plenty of funky sounds around then that I did like, and bought, but I did not want to hear them at all-nighters.'

So why did he go to Cleethorpes? Said Denny: 'The atmosphere was good, they did play *some* good Northern Soul, and we never saw any of the gangster-type incidents that occasionally took place outside the Casino or inside in the Casino's toilets.

'The coffee bar set-up was good for buying and selling records, much more room than the bar area at Wigan – and it may have been just me being lucky, but I always seemed to find more bargains at Cleethorpes – I used to think those guys were less knowledgeable about a record's popularity and value!'

Denny, now a father of two, is still enjoying collecting vinyl after all these years and brags about recently finding the following in a Johannesburg shop: a Terry Callier LP *Occasional Rain* (including 'Ordinary Joe'), price £1.20; and others at 10p each: Don Downing's 'Dream World', an instrumental version of 'Don't Depend on Me' on Phil. LA of Soul, Dobie Gray's 'Out on the Floor' on Inferno with a picture sleeve.

*Denny's all-time favourites include*

'These Chains of Love'  Chuck Jackson
'Catch Me, I'm Falling'  Little Esther Phillips
'You Don't Love Me'  Epitome of Sound
'Too Late'  Williams and Watson
'I Can't Help Loving You'  Paul Anka
'Girl Across the Street'  Moses Smith
'Lend a Hand'  Bobby Hutton
'Love Slipped Thru My Fingers'  Sam Williams
'Time Will Pass You By'  Tobi Legend

Among the regulars at Cleethorpes was Corinne Drewery, who later found fame as lead singer of the British group Swing Out Sister. Corinne, who was then living near Louth, Lincolnshire, first went to the Pier aged fourteen. She became a fan of Motown, and the more commercial end of soul music as a youngster and was attracted by the Northern Soul scene. She said: 'I went because it was the only place where they played decent music. It was the only place where you could go to where people didn't get drunk and fight. Nobody was interested in drinking, just dancing, although unknown to me at the time they did other things!'

There were the customary drugs problems associated with the all-night scene and soon the venue started to get pressure from the police. Drugs searches became the norm. Said Corinne: 'They used to frisk everybody as they went in, opening everything from bottles to tubes of toothpaste.'

Corinne never made it to Wigan Casino because of the travelling involved; but tried and enjoyed the Ritz all-dayers in Manchester, and stayed the course with the Cleethorpes events until they were stopped in March 1976.

'It was really exciting queuing up on the pier,' she said. 'The atmosphere and the music was great. The dancing was almost balletic. It was ballet for the masses. Watching the guys spinning, clutching their heart, it was so dramatic. This was their time and their stage.

'Sometimes if it was warm we would come out at 8 am and go

to sleep on the beach, we were so shattered.'

Corinne's favourite records of the time include Jimmy Radcliffe's 'Long After Tonight Is All Over' and 'Better Use Your Head' by Little Anthony and the Imperials. The music of her youth has played a big influence on her professional career. She said: 'There was a quality about the string arrangements and backing vocals, and a real feel-good factor in the records that I wanted to recreate.

'It's great just to look at some Northern Soul records. Every one of them on these small independent labels has had so much energy put into it. These weren't big corporations putting these records out – these small companies were putting everything into these songs.'

When Corinne met up with her eventual songwriting partner Andy Connell many years later, they found they had a common interest in the songs of Burt Bacharach (Bacharach and Hal David wrote 'Long After Tonight Is All Over' and a host of other classic tunes). Swing Out Sister was formed in 1984 and took their cue from soul, jazz and pop.

Corinne herself was influenced vocally by the Supremes, Dionne Warwick, and Dusty Springfield. Swing Out Sister's biggest UK hit, 'Breakout', stormed into the Top Twenty in November 1986. Looking around for future material, Corinne found another eerie link with the Northern Soul scene. One night she and Andy were visiting a Manchester club which they were aware was on the site of the long-gone Twisted Wheel. DJ Dean Johnson played Barbara Acklin's 'Am I the Same Girl' and they decided that would be a great song to record. It gave the group a minor UK hit and gave Northern Soul fans of the original something to ponder.

Despite having no record deal in Britain, Swing Out Sister have continued to have recording and touring success abroad. In the summer of 1999, their single 'You've Been Sleeping' was number two in the Japanese charts and an extensive tour followed.

The group are also involved with their own record label, Vivo. In another link with the Northern Soul scene, the Vivo release 'Expect a Miracle' by Jean Foster has been played at the

Togetherness all-nighters and at the Southport soul weekender.

Looking back to her Cleethorpes all-nighter days, Corinne said: 'It would be nice to think that, like the old American labels, we are creating little gems for people to find in the future!'

Anyone who walked into the famous Highland Room at Blackpool Mecca would have passed record and badge dealer extraordinaire Francis Terry Thomas, otherwise known as Mister Tee.

Everyone from punters to record collectors and DJs bought items from his familiar pitch at the tables on the left just inside the double doors. What may surprise many ex-regulars is that Terry is still in the same line of business – and doing a roaring trade to countries like Japan!

A staunch soul fan from Kidderminster, Worcestershire, Terry was a regular at clubs like the Up The Junction in Crewe and the Torch in Stoke. Then in about 1973 he began dealing more seriously in records, and started to buy a lot of new release material that was in vogue at the Mecca. In addition to selling new material to the dancers, his customers also numbered Ian Levine and Colin Curtis.

Terry was then working in the marketing department of a steel company, where one of the printers used to make button badges. Chris Burton had pioneered the first sew-on patches at the Torch, and they had proved incredibly popular. 'I remember going to the Torch the night he brought out his first badge,' said Terry. 'He was the first to recognize the potential of them and they were incredibly popular.'

Wigan Casino followed suit when the all-nighters began in 1973, and Terry saw a gap in the market. His first button badge was Soul Power '76, and from there he never looked back. He started to make patches for special events at Blackpool Mecca, the Ritz in Manchester and elsewhere, as well as churning out a range of lapel badges. He was also closely involved with the West Midlands Soul Club, being commissioned to do special badges for them too.

Wigan Casino, the Casino Classics and Inferno record labels were also clients, and in more modern times he is also doing badges for clients including Joe Boy Records and the Blackburn all-nighters. Terry himself can't belief he is still doing such a good trade nearly twenty-five years down the line. 'It was a craze which has never really stopped,' he said. 'The trouble with the patches nowadays is that they are so much more expensive to make than in the old days. If you wanted to replicate some of the early Wigan badges it would be impossible because they were so badly made! The machinery now is so sophisticated that they wouldn't look the same.'

A spin-off from the Northern scene was the Mod two-tone and scooter scene which sprang up again in the late 1970s. Terry made badges geared towards that scene and within twelve months went out and bought himself a Porsche. 'I find it amazing that I sold so many badges. It was just a spin-off from the Northern scene when people went in different directions. I think the dying embers were when the Mecca became totally disco and we lost the plot for a while.'

The 80s slump affected business, but Terry now finds the late 1990s a good time to be involved in the record and badge business. He has been astonished at the amount of interest from Japan, and Mister Tee tailored Mod and punk badges towards that nation when interest in all things British was at its peak. 'I have sold more Wigan Casino Night Owl badges to people in Japan than I ever did to Russ Winstanley! We did half a million Mod and punk badges to Japan in a year. I'm a hoarder by nature and so I kept all the artwork from the 70s. I have been able to find the original artwork and get them reprinted. I can't believe I'm still doing this after all this time.'

At one time Northern Soul was considered to be the exclusive property of the clubs in the north-west of England. History has proved this to be something of a myth, as up and down the country (and indeed in Scotland and Wales) there were thriving clubs all independently and unwittingly playing the same style of obscure black music.

One such example is the West Midlands, which has been a hotbed of Northern Soul since the term was first coined. In the early 1970s the seeds were sown for the West Midlands Soul Club, which grew from humble origins to a massive 80,000 members.

Up and coming DJ Steve Russell from Kidderminster was one of the men behind the WMSC. At the age of seventeen and armed with his soul collection, ranging from Okeh rarities to familiar Motown tunes, he took to DJing at the Nautical William pub in Kidderminster. Soon the playlist was 100 per cent Northern Soul and the packed venue boasted being the southernmost Northern Soul venue in the country.

Steve, together with friends Mick Flello and Joe Bragg, decided to create the WMSC with the aim of promoting events at bigger and better venues. They tried the Top Rank at Birmingham, but found out what others have since discovered too – that the city does not have a thriving soul community.

Then through another friend, John Carter, they decided to try all-dayers at Nottingham Palais. Suddenly they were cramming 1,500 dancers into the venue on a Sunday afternoon and it became the biggest all-dayer in the country. Derby Mecca and Leicester Mecca followed, along with soul nights at Coalville before Neil Rushton's Heart of England Soul Club took over.

But Notts Palais remained the most popular venue. Steve says no one involved had any thought of making money from the venture. 'It was quite scary at the time. I must have been only eighteen and we were trying to put on our first all-dayer. The licensing laws meant that everyone had to be a member and the only way you could put an event on on a Sunday was to give everyone some free food!

'We were doing it for the love of it. We tried other venues and could never make them pay, but Notts Palais was our premier venue. In those days all-dayers always used to start at 2 pm, but the queue outside the Palais was so long by then that we started to open the doors at twelve to get the people in.'

As the crowds started to increase, so did the DJ lineup's depth and quality. The local lads had useful contacts and turned up sounds which would eventually be picked up by other venues, especially Wigan Casino. Steve remembers selling records like Joe Hicks's 'Don't It Make You Feel Funky', and the Idle Few's 'People That's Why' to Russ Winstanley.

By the mid-70s, as more 'floaters' and disco-orientated material started to be played on the Northern Soul scene, the WMSC booked Blackpool Mecca's Ian Levine and Colin Curtis to balance their more modern playlists against the stompers-only sounds preferred by other DJs. 'We didn't try to stick 100 per cent with any particular kind of music. We wanted to give the crowd a cross-section of the music that was being played around the country,' said Steve.

Steve looks back on that period of his life with fondness. 'We enjoyed what we were doing. We were DJing and promoting at the same time. We never got rich, we would end up spending whatever we made on records.'

Craig Heyes of Irlam, Manchester, remembers: 'About early '74 in Little Hulton, the local youth club had a set of turntables anyone could use, you just had to bring your own records. It was usually girls bringing, say, the Rubettes or David Essex and dancing to them; the lads played table tennis and bar football. At this time lads did not dance at all, so I thought. Some lad, about eighteen years old, brought a box of singles, then he and about five other lads began to dance, spin and clap; all the decent girls were well impressed with these guys.

'I still remember the record, it was "Cochise" by Paul Humphrey (ABC). The story sounds familiar but that's just how it started. The first record I danced to, well halfway through it after plucking up courage, was "Where is the Love" – Betty Wright. It was at a local disco. Even now, pushing forty, hearing that record still gives me a buzz, as does "Breakaway" – Steve Karmen.

'In Little Hulton, at that time, Northern Soul was massive (just ask Dave Evison); everybody was mad for it! The first time I went to the Casino, I was just fifteen, I'd told my parents I was staying at my mate's house (the same mate I still go to gigs with), and him likewise. We caught the number 38 bus to Wigan, it was packed by the way, our plastic holdalls in tow. I will never, ever, forget literally squeezing into the Casino – through the doors, to be met by the guitar intro to "Sliced Tomatoes" – unbelievable – we danced still holding our bags.

'We were only young but we knew we had something unique and I don't think, looking back, we wanted to share it with anyone. It was a time in my life lasting only a few years, but at the time we thought it was for ever – I think it's because we packed so much into a short time and we grew up with it. I will never forget those days.

'I must also give the Ritz all-dayers a mention: we had some cracking times there as well. I particularly remember the red-hot year of 1976 – I don't think I missed an all-dayer that year, and it was incredibly hot, in fact I can remember one time it was so hot the fire exits were open and while that Sandy bloke was trying to win the dancing comp, we went for a swim in the canal at the back! Great times. When I hear "The Flasher" by Mistura, it always reminds me of the great dayers at the Ritz.'

*Top Sounds*

'My Sugar Baby'  Connie Clark
'You Didn't Say a Word'  Yvonne Baker
'To Win Your Heart'  Laura Lee
'Dance, Dance, Dance'  Casualeers
'Do I Love You'  Frank Wilson
'Better Use Your Head'  Little Anthony & the Imperials
'Too Many People'  Bobby Goldsboro
'Turning My Heart Beat Up'  MVPs
'Breakaway'  Steve Karmen
'I Travel Alone'  Lou Ragland

Here *Soul Galore* fanzine editor Dave McCadden relates a tale of one record hunt during the 70s heyday of Northern Soul. It illustrates how passionate and knowledgable the collectors were:

The next record I pulled from the box was Chapter Five's 'You Can't Mean It', a UK CBS demo. It was 30p – but I put it back in the box and moved on to the next one. I didn't buy it. And because of that one stupid act, born out of ignorance, it became one of the biggest sounds of '78. All because I didn't buy it.

This story began on a boring September afternoon in the backstreets of Moss Side, Manchester. In the company of Dave Withers I was scouring the junk shops for the rare sounds that fuel our scene. This particular area of Manchester had not been too kind to us in the past. Dave had found the odd 70s reissue and an occasional import of note, but all I'd ever had was a proposition from a local prostitute! Considering Moss Side had such a high black population there was a distinct shortage of soulful vinyl to be found. We made our usual stop at Johnny Roadhouse, a large second-hand shop (whose massive sign I BUY I BUY I BUY I BUY I BUY could be seen for miles) and checked out a sad smattering of 45s in the back room. Didn't we have anything better to do?

Walking back along Oxford Road Dave remembered an encounter with an old mate that sounded interesting. This guy had been in a recording studio near Granada TV and had found loads of boxes of records in a back room. Loads of boxes of records! This was getting interesting. Apparently he'd only flicked through one of the boxes and had just bought a single 45. 'What was it?' I asked. Dave kicked a Coke can along the gutter and coyly replied 'Doris Troy – "I'll Do Anything" on a British Cameo-Parkway demo!' My pulse raced. Let's go to work.

As luck would have it Dave had remembered the name of the studio, so we decided to give them a ring to ask if they had any records for sale. We weren't really hopeful. It all sounded a bit unlikely. But sure enough the girl on the switchboard told us we could come down the next day and have a look.

Even at this point we still had no idea what was lying in wait for us. I had visions of a few boxes of ex-chart sounds and maybe the odd obscurity for us to take a chance on. Boy, was I in for a shock. We decided to take along the other member of our Mancunian triumvirate, Rod Shar. The three of us regularly went hunting as a pack. We often descended on faraway towns in the search of rare vinyl: our combined knowledge enabled us to strip a town dead in just a few hours.

'You the guy that phoned?' she asked, chewing away (most unprofessionally) on a Bazooka Joe bubble gum. I noticed she still had the cartoon joke in her hand. 'That's right, love. We've got a market stall and we're looking for new stock,' I swiftly countered. Rod looked at me and slowly shook his head. Some people have no sense of the dramatic! We were shepherded along a narrow passage and up some stairs, Miss Gum-Chew pointed at a door and threw a 'They're in there, and they're 30p each' at us. She had gorgeous tits. We watched her arse wiggle its way back down the stairs before Rod whispered conspiratorially, 'You'd have to gag her first!'

The yellowing sign on the door said 'Do not leave your pets in here'. 'No chance of finding the Pussycats then!' I ventured. It was a sad collector's joke. Rod looked pained and pushed past me into the room. Dave and I followed. There was little room to move. The majority of the floor space was occupied by green tin boxes. There must have been a couple of hundred of them, and each box held around 300 singles. We each moved automatically to our own space and began ploughing through the boxes. We were close enough to touch each other, but not near enough to inspect our neighbour's boxes. Rod scored first. 'Flippin' heck. Garnet Mimms. Demo!' Dave and I wheeled our (green) heads in his direction. 'Let's have a look,' we shouted simultaneously. Then Dave found Shane Martin. A British demo – they were all British, and nearly all demos. Rod whooped with delight as he waved a Carol Keyes on Columbia in the air.

We were making our own piles. I'd stopped shouting them out, and eventually the other two followed suit – unless it was something really special. One of the biggest sounds at that time was John E Paul's 'I Wanna Know' on UK Decca, which prompted me to ask, 'Who's gonna get John E Paul?' As it happened it turned up in one of the boxes scoured by Dave Withers – and there were two copies to be had, both demos of course!

It was like shelling peas. All the known UK releases just fell into our laps. April Stevens, Fascinations, Gene Chandler, Lou Johnson, James Carr, Bessie Banks, Bobby Paris, Human Beinz, Kenny Chandler, Patrice Holloway, Artistics, Candy + Kisses, Thrills, Alexander Patton, Rufus Lumley, Incredibles, all the UK Motown rarities . . . the list just goes on and on. What was there? You might well ask what *wasn't* there. Strangely enough there wasn't a single Major Lance record in sight. And of course Doris Troy's 'I'll Do Anything' was missing. But every other known UK rarity was there for the taking.

When we first started to flick through the boxes it was every man for himself. But eventually we realized we'd hit upon the mother lode, and it would be impractical to carry on in this manner. In our efforts to outdo each other we'd all begun to flick through the boxes faster and faster. We cast envious glances at the guy with the biggest pile. We were in danger of missing things. Practical Dave made the decision. 'Hang on. This is getting daft! Let's all put them together and we'll share them out after.' Even though my pile was the largest I was forced to agree. After all, Dave had found two copies of John E Paul and I was desperate for it.

All our piles became one mass of rarities in the middle of the floor. It would have been a bizarre sight to behold. We tossed record after record into this ever-growing pile as we shouted out the artist's name: 'Bobby Bland, Mattie Moultrie, Hoagy Lands, Kim West, Bobby Sheen.' I got the devil in me. I picked out a Marmalade record, skimmed it across the room till it smashed against the wall and shouted out, 'Shane Martin. Oh shit!' You should have seen their faces! But by now we were off our heads. Finding a UK rarity was hard enough, even in 1978, but to find a whole roomful was too much to take in. We were getting giddy. We started tossing across the room any record we didn't like. Rod spat on Dennis Dell on CBS and chucked it in the corner. I was over there in a flash. 'Fuck off, Rod, that's brilliant.' Dave Withers calmed things down. 'Look, they're only 30p, so anything worth a coupla quid's worth getting. Stop getting carried away.'

The boxes were more or less in alphabetical order. As chance would have it I happened to be fishing through the box which contained some of the 'C's. I scrutinized a Chapter Five record on CBS. Didn't know it. I shouted to Rod: 'Chapter Five, Rod. "Anything You Do is Alright" – know it?' Rod was busy. He was in the box with all the S's and was making an extensive pile from Dee Dee Sharp, Sharpees, Bobby Sheen, Bunny Sigler, Soul City etc. 'Has it got "One in a Million" on the flip?' he asked. 'No, it's "You Can't Mean It".' I'd already chucked 'One in a Million' on the pile, and told him so. 'Dunno then.' Hey, we were busy and didn't have time to start looking for unknowns. So I slipped the Chapter Five record back in the green tin box and moved on. A move I'd always regret.

By the time we'd finished we had a decent pile of records to carry down the stairs. To be honest, we were shitting ourselves. We didn't really think we could just walk out of there with the cream of Northern Soul, all on UK demos and only be charged 30p each. It couldn't be that easy, could it? But it was. I can't even remember how much the bill came to. I only had about £2 on me, so Dave and Rod made up the difference. We floated up King Street to a café on Deansgate. It was share-out time.

'How should we do it?' someone asked. Good point – where do you start? After a bit of argy-bargy we agreed to take a record each in turn. Dave Withers ended up with the first choice and picked the Shane Martin demo. Good. Although it was rare it had become a played-out sound by that time, though none of us realized how much it would be worth in the late 90s. I was next, and joyously kissed my John E Paul demo. Whatever happened I'd got the biggie. By a strange turn of fate I could have had both copies of John E Paul. When my turn came around again the second copy was still up for grabs. I ignored it and plumped for a white Tamla Motown copy of

Kim Weston's 'Helpless'. We continued to divide the spoils until there were only three records left. I can't speak for the others but I remember my last record was a Vocalion demo of Bobby Bland's 'These Hands (Small but Mighty)'. The café owner was starting to get pissed with us. He wanted to sweep up. I couldn't see the problem. Why didn't he just sweep underneath us – we were so high we could have bumped our heads on the ceiling.

It was dark when we left the café. I had to walk to Albert Square to catch my bus. Struggling along with my big pile of records I was frightened to death I was going to drop them, or I'd be mugged by a passing Brian Rae. Standing under the shadow of the huge Town Hall I felt extremely conspicuous. I made sure the top record on my pile was the least rare – it was the Bobby Bland demo – and I sighed inwardly as my bus finally rounded the corner and pulled up beside me. Safe at last. Or so I thought. It suddenly dawned on me that I didn't have a penny in my pocket. There was no option but to walk the three and a half miles home. Unless the driver wanted to buy an original 'Queen of Fools' demo (yes, I got that one too). It was the longest walk of my life, through the shadowy streets of Salford and Cheetham Hill clutching a pile of rare 45s in front of me. No carrier bag, too many records to stuff in my jumper and nobody at home to pay for my taxi. Life is a song worth singing. Get walking.

Over the course of the next few months I sold the lot, and proceeded to squander the money in a spectacular fashion. Only two purchases of note came out of the affair. I paid for my brother's wedding ring and I bought myself a full-length black leather coat. The coat was £65 (it was 1978!) but reduced to £60 by the legendary M/c N/Soul DJ Stephen Sale (Siz) who worked in the Stolen From Ivor shop. Just three months later I would leave it in the Black Lion pub after a Northern Soul session on a Sunday night – pissed as usual. Money talks, but all mine says is 'goodbye'.

After our windfall, and confident that we'd left nothing behind of note, we showed off our finds to another Manchester buddy called Richard Searling. He was famous for not having any decent UK issue, so naturally we wanted to rub his face in it. Good-naturedly, of course. He bought one of my John E Pauls and swapped me a Shawne Robinson Minit DJ for my Pye acetate of Billie Davis's 'Just Walk in My Shoes'. Richard being the guy that he is couldn't resist the idea of going down to have a look for himself. We told him he was wasting his time. 'Forget it, mate, we left nothing behind.' But if he wanted to feed on the crumbs from our table then good luck to him. It may be hard to fathom these days, but back in the 70s Richard was well known as a collector of UK issues. His knowledge was legendary. But we didn't care. As far as we were concerned there was nothing left to be had – let him sift through the dross we'd left behind. Our arrogance was rewarded with the kick in the pants it deserved.

I can't remember everything he came out with, but the ones I do remember are worth noting: Evie Sands's 'Picture Me Gone' demo, Originals' 'Goodnight Irene' demo, Four Tops' 'Shake Me, Wake Me' demo and something by the Chapter Five called 'You Can't Mean It'. Another demo, of course. History shows that it became one of the biggest sounds of the next ten years, and is still so popular that it was recently reissued on Goldmine's classic Sevens series. But I sometimes wonder what would have happened if I'd bought it that day, and Richard hadn't picked it up. I'd probably have asked two pounds for it, as it was an unknown, and it may have been another ten years before a top jock started playing it.

In today's climate we'd have been sitting on a small fortune. But back then, UK records simply didn't command the same prices as they do today. (This is more than a little embarrassing but we actually laughed out loud at the Beatles' demos. We didn't buy them either!) If we found the same records in 1997 I'd probably be able to buy myself a new car; but knowing me I'd probably end up leaving that in a pub as well!

*Reproduced by permission of* Manifesto, *a Northern Soul fanzine.*

# Part IV

SOUL PROMOTIONS PROUDLY PRESENTS

 ## THE VERY FIRST REGULAR

# Northern Soul All-Nighter

## SINCE THE DAYS OF WIGAN CASINO
## THIS FRIDAY & EVERY FRIDAY
## 11.00p.m. - 9.00a.m.

PLUS OUR OLDIES ALL-NIGHTER FOURTH FRIDAY OF EVERY MONTH

## at the
# CENTRAL PIER MORECAMBE
## The Very Best of Northern Soul Old & New

| STAR D.J.'S IN THE MAIN HALL | IN THE STARLIGHT ROOM |
|---|---|
| | SPINNING THOSE OLDIES |
| RICHARD SEARLING | |
| SHAUN GIBBONS | STEVE WHITTLE |
| PAT BRADY | STUART BRACKENRIDGE |
| JOHN VINCENT | DEREK SMITH |
| BRIAN RAE | KEITH BRADY |
| MARK FARLEY | |

* * * * FULLY LICENSED BAR TILL 2.00 A.M. * * * *

ADMISSION FOR MEMBERS £2.00     GUESTS £3.00

ENQUIRIES & COACH ORGANISERS TEL. LANCASTER 39230

SEND FOR FREE MEMBERSHIP NOW AND SAVE A £1.00 ON THE NIGHT!

I AM OVER 18 YEARS OF AGE; PLEASE SEND ME A MEMBERSHIP FOR SOUL PROMOTIONS

NAME .................................................................................

ADDRESS ..............................................................................................

SEND S.A.E. TO SOUL PROMOTIONS, CENTRAL PIER, MARINE ROAD, MORECAMBE, LANCS.

# 8

# The Panic is On

*'In 1981 the Northern Soul scene unofficially died when
Wigan Casino closed.'*

The 80s proved a watershed in the Northern Soul scene – and it
was all to do with the demise of Wigan Casino.

Mass unemployment, a general recession and rocketing fuel
prices meant that many hundreds of soul fans no longer had the
disposable cash they once had. Attendances at the Casino had
noticeably tailed off in its last year – apart from the monthly
oldies all-nighters, where they were virtually packed to the
rafters. Many fans who discovered soul music in the boom years
of 1973–5 were now of course growing up.

The end of an era in Wigan's book also became the signal for
many soul fans to 'retire', move on to the jazz-funk scene, or
consign the halcyon years to happy memories.

DJ Kev Roberts said: 'In 1981 the Northern Soul scene
unofficially died when Wigan Casino closed. A lot of people got
into more contemporary musical styles. The DJs had disappeared and moved on to pastures new. The promoters had also
disappeared. It was left to the real collectors to discover records
and organize the events.'

The scene lost its focal point, and without the Casino it was
hard for all but the die-hard fans to maintain their interest. As far
as the general public was concerned, Northern Soul had been
and gone. In fact, many people thought the Casino had closed
long before it did, which suited the insular soulies just fine.

There were no Northern Soul records in the charts any more,

few magazine and newspaper articles, and the music industry was looking around for the post-punk Next Big Thing. The 80s would mark either the return of the Northern Soul scene to its roots, or its death knell. In the event, it was a bit of both.

As soon as the legendary Station Road venue closed in late 1981, the nationwide search was launched for its natural successor. In reality, people are still looking now. Richard Searling and Bernie Golding, alias the SAS of GB, opened the occasional Wigan Tiffany's all-nighters soon after the Casino's closure. This smart 1,000-capacity venue provided some excellent nights, attracting a huge number of ex-Casino-goers looking for the right venue. It was relatively short-lived, however, and even passed into the hands of Russ Winstanley for a time before the events fizzled out.

Clifton Hall at Rotherham was a fine venue – a large ballroom dominated by a massive dance floor and circled by a balcony. Comparisons with the Casino were obvious – and the DJ lineup often closely mirrored the Casino's, too. But the music policy was more progressive and oldies were in the minority at Rotherham.

Richard Searling and (to a larger extent) Soul Sam and Arthur Fenn kept the modern-thinking policy moving forward. The fortnightly Rotherham events again attracted up to 1,000 soul fans from all over Britain, but again this was no Casino. And unusually, the event could even empty halfway through the night. Testimony to the fact that you could take virtually the same crowd, much of the same music and the same scene and never recapture what the Casino had. Things had to move on . . .

Said Richard: 'The scene found it very difficult to get over the loss of Wigan. Attendances and the records dropped dramatically. In the 80s, Stafford apart, there was a real lack of class material.'

Collectors and DJs began selling their Northern Soul 45s, and moving into other areas. Richard was not immune from this himself and cringes at the memory of selling his copy of the ultra-rare Del Larks' 'Job Opening' for just £40 at a gig in Burnley one night. A mint copy now would fetch at least £800.

Richard's original copy of Larry Clinton's 'She's Wanted in

Three States' went to fellow DJ John Vincent for £80. 'Record prices dropped dramatically in about 1981/82,' said Richard. 'The feeling was that when Wigan closed the scene would shrink in size.'

One of the many soul fans who felt a sense of loss in the post-Casino years was Lancaster's Shaun Gibbons. He experienced first hand the dwindling attendances and apathy that was creeping into the Northern Soul scene as it searched for the new 'big' venue. 'Those first couple of years after the Casino's closure really were wilderness years. I distinctly remember going to venues, when you could literally count the number of people in there.'

Shaun had co-promoted an all-dayer with some friends at the Central Pier at Morecambe in 1977. It was a success which he wanted to repeat, but his colleagues weren't so keen. The Victorian pier came back to the forefront of Shaun's mind in 1983 as he thought about promoting his own venue.

In April he took the plunge and hired a posse of ex-Casino DJs (some reluctantly) for a Casino revival all-nighter. Shaun accepts now that hiring a 2,000 capacity venue at a time when average attendances were just a few hundred was perhaps a little foolhardy. But 650 turned up for the first of the monthly all-nighters. The following month attendance rose to 800, then 900, and by the first anniversary the pier was pulling in capacity crowds.

Shaun set out initially with an oldies-based format, but quickly encouraged the DJs like Richard Searling, Brian Rae and Mark Farley to introduce little-heard and newer sounds to keep it fresh. The Morecambe crowd loved the mix, and its reputation grew and grew.

Said Shaun: 'I think we re-enthused people and helped them find their enthusiasm again for Northern Soul and modern soul. I always loved oldies, but I loved the more modern stuff as well. Some DJs and venues went too far too fast – they just dropped the Northern stuff overnight and started playing the newer stuff. We waited until we had the following and then gradually introduced the modern stuff.

'I invested thousands in records. I remember things like Sydney Joe Qualls' "I Don't Do This" going down a storm. I was very impressed with the music that all the DJs played. There was no way I could have competed with the Casino when that was going, but I believe we promoted the best venue of the 80s with the best music of that time.'

Shaun's ambition grew and by the end of 1983, he had booked a live appearance by Gene Chandler. Despite massive overheads to pay for the legendary 60s soul man and a five-piece backing band, he took the risk and was rewarded with a sell-out attendance. Shaun recalled how in rehearsals Gene went through all his repertoire of Northern Soul favourites – 'I Can Take Care of Myself', 'Mr Big Shot', 'There Was a Time', etc., like the true professional he was. 'I spent a good hour talking to him and he was an absolute gentleman. He was amazed at the interest in his records, stuff that he had almost forgotten about. He was a great showman, and asked me what was the biggest record of his that people would know. I told him it was "There Was a Time".'

Come the night of the performance, Gene had the capacity crowd in raptures. As he concluded his set, he still hadn't performed 'There Was a Time'. He asked the crowd if there was any song he hadn't done. They all screamed 'There Was a Time'. Gene turned to the band and joked 'Hell, we haven't rehearsed that one, have we?', before taking the roof off with a grand finale of the Morecambe faithful's favourite song.

Other live acts to grace the stage of the pier and Shaun's later Morecambe venue, the Carlton Inn, included Bunny Sigler, Chuck Jackson, Sam Ward, Frances Nero and Lou Ragland, and Prince Phillip Mitchell.

By 1986, however, the ageing pier was starting to deteriorate structurally. A safety order was slapped on the building as it literally became unsafe and needed massive structural repairs. The council would not pay and the all-nighters had to end.

Shaun said he was proud that his venue was now seen to have played such an important part in keeping the fire burning after the Casino. 'I could have gone on for three or four years if it wasn't for them physically closing the building. They were three very special years and I remember them with great affection.

'If someone was to do a Morecambe Pier compilation CD, I think they would be surprised at how many sounds we actually made big in those days.'

Shaun eventually turned his 'hobby' into a profession, running all-nighters at the Carlton Inn, and in Newcastle, Colwyn Bay and Nottingham. In the 1990s he turned to organizing rave venues.

The problem that forward-thinking venues in the early- to mid-80s encountered was that current music was becoming more synthesized. Strings and real instruments were being replaced electronically, and the sound was anything but soulful. Coupled with what many saw as the drying up of the wealth of class 60s soul material, it was a confusing time.

Richard Searling admits that much of the new 80s material that he was playing at the time now sounds less than impressive. He said: 'Synthesizers could never replace real musicians. All the great records of the 60s were made with great musicians and a full orchestra. It has got steadily worse and worse. We have all been short-changed.

'I listen to some of the 80s records and they sound awful. The 60s stuff has never been bettered. The production is everything. When you listen to something like "Too Late" (Larry Williams and Johnny Watson), the production is a masterpiece.'

So the Northern Soul scene began to lean more towards 60s and 70s material, but the frantic-paced rarities were becoming fewer and fewer. The answer was the beat ballad, the mid-tempo stomper, and the 70s floater.

Richard said that although the Morecambe all-nighters began basically as an oldies venue, the music mix became more and more adventurous. The diversity of the music places Morecambe as the most important venue of the early 80s in his eyes.

When the Top Of The World all-nighters in Stafford came into their own after the Casino's closure, the gradual meta-morphosis of the scene was complete. The buzzwords were now 'rare soul' rather than Northern Soul, to show that the scene had moved on. Records that would have bombed at the Casino or be considered too slow were happily accepted at Stafford, and the accent was firmly back on *soul* rather than *dance*.

The guiding hand behind the Stafford events was Dave Thorley. The former Gloucester-based soul fan, record collector and later DJ and promoter was a regular at Wigan Casino from 1974 to the day it closed. His open-minded soul music tastes were influenced by regular visits to the Yate all-nighters in Bristol, which he frequented in between making the trek up north to the Casino. He found Yate's music policy a little more broad-minded than the 60s-based rarities being championed at that time by the Casino. 'Because I didn't come from the north I wasn't surrounded by the baggage of Va-Va's and all that. Some people had become very set in their ways.

'Yate, and St Ives, were much more broad-minded. A lot of people went just for fun. There was a fully-fledged Saturday night disco crowd in there sometimes, which made the music much more contemporary. People would go in fancy dress. Wigan never accepted that. There was a seriousness about Wigan, that it was like the holy grail.'

Becoming firm friends with Casino DJ Richard Searling, Dave secured several slots DJing at Wigan before its closure. By now he was also friends with, and shared the same musical outlook with, the likes of Gary Rushbrooke, Dave Withers, Dave Greet, and Rod Shard. He always wanted to be playing something new, or recently discovered.

Dave describes himself in that period as a 'soul fascist'. The extreme soul fascists in his book were Guy Hennigan and Keb Darge, who would later form part of the Stafford team. Their view, said Dave, was that soul music died in 1969, and nothing after that period would be considered.

This new gang of DJs and collectors decided to investigate running their own all-nighter and after scouring Mecca venues all over the north, they found the Top Of The World management in Stafford agreeable.

After a short period in 1980 running the venue with ex-Torch and Casino DJ Keith Minshull, Dave Thorley became sole promoter of the all-nighter. It was his vision that moulded Stafford from that moment on, with a main room playing upfront rarities and newer release material.

The ex-Wigan DJs, including Richard Searling, carried on where the Casino left off, with some of the best recent discoveries. Dave Withers turned up some mouth-watering Motown tapes, and oldies fans were catered for in the second, smaller room.

'For the first year it was a roaring success,' said Dave, 'but the format was very, very mixed. Richard and I would be playing lots of 12-inch releases as well as 60s stuff.'

When Richard, Dave Withers and others bowed out after about a year or so, Dave Thorley formed a closer alliance with Soul Bowl's John Anderson, who had turned up so many 'monster' records for Wigan Casino and other venues. Dave soon came into possession of some stunning 60s obscurities like the Empires' 'You're on Top' and the Ringleaders 'All of My Life'. He was also impressed with the completely fresh 60s playlists of Guy Hennigan and Keb Darge and added them to the DJ roster.

'They were brilliant,' said Dave. 'They had all these new 60s things and almost by chance the main room became 60s-orientated. The whole thing shifted from being up-tempo to being very much underground and more obscure. Within six months the whole format of Stafford had changed.'

A key factor in the success of the all-nighters was their fortnightly format. Dave believes this was vital to break and keep faith with new discoveries. The average attendance of around 700 was boosted to 1500 on the first anniversary when Harold Melvin appeared live. Dave recalls: 'In most people's opinion that was the best night ever. It was awesome – it was one of those nights when I didn't care whether we lost money, made money or whatever, it was brilliant.'

Ironically, Dave reckons Stafford's most creative time was when the crowds started to tail off a little in around 1982. The average attendance fell to around 400–500 as the Northern Soul scene generally went into a decline.

By this time Stafford had three rooms, featuring everything from 60s obscurities to modern soul served up by London-based Terry Jones and company. But the Top Of The World changed hands twice and Dave's relationship with the new owners was not as comfortable as in the past. In 1984 he decided to end the all-nighters.

He says: 'It had run its course and it had done its job. I didn't set out to redefine the Northern Soul scene. I set out to come up with the rarest and best soul we could find. I wanted people to come in off the street and hear music they could relate to, which included new release things of the time.'

Like many DJs and soul fans, Dave put Northern Soul on the back burner in the mid to late 80s and sold a lot of his 60s rarities. He moved on to pastures new and favoured contemporary soul music for many years, before the Northern Soul boom returned in the mid-1990s.

Now sales director for a furniture company, Dave enjoys regular trips to the USA, and counts among his friends legendary Detroit producer Richard 'Popcorn' Wylie. Dave is still in demand as a DJ in modern soul rooms all over the country. 'I'm viewed more as a contemporary DJ, which is a shame because I have loads of other stuff which has never been played!'

One of the new 'eighties' soul fans was Mark Freeman, of Nuneaton. He only managed to make it to the Casino as a 16-year-old in its final days – his best years on the soul scene were yet to come.

'Wigan will always have a place for me as it was a one-off and for me will be unrivalled anywhere for atmosphere. When it actually closed I started to go to venues regularly as did most others of my age but the old guys were resigned to the fact that the scene was over now that Wigan had gone.'

It was a feeling shared by many. When you had lived through the years of the greatest-ever, largest and most charismatic venue of them all, what was there left to surprise you?

Chris King tried to surprise everyone at Hinckley Leisure Centre in Leicestershire, and succeeded in drawing in vast crowds. By 1983 the venue was staging the ambitious Ric Tic revue, featuring J J Barnes, Al Kent, Pat Lewis, and Edwin Starr.

Mark recalled: 'There were lots of live acts at this venue, Junior Walker, Eddie Holman, Gene Chandler amongst others, but the two mega nights (apart from the 1st anniversary) were

Major Lance and the Ric Tic revue (which for me to this day was the biggest all-nighter ever). I have never seen so many people at a venue. One night Martha Reeves was due on there but for some reason they couldn't get the hall so she did a show at the Regent Club, a right old run-down club, but she kept 700 soulies very entertained. Chris King deserves heaps of praise for this time as he made it happen and put Hinckley as a top venue, like others before and after, never appreciated until it's gone.'

After spells at other all-nighters like Leicester Oddfellows ('a cracking venue'), Mark found his way to the Top Of The World at Stafford. 'I went to all the early Staffords, including the first room which was at the bottom then gradually we went to the top room and then the main hall.

'In the early days I believe it took over where Wigan left off, playing the rarities that were at the Casino at the end. Richard Searling was DJing; so was Gary Rushbrooke and Dave Withers and the quality was very high. There was the right mix I felt of rare 60s soul amid good-quality oldies.

'Searling left, Withers packed in the scene and attendances started to drop. This venue then took a turn maybe for the worse but ultimately for the better. Keb (Darge) and Guy (Hennigan) came on the scene and the venue went fortnightly with a view to new discoveries being played in the main hall – a bit risky looking back, especially at the time as there were more people on occasion in the small oldies room than in the main hall.

'I remember sitting in the main hall listening to "Spanish Maiden" thinking what the hell's this rubbish? But this was a classic case of not being prepared to listen to new things.

'The policy that Keb and Guy undertook paid off as the other DJs, Dave Thorley and Pat Brady etc., also contributed to play rare undiscovered 60s monsters.

'The biggest record, make no mistake about it, from Stafford was "Suspicion". This was massive and I really believe started to make people come back, others included "Peanut Duck", Tony Galla "In Love", Romance Watson – "Where Does That Leave Me" etc, soon the in word was rare soul! And it was great.

'For me, I had the best of both worlds at Stafford – all the best in new stuff and a great oldies room with the old Wheel, Torch and Wigan DJs Esher, Dave Alcock, Nick Marshall, Steve Whittle, Dave Evison etc. The difference being that they were playing stuff that didn't get played at the normal all-nighters, all up-tempo oldies. I learned my stuff at this venue.

'I also saw some good acts at Stafford, Harold Melvin at the 1st Anniversary, Eddie Holman, Gene Chandler, but the best was Eddie Parker and Lorraine Chandler . . . sensational.'

Mark added: 'I attended lots of other nighters in the 1980s, often trying to capture those early magical days, but saw some very poor attendances at some venues.'

*Mark's all time Top Ten*

'I'm Gone' Eddie Parker
'Stop, Look, Listen' Intros
'Suspicion' Monitors
'Village of Tears' Ben Zine
'No Second Chance' Deadbeats
'It Rained 40 Days and Nights' Jimmy Scott
'I Can't Let Him' Cheryl Ann
'You've Been Away' Rubin
'You Can Split' Youngblood Smith
'Cheatin' Kind' Don Gardner

Carole Thornley of Blackburn recalls: 'For me, life really did begin after Wigan. The Casino was just the start. I used to come up for the Wigan oldies all-nighter from Cornwall, where I was working the summer season, having a quick brew with Mum and Dad in the morning in Horwich, near Bolton, a quick shower and then trucking back down the motorway to stop off at the Yate all-nighter on the Saturday night with the Cornwall crowd (Dave Warr, Chico, Graham Bigford) before starting work on Sunday evening serving the holidaymakers their evening meals.

'But, even as a very eager 19-year-old soulie, the pace had to change eventually, and the bombshell of Wigan closing soon had me searching in other directions.

'Thanks to Ste and Kim Whittle going to the Top Of The World in Stafford, where Ste was DJing in the oldies room, the buzz continued, the records were excellent, but very much a different atmosphere to Wigan. Everyone seemed to have matured. The beer-towel brigade were nowhere to be seen!

'It was a very healthy, thriving scene where strong friendships were made, including meeting my future husband Shaun Pawsey. Through going to venues with the Whittles, like Hinckley, the 100 Club in London, Keele, Weston-super-Mare, the Great Yarmouth weekenders (playing Scrabble with Marv Johnson and Richard Popcorn Wylie after the nighter), lots of new friends were made, and there was life after Wigan!

'I think most people would agree that after Stafford, the scene dwindled to a certain extent, or was that the fact that we were all getting married in the mid-80s? And as for Northern venues, the Bankhall Miners in Burnley and soul nights locally and in Doncaster and Stoke were as far as I ventured. But then a complete upturn in the mid-1990s, the scene is stronger now than ever. Life after Wigan, life after divorce, is brilliant. Let the good times roll! There's plenty of soul left in those old shoes.'

*Carole Thornley's Top Ten*

'Just Loving You' Ruby Andrews
'Are We Ready for Love' Patti Austin
'Love's the Only Answer' Kelly Garrett
'Heartaches Away' Christine Cooper
'I Need My Baby' Jacky Beavers
'Do You Love Me, Baby' Masqueraders
'One In a Million' Maxine Brown
'What's That On Your Finger?' Willie Kendricks
'Dearly Beloved' Jack Montgomery
'Got Hung Up Along the Way' Jay and the Americans

*Twenty selected Stafford floorshakers*

'Naughty Boy' Jackie Day
'Too Late For You and Me' Gladys Knight
'Baby Have Mercy On Me (Suspicion)' Originals
'Hurt' Victors

'Please Keep Away from Me'  Elbie Parker
'I Won't Let Her See Me Cry'  Big Frank & the Essence
'Stop Overlooking Me'  Cairos
'Somebody Help Me'  Donald Jenkins
'Where Does That Leave Me'  Romance Watson
'I'd Think It Over Twice'  Sam Fletcher
'Come See What's Left of Me'  Bobby Hutton
'Like My Love for You'  Four Tracks
'King for a Day/Angelina'  Stewart Ames
'Three Lonely Guys'  Brilliant Korners
'Something About You Sends Me'  Royal Robbins
'Think It Over, Baby'  Groovettes
'Say Something Nice to Me'  Bobby Kline
'I Won't Be Coming Back'  J D Bryant
'Pyramid'  Soul Bros. Inc
'Sleepless Nights'  Paris

Even before Wigan Casino closed its doors, an all-nighter at the opposite end of the country was setting itself up as a smaller alternative venue with a fresh music policy. The 100 Club in London's Oxford Street now hosts the longest-running all-nighter in Britain. Ever since 1980 the monthly events, championed by Ady Croasdell, have pulled in a mixture of old and new faces. The famous jazz venue only holds around 300, but its reputation and DJ line-up pulls in crowds from all over the country. And, being in London, it attracts a slightly different crowd from the usual events up north. After a period in the wilderness, Northern Soul is back in fashion in the capital.

Ady, a long-time soul fan and now label boss of Kent Records, said the 100 Club events started basically as a reaction to the out-and-out Northern Soul played at venues like Wigan Casino. In 1979, he and a group of friends launched the 6Ts' soul nights in London, which introduced a broader music policy, with the accent on quality rather than rarity. And records did not necessarily have to be 100 mph stompers. Old Twisted Wheel favourites like Bobby Bland and the Impressions were back in vogue.

Using venues like Henri's at Covent Garden, the Starlight

Room in West Hampstead, and the Last Chance in Oxford Street, the 6Ts soul club attracted a mixture of soul stalwarts and Mod revivalists.

Then Ady got the venue that appealed to him most – the 100 Club. Small, atmospheric and with a wealth of musical history from blues and jazz to beat groups. The all-nighters began in August 1980.

Ady said: 'It's a basement venue, which I like, and it has a terrific history. It has a nice size dance floor, although possibly a little small for an all-nighter, and it's ideal for me. I don't particularly like the big monster all-nighters.'

The neatly-sized venue did not suffer from the same drastic fall-off in attendances as suffered in the north in the 1980s and was able to press ahead with its progressive music policy. Like the Stafford all-nighters, the 100 Club is famed for its love of 'new' 60s discoveries, mid-tempo items and beat ballads.

Said Ady: 'Being in London we have always had a slightly trendy aspect, sometimes we're in fashion and other times we're out of fashion, but we've always had a very loyal following and a high standard of DJs.'

Its current resident DJs of Butch, Mick Smith, Shifty and Ady have ensured the 100 Club has a reputation as a connoisseurs' venue. Its location in the capital means that showbiz celebrities occasionally drop in. Liam Gallagher of Oasis once paid the 100 Club a visit before the band achieved world fame, and Shane McGowan used to work in the cloakroom. Once when soul singer Doris Troy was appearing at the venue – a promotion on which Ady lost money – a fan tried to jump the queue for autographs. A slightly ill-tempered Ady told him to get back in line. The fan was Van Morrison.

Regulars come from all over the south, Midlands and Wales, with French visitors hopping on to the Eurostar to enjoy the all-nighter. The 100 Club had the first female Northern Soul resident DJ in Val Palmer, and also pioneered the 'guest nights', when punters can go along and be a DJ for the night.

After twenty years the 6Ts crowd show no signs of veering towards ultra-modern sounds. The golden era of soul music is what interests the 100 Club faithful. 'There is more acceptance of

70s soul now but it is a small percentage,' said Ady. 'It's still basically 60s soul mixed with old obscurities and some crossover things. There is no sign of things drying up. More and more acetates and unreleased tapes have turned up over the last ten years. DJs are still finding different things, like Nolan Porter ("If I Could Only be Sure"), which has been around for ages. Someone plays it a couple of times and suddenly it's a monster.'

Regular media attention – the *Guardian* colour supplement published just one of the features done on the all-nighters in recent times – has ensured the club stays packed and keeps attracting new faces. 'We tend to get a lot of media coverage because of where we are, but we are the longest-established club so we probably deserve that extra bit of attention,' said Ady.

He certainly sees no problem with the 100 Club all-nighters continuing well into the next century. The longevity of the 100 Club itself, and the Northern Soul scene as a whole, may have been questioned in the 80s, given the vanishing crowds, but the Northern Soul revival in the 1990s brought thousands of new and old devotees out of the woodwork.

Suddenly the buzzwords were Keele, Blackburn, the Ritz (again), Lowton and Togetherness . . .

# 9

# Time Will Pass You By

*'Let's all be elitist like we used to be twenty-five years ago.'*

Picture the scene. It's 1971 and a British teenager stands alone in the middle of a record warehouse the size of an aircraft hangar in Philadelphia, USA. The long-haired Richard Searling stares up at pallet after pallet of American 45s and wonders about the huge size of the task ahead.

His mission: to seek out rare soul recordings abandoned and forgotten by everyone except a growing band of British soul fanatics. Clutching a wants list provided by his employers, he will spend the rest of the day with just his sandwiches for company, scouring thousands upon thousands of vinyl recordings for those with the essential Northern Soul ingredients.

His American hosts are bemused by the knowledgeable lad's enthusiasm for recordings they consider only fit for junk shops. They happily load stack after stack of 'worthless' 45s on to a truck for collection. Some recordings are one-offs, others are in batches of 100 and 200, but all these 1960s soul productions are heading for the same destination: the record shops, the clubs and the record collectors of the north of England. They will fetch 10, 20 or 100 times the price paid to the warehouse, but don't tell the Yanks.

Fast forward twenty-eight years and the same Richard Searling is still at work furthering the cause of Northern Soul. Now he has swapped the grim interior of a dusty warehouse in Philadelphia for the comfort of a high-tech studio at the radio station Jazz FM in Manchester. The long locks which the now folically-challenged Richard remembers with fondness have vanished, but the records he salvaged on that day in 1971 live on in the hearts and minds of thousands upon thousands of soul fans. And a new generation of younger fans are enjoying for the first time the music that he and other British fanatics snatched from under the Americans' noses two decades previously.

It's 12.30 pm on a Sunday afternoon and Richard, one of the most influential DJs and gurus of the Northern Soul scene ever since the 1970s, is presenting his weekly soul show. From the plush new Jazz FM building in Exchange Quay, Manchester, his four hour show attracts up to 35,000 listeners from an area stretching from the North Lakes to Wolverhampton.

Dressed casually in white T-shirt and black tracksuit bottoms, he leaps around the small studio, switching expertly from cueing-up records, popping in CDs, juggling listeners' letters and club information, and playing the obligatory ads and jingles. He's alone in the small, modern studio but outside, by their radio sets, armies of Northern Soul fans wait to listen to their favourite tracks, hear a familiar name mentioned, or find out where the best Northern Soul nights are happening.

The first two hours of Richard's show are laid-back and based on current releases and 90s soul output. The third hour – *A Cellar Full of Soul* – is tailored to Northern Soul fans. Fast, driving 60s and 70s black American recordings which still pack the dance floors every weekend of the year.

Hanging from the ceiling are two speakers belting out the sounds. The volume is adjustable. Richard wants it loud. A listener's request, Gloria Scott's 'A Case of Too Much Love-making', blasts out in full glorious, crystal-clear digital stereo.

'I never get tired of hearing this,' he says, cutting the volume in the studio for seconds before cranking it back up again. Then he's back flicking through vinyl, scouring listeners' letters and dashing across to his record box to choose another track.

Richard's show has become a focal point for many Northern Soul fans who tune in to find out who is doing what and where, and is just one example of how the profile of Northern Soul has been raised since its underground days. Once the exclusive property of 'hip' youths in seedy little-known clubs is now broadcast across the North-West weekly on the upmarket, almost yuppy-ish, Jazz FM.

When the *Cellar Full of Soul* kicks in for the third hour of Richard's show, soul fans are transported back in time to the glory days of Northern Soul and are brought up to date with the current discoveries that are still setting the dance floors alight. Those callow youths that misbehaved and took lots of illegal substances twenty years ago are now respectable parents and spouses. So the dedications on Richard's shows are for fortieth birthdays, 'best wishes to Dad from your loving kids', and silver wedding anniversary messages. Ouch! How time catches up with us.

Club information is also hugely enjoyable, ranging from official Jazz FM soul nights at the splendid King George's Hall in Blackburn (with Richard and a host of top-name DJs), to a Northern Soul night at the Whippet and Ferret Breeders' Social Club in Rawtenstall (£3 admission with Jim, Ted and Bill DJing and free pasties to the first 100 through the door). That last event, by the way, is fictional, but you get the picture.

It's all a far cry from the mid-70s when the best you could hope for was Richard and Casino main man Russ Winstanley guesting for a short while on Andy Peebles' *Soul Train* show on Piccadilly Radio in Manchester. That gave Richard a taste for radio work which he has relished ever since. He and Russ would go along on a Sunday night and play a handful of current 'biggies' from Wigan Casino at the end of Andy's soul show. It was always well listened to by Northern Soul fans and was a welcome livener for all those recovering from the previous night's Casino all-nighter.

Richard's contacts with radio continued in 1976 when he got a job with RCA records as 'plugger'. He would serve all the local radio stations with current RCA releases and try to ensure air play for all the company's products. He built up some useful contacts and by 1980 he was lending one of the presenters at Radio Hallam in Sheffield some rare soul records to feature on his show. The presenter went on holiday – and the station bosses asked Richard to step in.

With no previous experience as a radio show host, Richard

was terrified but delighted. 'I can't remember ever being so nervous,' he said. 'Luckily a guy I used to go to school with, Martin Kelner, showed me the ropes. I must have done reasonably well because they said "You can keep on doing it if you want."

'I thought I would just be doing it for two weeks or so, but I ended up spending five years there. It just goes to show you should never go on holiday!'

By 1983 he was doing a spot on Radio Hallam on Saturday and Red Rose Radio in Preston on Sunday, as well as continuing his DJing work and holding down a full-time job.

'I felt good doing radio,' said Richard. 'I've tried writing articles for magazines and such and to be honest I always found it hard work. Sitting back and playing the music is for me a lot more relaxing and enjoyable.'

The Hallam show ended in 1985 and Richard later joined the ill-fated black music orientated Sunset Radio in Manchester. 'The format was great and the music was great, but it just didn't take off,' he recalled. 'But it was a great learning curve and I stayed there for a couple of years before joining Red Rose Gold in Preston. After a year at Red Rose I left and then I had a period when I didn't work.

'The problem with radio is you are judged solely by your listening figures. DJs don't get a second chance. Every station should have a soul show. There's always room for specialist shows but sometimes the stations don't want to take the chance.'

Then in 1995 the jazz, soul and blues orientated station Jazz FM decided after the success of its London operation to open a northern branch. Manchester was the chosen site and Richard was approached to do the Sunday morning soul show.

'The show has come on well, it's on at a good time and the format works well,' said Richard. 'The first couple of hours is mine and the middle hour (*A Cellar Full of Soul*) belongs to the listeners. It's their dedications and their requests. The show has helped enormously in raising the profile of Northern Soul and getting it back on the agenda for a lot of people.

'People thought nothing was happening on the scene and now it is. Coupled with the fact that you can get most of the records on CD it has helped the revival. You can take a trip down to Goldmine Records and spend £500 and get a good collection together. Years ago it would have cost you thousands and thousands of pounds to get all the vinyl originals.

'The choice of gigs that's available to people nowadays is absolutely unbelievable. There are perhaps four or five gigs on in the North-West every weekend. There are lots of fanzines and Northern Soul has a higher profile now than we have ever had. There were never as many clubs in the heyday as there are now.'

Tamla Motown has never been far away from the hearts of Northern Soul followers and it is certainly back with a bang as the new millennium dawns. All-nighter DJs have always played a selection of the rarer Motown tracks with the essential driving beat. Now they can treat fans to previously unheard tracks straight from the vaults of the famous Detroit label.

The man at the forefront of the resurgence of interest in Motown tracks is Midlands-based DJ Chris King. His two CD compilations for Debutante turned the whole culture of Motown Chartbusters-style reissues on its head. For the first time each CD – *This is Northern Soul* Vols I and II – brought together an eclectic mix of well-known, rarely heard and never-previously-released Motown recordings.

The first compilation in 1997 ranged from long-established dance floor favourites like Frank Wilson's £15,000 stormer 'Do I Love You' and Gladys Knight's 'Just Walk In My Shoes' to the recently reactivated Supremes' 'He's All I Got' and the unreleased and massively popular 'This Love Starved Heart of Mine' by Marvin Gaye.

Healthy sales and rave reviews in the music press brought about volume two, featuring such gems as the Stafford anthem 'Suspicion' by the Originals, Junior Walker's 'Tune Up', Martha and the Vandellas' 'One Way Out', and more mainstream tracks like the Isley Brothers' 'Tell Me It's Just a Rumour'.

For Chris King it was the culmination of an ambition to be associated with what many regard as the greatest soul label of them all. The Motown fan had been trying to license various rarities through his own record company for many years without any success. The answer to his prayers came via UK-based Debutante, a budget label specializing in reissuing a wide range of musical tastes. The label is now owned by Polygram, which owns Motown. They asked Chris if he would put together a compilation for them with Motown's blessing, and he grabbed the opportunity with both hands.

Using a variety of master discs, acetates and tapes from Motown's vaults he put together a listing for a 24-track CD that stunned Motown's New York staff. Where were 'Baby Love', 'Where Did Our Love Go', 'I Can't Help Myself' and dozens of other guaranteed best-sellers that always featured on Motown compilation tapes? Instead Chris was putting out Brenda Holloway's 'Reconsider', Gladys Knight's 'It's Too Late', the Monitors' 'Crying In the Night', etc., which were all Northern Soul anthems.

Said Chris: 'Nobody at Motown had a clue what they had in the vaults. They couldn't understand why anybody would be interested in some of the tracks because they lost money. In some cases it cost more to record the tracks than they actually made on them, and quite a few of them never saw the light of day.'

Tens of thousands of sales later, Debutante and Motown were delighted enough to do Volume II. At the time of writing, a Volume III, again compiled by Chris, is ready for release.

Through his record hunting trips abroad in the 1970s and 80s, and through his current good relationship with Motown, Chris has amassed literally hundreds of unreleased tracks. Some have already appeared on the CDs, and others have set dance floors of the Northern Soul scene alight in recent years. Two previously unheard Gladys Knight tracks, 'Pieces of My Broken Heart' and 'Never Let Go', along with Jimmy Ruffin's 'He Who Picks a Rose' and J J Barnes' 'Show Me', are among the most requested tracks at venues all over Britain.

Chris said many of the latest mouthwatering discoveries actually dated back to his trips to Detroit between 1979 and 1985. He and fellow collector and DJ Guy Hennigan walked into the Eight Mile store in Detroit after hearing it was a goldmine of Motown material. The owner puzzled the two Brits by apparently telling them he had bought a vast amount of records, tapes and acetates off a certain 'Joe Betts'.

It transpired he had actually bought the Jobete library – Motown's publishing company. Chris and Guy couldn't believe their eyes as stacks of Motown demos fell into their laps at 10 for a dollar.

This same store was the source of British DJ Pete Lowrie's famous acetate collection – which included 'Reconsider' and others. Said Chris: 'There were handfuls of great records. There was more good stuff in the acetate section than anywhere else, but we had so much stuff we never even bothered.'

Chris also acquired stacks of four-track tapes, not knowing what most of them were. If he pulled out a box saying 'Lonely Boy by Shorty Long' on it, it turned out to be Brenda Holloway. Sometimes there were two different artists on the same recording. He found a version of 'Oh, I've Been Blessed' by the Four Tops, which clearly has Martha Reeves singing on the last line.

Chris said: 'As we listened to them we had to guess the artists and work out the real title. It was nice, years later, to be able to put real names to everything and find the master tapes.

'I've had some of these tracks for years, but the time wasn't right before. People didn't accept them like they do now. It was a different culture fifteen years ago – some of them would have been considered too slow then.'

Chris disputes his status as the 'Mr Motown' of the British soul scene. He said: 'There are people out there that know far more about Motown than I do. It has been nice to be involved and the pleasure comes from being able to hear things we have never heard before.'

Hot on the heels of Debutante, Motown put out its own rarities collection – *Motown Sings Motown Treasures*. Twenty-one tracks of mainly 'alternative' versions of well-known Motown hits, but by different artists. Thus the world was treated to David Ruffin's version of 'I Want You Back', Kim Weston's take of 'Stop in the Name of Love', the Originals with 'Come See About Me' and the Supremes doing 'Can I Get a Witness'.

There is no doubt that the interest shown by British Northern

Soul fans has awakened Motown to the gems it never knew it owned.

After 130 CD compilation releases, Goldmine/Soul Supply reckon they know their market. Label manager Kev Roberts says the majority of Northern Soul punters want to hear familiar tunes. Compilations featuring what some esoteric DJs and collectors would term 'massive in-demand' tunes just don't sell well. 'The whole Northern Soul scene is more of a lifestyle thing now,' said Kev. 'It isn't about records as much any more. People just don't take it that seriously. We in the business, and the DJs, take it very seriously because we are into it, but most people just want to come and have a good time.'

Goldmine is the leading Northern Soul CD reissue compilation company and is based in Todmorden, Lancashire. It was formed in 1990 by Canada-based Martin Koppell and British-based Tim Brown, both fanatical record collectors, with Kev brought in as label manager.

After some less than spectacular early sales on a limited budget, Kev and the partners decided to take a slightly different tack. He saw that their main rivals Kent were collaring the 'serious' soul collector market. Goldmine would be better concentrating on the less serious soul fan, the fan who wanted to play a CD on a Sunday morning that had well-known items.

Sales started to pick up, and the company invested heavily in securing the rights to many classic tunes from the 70s golden era of Northern Soul. Kev compiled a list of hundreds of top tunes and set about leasing them. Themed compilations like *The Wigan Casino Story*, *The Twisted Wheel Story*, *The Torch Story* and *The Blackpool Mecca Story* were massive sellers. In addition to the hard-core soul fans, Goldmine was finding great interest from the causal punter who might wander into his local record store and find a CD containing all his old favourites.

More sales, however, often resulted in record companies demanding more money from Goldmine to license tracks which they owned. Says Kev: 'We are victims of our own success. You might go to one record label and ask them for a track and they will say "You can't have that for less than five grand – Northern Soul is massive now."'

In order to recoup what might amount to a £10,000 investment in a compilation, Goldmine has to be sure it will appeal to more than just a few thousand people in the north of England. Therefore, if the company is dealing with RCA, something like Beverly Ann's 'You Got Your Mind on Other Things' would represent a better investment than unreleased masters of unknown material.

The company has since done two *Soul Time* compilations for Sony Records, taking in the Columbia, Epic and Okeh labels. But it can't get its hands on the Atlantic, Warner Brothers and Atco stables, which is a source of regret for them. Kev said that of the 1,000 or so records he had on his 'hit list', Goldmine had secured the rights to about 80 per cent of them. 'There are a couple of big tunes that we just can't get our hands on, but a lot of the real dance floor winners have been released.'

The market for CDs is seemingly endless. As well as the specialist labels, major record companies are waking up to the potential great sales they can achieve just by reissuing Northern Soul classic tunes which the rest of the world has overlooked.

Sony has issued three volumes of its *Soul Time* compilations, featuring the best 60s output on labels like Okeh, Epic, Columbia and Date. Shirley Ellis, the Spellbinders, Nancy Ames, Lynn Randell, and Lee David are just some of the names featured in crystal-clear digital sound.

RCA, acting on a suggestion from Richard Searling, has reissued its 1970s vinyl offering *Jumping At The Go-Go* in CD format, with some additional tracks thrown in for good measure. Previously unseen studio photos and extensive sleeve notes all add to the appeal of tracks by the likes of Roy Hamilton, Lorraine Chandler, Herb Ward, Dean Courtney.

Compilations for Stateside and MCA/Universal are just two of the other projects that Richard has been recently involved with. Richard said hunting down and gaining the rights to in-demand tracks was sometimes exasperating but ultimately rewarding. Try as he might, he was unable to secure the rights to include Nolan Porter's 'If I Could Only be Sure' and Jackie Lee's 'Darkest Days' on the Universal compilation.

Kent Records have been in the soul compilation market since 1982. London-based soul expert Ady Croasdell was hired for a one-off deal to compile a vinyl LP of the best of the collectable Kent and Modern labels.

*For Dancers Only* sold by the lorryload and Kent Records was established as a major force. After 97 vinyl album releases and around 100 CD releases, Ady is now label manager and lovingly compiling CDs of some of the best-known and unknown 60s soul material.

The Kent label is seen by many as catering for the more specialized soul tastes, with 24-track compilations on legendary American labels including Okeh, RCA, Chess and Shrine. The accent is mainly on dance, but slower items find their way on to the albums.

Ady says the concentration on one label was not always by choice as the logistics of licensing recordings from different sources could be very difficult. But when Kent chose to devote its attention to one label, it liked to do thorough background sleeve notes to complete the picture. A typical example was its aptly-named *Okeh – A Northern Soul Obsession*. The CD features 24 tracks from the legendary Chicago-based label, many of which have sent dancers at the Torch and Wigan Casino into a frenzy and cost them a small fortune to own on the original vinyl. The sleevenotes on the accompanying 10-page booklet gives a unique insight into the musical history of each track.

Said Ady: 'We are already like soul music historians in this sense. It's such an opportunity that when it comes we shouldn't let it go without recording the whole thing for posterity.

'There are always frustrations when dealing with the major companies. The Okeh CD went reasonably smoothly, but the Atlantic compilations we are doing will have taken five years of negotiations before they eventually come out.'

Like other companies, Ady and Kent are constantly seeking new avenues for releasing soul gems never released before on CD, or never previously discovered. Said Ady: 'There are quite a few more great tracks out there. The Motown compilations have been patchily done to put it at its best. We would love to give it the treatment it deserves.'

Kent's best-seller to date is ironically a selection of slower items compiled by ex-*Blues and Soul* journalist Dave Godin, *Deep Soul Treasures* Volume One. 'It was a pleasant surprise for all of us,' said Ady. 'But knowing Dave's reputation it shouldn't surprise us that much. He did such a definitive package.'

Ex-Wigan Casino founder and DJ Russ Winstanley has the privilege of having compiled the best-selling Northern Soul CD of all time. The Telstar-produced *Soul Survivors* CD has now sold close to 100,000 copies, grossing a massive £1.7 million. The 1997 compilation was meant to be an entry-level introduction to Northern Soul, featuring the more commercial end of soul with songs like Curtis Mayfield's 'Move On Up', Marvin Gaye and Tammi Terrell's 'Two Can Have a Party', and Arthur Conley's 'Sweet Soul Music'. Then Telstar decided to subtitle it *Wigan Casino Anthems*, and Russ raced around trying to get 'deeper' tracks like Jack Montgomery's 'Dearly Beloved', and the famous 'Three Before Eight' to give it a Casino flavour.

TV advertising ensured booming sales, and Volume Two has

to date sold an equally impressive 70,000 copies. The two CDs have brought Northern Soul to a wider audience, including many younger fans who were unaware of the scene. Russ said: 'I was surprised with the sales, but I knew it would happen if everything went right. I have hundreds of phone calls from people asking how they can get back into the scene. At the Brighton Beach soul nights in Leeds it's amazing the number of people there in their teens and twenties who bring along their *Soul Survivors* CDs and books and say that's what got them into the music.'

CDs may be here, but the post-Wigan era has done nothing to dampen the enthusiasm of the committed record collector.

Steve Guarnori gave this insight into the soul fan's vinyl hunting mentality in an article for the Northern Soul fanzine *Manifesto*:

My job has taken me to the USA nearly forty times. Although hard work, I often manage to find a couple of hours (normally between a 4-5 pm finish to the working day and 7.30 pm-ish dinner) to hunt down records. It's getting harder now, and real 'hits' are getting fewer. Everyone who's been regularly to the USA can recount tales of good fortune. Here is a modest tale of mine which was so odd that I can remember it like it was last week, even though it happened in August 1990.

I had finished work at 4 pm, gone back to my hotel in Century City, changed from my suit into record-hunting clothes, and cabbed off down to Record Surplus on Pico Boulevard. A favourite LA stop for everyone because of its cheap prices. What would I find this visit? Like every collector, I was drawn upstairs to the racks of '10 cents each' 45s. At that price everything was worth buying.

Time stopped. I had amassed a healthy pile of 45s, when I glanced over the balcony. Some geek, who in physical appearance resembled the bad guy who hijacked the kids' schoolbus in *Dirty Harry* was downstairs with a big box of records – what looked like hundreds of them. I could see a distinctive MGM yellow demo copy of something – 60s records! He had an exchange of words with the store salesman, and then picked his box up from the counter and proceeded to leave.

I ran downstairs and asked the salesman what that guy was doing. In typical southern California take-it-or-leave-it style he told me, 'Oh, he's trying to sell some old 45s – I had a look through; there's nothing of interest there. I offered him 50 dollars he wants 100, so I told him no. That's the way it goes, man.' I agreed but in total contradiction then left my pile of vinyl on the counter and rushed out after the man with the records. The lure of an MGM demo! Outside on the sidewalk I stopped him.

'Excuse me, are those records for sale?' I asked.

'Yes,' he replied before proceeding to tell me how the store man hadn't offered him enough dosh.

'Can I have a look?'

'Sure, help yourself.' We placed the box on some innocent's car bonnet. The MGM demo was Dottie Cambridge, but the second record was Ty Karim 'Lighten Up, Baby' on Car-A-Mel. I struggled through a few things like Timmy Willis on a Veep demo, and some James Brown King demos, not really focusing, blood rushing to my head, then re-checking – no, I wasn't dreaming – that Ty Karim was real. 'Oh well,' I said nonchalantly, 'I'll take that one', pulling out the Ty Karim, careful not to show the slightest sign of excitement or over-interest.

'Sorry pal, I'm not selling them one at a time, take the whole lot or nothing.' Here I made my first mistake – I tried to up the ante, and hardball him with untrue words.

'Maybe, but I'm not interested in most of this stuff.'

'OK, take it or leave it,' he double-bluffed. Bollocks, I was suddenly outmanoeuvred and wrong-footed.

'Well, let's have a look through – see what else is in there,' I retorted, regaining the initiative. As I dug deeper more bits of interest appealed, Prince Philip Mitchell on Smash, some Okeh demos, what looked like another version of 'Gone With the Wind Is My Love' on Mojo – another on Mojo, bloody hell Virginia Blakly. By now my pulse was beginning to race, there was no way I was going to let him leave with this box!

'OK – there are a few bits in here – how much for the box?' I asked, keen to appear only mildly interested.

'100 dollars.'

'Will you take 80?' I replied – my second mistake. His face turned to one of scorn, and like some spoilt child he told me that maybe the records are not for sale after all.

Anxious not to lose out I hit back. 'OK, 100 dollars is fine – no big deal' and proceeded to get my wallet out.

'Well,' he said, 'I was taking them to a guy in Orange County who was going to buy them, I only really stopped at Record Surplus to see if they wanted them. In fairness I should call this guy to see if he wants to make me an increased offer before accepting 100 dollars from you.'

Oh no. No, no, no. Keeping a cool demeanour I told him I had not got all day to hang around the sidewalk negotiating, and in any event I had to go back to my hotel to meet some people for dinner.

He suggested that he'd see this guy in Orange, and if he didn't want them he'd bring them by my hotel later. No way Jose; those records were not leaving my sight. Instinct told me if he disappeared off into the evening I'd never see the records again. I suggested we find a payphone and he call the guy down in Orange.

Hesitating, he said, '120 dollars and they're yours.' I agreed.

He then had second thoughts again. 'Maybe I should give the other guy a call anyway, he may offer more.' By now I was losing patience fast. I was being pissed around royally.

I carried the box up the road until we found a payphone, but he wanted me out of earshot while he dealt with the guy in Orange. After a few minutes he returned.

'So what's the deal?' I barked.

'Well the guy in Orange says he wasn't that bothered anyway; it's 100 dollars or nothing; he has 50,000 records, so doesn't mind if he doesn't get these.'

'OK, 120 dollars?'

'Er ha-ha, no – 140. They're not my records; they belong to a friend. I'm just selling them so he can get a car,' he replied unconvincingly.

Beaten, but also knowing a gift horse when I see one, I gave him 140 dollars. We traded the records and then I headed for the payphone to call for a cab. Something told me he'd change his mind, and want the records back, he was that kind of creep. I crossed the road to get away from him and waited on the corner of Pico and Sepulveda, keeping an eye on him until he had eventually disappeared from sight. It seemed like an age before the cab arrived and as I travelled back, now late for dinner, the bad part of me mused how I wanted to give this clown a good kicking for messing me around so much. But there again to find two monster rarities in a box of 500 takes some beating! And what of the guy in Orange County, sitting there waiting for someone to turn up with a box full of records, only to get a call saying more money is needed or the deal's off? Ha! If you're reading this, pal, you should have believed him and offered the money!

As I entered the grand entrance of the Century Plaza, I passed the doormen in Beefeater outfits – it's that kind of place. I caught sight of my dinner hosts, all suited up, waiting for me. I scuttled past towards the lifts. 'Hi, guys; just dropping this off in my room – back in a couple of minutes.' Quick-change artist and out to dinner. I cannot remember anything about the dinner, but remember I rushed back to my room afterwards and trawled through the entire box – 500 records. 350 were soul, nothing less interesting than Arthur Conley Atco demos, and plenty of £15–50 collectables (Veep, Mercury etc.). All were mint and in their original sleeves. There were several on Date (including Sweet Things, Glories and Charmaines). There was a nice little handful of Okeh demos including Johnny Robinson 'Gone But Not Forgotten', Sandi Sheldon and Major Lance 'Without a Doubt'. The percentage hit-rate of rare soul was really very high in this box. Curiously, virtually everything dated from 1968, which got me wondering whether the geek's friend had more boxes of similar stuff. Too late now; they'd be someone else's find.

The other 150 records were obscure West Coast rock bands

by the look of things. I sorted them out and took them back to Record Surplus the next day in a big carrier bag. With all my other records I'd found I couldn't be bothered to hike 150 surplus rock 45s halfway round the world.

Back at Record Surplus the same salesman from the day before took a look through the bag. 'Weren't you in here yesterday? Yes . . . there's some kinda nice interesting things here; I'll give you 45 dollars for them.' I agreed, deal done. I even managed to find the records I had originally dug out the day before, which had been re-filed clumsily en-masse in the same order I had pulled them out. Life can be kind when you're on a roll!

The moral to the story is that it's not just about who you know, it's about being in the right place at the right time.

Dave Rimmer, of Dudley, West Midlands, founded the soul fanzine *Soulful Kinda Music* in 1989. The usual sort of issue will contain anything between 40 and 50 A4 pages, and normally takes Dave about two hours of working in the evenings and at weekends to put together. Dave has found that this workload has reduced greatly over the last couple of years as the greater use of personal computers has meant that articles now arrive on disk, or even over the net, so all the retyping of handwritten articles has gone.

He started the magazine as he became increasingly disenchanted with the content of the soul fans' 'bible', *Blues and Soul*. Dave explained: 'I felt I could produce something which would contain the same type of articles that *B & S* used to do, of interest to 60s soul fans. This also coincided with my own, continuing, desire to learn more about soul music. I am also a compulsive reader, and will read anything! Having seen some of the other magazines around at the time I felt I could do as good a job, if not better. My command of the English language is reasonably good, I enjoy doing research, and nowadays enjoy playing with computers. So why not combine that with my other hobby and produce a magazine about soul music?

'I also get a very great sense of satisfaction in producing the magazine – a sort of "I did that" feeling.'

In common with many passionate followers of the Northern Soul scene, Dave has definite opinions on the current boom and reawakening of interest on the scene. 'The oldies scene, with its huge venues and loads of punters is entirely regressive. Loads of people who want to hear the same records they heard twenty years ago. Most of the punters are recent returnees to the scene. Where will the scene be left when they are bored again and all leave?

'The real scene is the one that happens every weekend, at places like the 100 Club, the Wilton, Bolton Pigeon Club, Albrighton, even Winsford. The real scene belongs to the people who attend nighters every weekend, not once every three months. This is the scene that will continue after the Ritz/ Togetherness/Trentham Gardens venues have shut again. I also have to point out that I attend all of the above venues, for different reasons perhaps, but I do attend all of them.'

Dave is also one of those purists who when DJing refuses to play anything other than a record in its original vinyl form. He is equally intolerant of pressings and (heaven forbid) CDs. He cheerfully admits that some will see him as an elitist snob, but defends his stance eloquently: 'It's not that I won't tolerate CDs or pressings, I have hundreds of CDs at home, and even a few pressings. I also have no problem with other people buying pressings, and even having whole collections of pressings and reissues. What I won't tolerate is people DJing with CDs or pressings. I spend a lot of time and money chasing rare American singles, so that I can DJ at top venues.

'Why should someone who popped into HMV and bought a CD that afternoon be able to DJ before me, play one of the rarities I have on original, thus stopping me from playing it? Perhaps there is a certain amount of snobbishness there, but when I DJ I would not dream of playing someone else's big sounds off CDs, so why should I tolerate someone else doing it to me? You should either do it right, or not at all.'

Warrington-based soul fan Andy Love launched the fanzine *Love Music Review* in December 1995 with an 'across-the-board' music policy similar to his own tastes. Ex-Wigan Casino-goer Andy says *Love Music Review* is not just about Northern

Soul, but about all forms of good soul music from whatever era. 'For far too long many so-called soul fans have been listening to only a limited diet of Northern oldies from the 60s, while all around them soul musicians have carried on making good records.

'The early days of the Wheel, Torch, Wigan, St Ives, Cleethorpes, and Blackpool Mecca continued to play new recordings alongside the rarities and they were accepted. Nowadays people call you elitist if they don't know the tracks you champion from the heyday of Northern Soul. My aim has been to try and educate these people into hearing new sounds and give the more open-minded a chance to hear something different and good.'

*Love Music* is scheduled to come out every three months or so ('but I rarely manage to be that regular,' says Andy). In addition to his own writing he uses a wide variety of contributors on new and old releases and events up and down the country. His labour of love means he has to put in many hours after work at night laying out the magazine and compiling the cassette tape which normally accompanies it. 'Although it's hard work and very time-consuming, I get a kick when people take time to ring me and tell me how much they like the mag, and the fact that its unblinkered attitude is refreshing.'

The open-minded music policy that Andy champions he feels is vital to the continued healthy state of the Northern and Modern Soul scene. 'In the past, all the best all-nighter and Northern Soul clubs played across the board. As long as it was real, good-quality soul music, it would see turntable action. I want to go to a club and hear a wider variety of soul from all eras. I want to hear records for the first time, not necessarily brand-new tracks, but unknowns from the 60s, 70s, 80s and 90s in one room.

'Let's all be elitist like we used to be twenty-five years ago. Modern soul is twenty-five years old now and an awful lot of those "disco" tracks have infiltrated into the Northern oldies room without a blink of the eye from the so-called dinosaurs, so there is hope!'

> Right about now . . . The funk soul brother.
> Check it out now . . . The funk soul brother.

Yes, it's a long way from the Torch to the close-of-the-century pop charts, but those few words and a generous sample from a Northern Soul instrumental certainly did it for Norman Cook. Recording as Fatboy Slim, the former Housemartin stunned thousands of Northern Soul fans when he released 'The Rockafeller Skank' in the summer of 1998. How many of us turned up the volume and listened incredulously as the strains of 'The Rockafeller Skank' came over the airwaves for the first time?

'It sounds like . . . no it can't be. It bloody well *is*. It's "Sliced Tomatoes"!'

Quite how Norman stumbled across an obscure instrumental like 'Sliced Tomatoes' by Just Brothers is as intriguing to Northern Soul fans as how Rubin's 'You've Been Away' came to be used on the Felix cat food adverts on TV.

The 'Rockafeller Skank' became just about *the* dance floor anthem of 1998, with hundreds of thousands of youngsters hooked by its great rap and irresistible dance beat. But how many of them knew the song had its origins in the sweaty Northern Soul clubs of the early 1970s? To the author's knowledge, this fact has never been publicly acknowledged other than in minute print on the credit sleeves of the LP and the single.

The dance floors of the north have rocked for more than twenty-five years to the manic, guitar-led strains of 'Sliced Tomatoes', a 1972 recording on the Music Merchant label, which became a firm favourite with the Torch crowd.

Those familiar strains still form the backdrop of Norman's 'The Rockafeller Skank' with an added 'surf guitar'. The classic rap 'Right about now . . . the funk soul brother' added the seal of approval to its soulful roots and turned the single into probably the most memorable pop song of 1998. It is even featured as background music on Sony Playstation's FIFA 99 CD-Rom, as the author's young son can gleefully confirm.

Bromley-born Norman attended college in Brighton and

demonstrated his love of music by DJing around the resort. He shot to fame with his old schoolchum Paul Heaton when they formed the Housemartins. It was Paul who had opened his eyes to soul music when he brought home the Atlantic compilation album *This is Soul*. Suddenly the two friends were enjoying together Otis Redding, Sam and Dave and other classic 60s output.

This inevitably led Norman to hearing rarer recordings and dabbling in Northern Soul. 'I've always had fairly eclectic tastes in music,' he said. 'I've never just concentrated on one particular style. I would always be getting into Northern Soul and then going back to blues and R & B and stuff.'

By the early 80s Norman was DJing in the Brighton area and regularly featuring some of his Northern Soul collection. One track that stuck in his mind was 'Sliced Tomatoes' by Just Brothers – 'I think it was on the B-side of one of the Inferno re-releases,' he reflected. 'I suppose to the serious Northern Soul fan I was just sticking my toe in the water, but I loved the music and was playing rare groove, funk and Northern Soul.'

The Housemartins' love of soul was illustrated in 1986 when they had a number one hit with their a cappella version of the Isley Brothers' 'Caravan of Love'. The band broke up and Norman, deciding he loved dance music too much, went back to Brighton and forged a career as a remixer.

He then formed Beats International, who had a number one with 'Dub Be Good To Me'. A period of personal trauma followed, and Norman didn't work for two years. Then one night a friend took him to a club and gave him some Ecstasy, and everything changed. He formed Freakpower with trombonist Ashley Slater and notched up another Top Ten hit with 'Turn On, Tune In, Cop Out', a tune loved by many modern soul and broad-minded Northern Soul fans.

Freakpower's second album *More of Everything for Everybody* was in the same vein but it bombed. That's when Norman started making records under a variety of aliases – Pizzaman, The Mighty Dub Kats, Fried Funk Food, and in 1995 Fatboy Slim for Skint Records.

According to Norman, the name comes from a Louisiana

blues singer from the 1940s, famed for a song called 'Baby I Want A Piece of Your Pie', and the Fatboy Slim sound from 'trip hop records played at 45rpm'. His first single was 'Santa Cruz' – 'trip hop you can dance to', says Norman. Through London clubs like the Sunday Social, where the Chemical Brothers were resident, and Big Kahuna Burger, he discovered dance audiences who loved 'Santa Cruz', and was persuaded to come out of his DJ retirement.

Fatboy Slim's second single was 'Everybody Loves a 303', which borrowed from Edwin Starr's 'Everybody needs Love'. It was another dance floor smash, and buoyed with confidence, Norman had smash remixes with Wildchild's 'Renegade Master' and Cornershop's 'Brimful of Asha'.

Which brings us to 'The Rockafeller Skank'. '*Hawaii 5-0* on acid' is how Norman describes that track. 'A Northern Soul instrumental with a rap,' is how many soul fans will remember it. Norman got the idea for using 'Sliced Tomatoes' as he DJ'd at a club in 1997. He had got into the habit of playing more unusual tunes to warm up his regular dance spot. He would usually feature a couple of Northern Soul tracks 'to wake people up', and 'Sliced Tomatoes' was one of them. Norman said: 'You could see people loving it and at the same time thinking "I don't normally dance to this kind of stuff." I logged it in my brain for future reference.'

Some time later, Norman was playing around with the soon-to-be-famous rap 'Right about now . . .'. He found that it only seemed to work over a 160-beats-per-minute backing track. Northern Soul had that kind of speed, and in a flash of inspiration Norman remembered 'Sliced Tomatoes'.

The Lord Finesse vocal wasn't in fact a made-to-measure rap, it was a spoken intro to an obscure album. Norman cut it up to come up with the immortal lines 'Right about now . . . the funk soul brother' and laid it on to the basic Just Brothers instrumental track. He already had the ingredients for a dance favourite, but he felt it still needed something else – and the final ingredient came to him while he was DJing in Bali.

'I was watching all these surfers with the song going through my head and that's where I came with the idea of the twangy guitar,' he said. The original idea for 'The Rockafeller Skank' came to him in just three hours, but it was three months of working on and off before Norman came up with the finished product. 'We wanted it to be right because it was going to be the first single from the new album (*You've Come a Long Way, Baby*). The funny thing is, that by the time I have finished producing and remixing something I am usually fed up of hearing it. When we had finished "The Rockafeller Skank" and played it back I thought "I quite like that". It seemed to be an instant thing amongst everyone who heard it. We hoped something would happen for it, but I never thought it would be a Top Ten single up there with the likes of George Michael and Madonna.'

The video was in keeping with the intended surfing feel of the track. Skint Records proclaim 'The Rockafeller Skank' as *the* summer anthem of 1998, and who could argue: a record that surfed to sales in excess of 190,000 in the UK alone and set dance floors alight all over Europe. The single probably did a lot to earn Norman the Best Dance Act award at the Brits.

As far as the original artists are concerned, Norman says Just Brothers were 'handsomely rewarded', receiving about 70 per cent of royalties. So their under-appreciated efforts have finally earned them substantial amounts of money almost thirty years later.

And most Northern Soul fans seem happy with his treatment of one of 'their' classics. 'I'm so glad about that,' said Norman. 'I can imagine that this sort of thing might piss off the purists. I always like to select tracks that haven't been in the charts before. To most people "Sliced Tomatoes" is pretty obscure, but to Northern Soul fans it's a classic. It's a bonus if by listening to my work, people then get into other things by the original artists.'

Soul fans enjoying the *You've Come a Long Way, Baby* album were in for another surprise. Norman also sampled the Olympics' Mirwood stomper 'I'll Do a Little Bit More' for the track 'Soul Surfing'.

With further singles, 'Gangster Trippin' hitting the charts and 'Praise You' zooming straight in at number one in the UK, Norman seems to have found the winning formula (with a little help from the Torch DJs who stumbled across 'Sliced Tomatoes' twenty-six years or so earlier!).

Now there is talk of a compilation album of original tracks that Fatboy Slim has sampled in recent years – which will mean more exposure and money for artists like Just Brothers and the Olympics. And Norman is still listening to Northern Soul tracks with an ear to giving them the golden touch. As for which ones, he is not saying. 'I don't want to give too much away,' he said mischievously.

In 1983, a well-known recording artist wrote to an aspiring young bass player who was auditioning to join his new band. The lad showed promise, but needed to work more on his technique. 'For great feel and space in the music, check out some old Booker T and the MGs records,' was the star's advice.

Who was the artist? An American soul star? A blues or R & B specialist? No, the man in question was none other than British singer-songwriter Paul Weller.

The ex-Jam member is not the first name that comes to mind when one thinks of the influence of 60s soul artists on today's music, but his admiration for the musicians and singers of black America is demonstrated by his Booker T tribute and some of his recordings.

When Weller left the Jam he went on to front the decidedly soul-influenced Style Council. But take a look back at his teenage years and you find a passion for Northern Soul and early Jam cover versions of soul standards Martha and the Vandellas' 'Heatwave', and Curtis Mayfield's 'Move On Up'.

By all accounts, the young Weller was born to be a Mod. It was the Who's anthem 'My Generation' that turned him on to the 60s Mod scene. Paul was already the school's sharpest dresser and his encounter with 60s R & B and soul only served to enhance his wardrobe of Ben Shermans, smart suits, brogues and all things Mod.

He attended Northern Soul nights in his home town of Woking, Surrey, and at the nearby Bisley Pavilion. These sweaty, packed events were where he learned to appreciate the harder edge of soul music and although the Jam later developed a full rock sound and went on to become synonymous with the punk boom, they could still surprise audiences with their Curtis Mayfield and Martha and the Vandellas cover versions.

When he was just eighteen, Paul recorded a stomping song for the Jam's debut album called 'Non Stop Dancing'. It included the telling lines:

> When you're dancing all night long
> It gives you the feeling that you belong
> Non stop dancing
> I'm truly out of my head
> But I ain't sleeping baby
> You'll see me dance right past my bed.
> Things are really getting wild
> The kids are screaming for the James Brown style.

When the Jam scored their third number one hit in 1982 with 'A Town Called Malice', soul fans immediately heard the Motown influence and compared it to the Supremes' 'You Can't Hurry Love'.

When he formed the Style Council, his soulful musical roots came to the fore. By 1983 his new group was recording out-and-out 70s-style dancers like 'My Ever Changing Moods', and mid-tempo items like 'Long Hot Summer' and 'You're the Best Thing'. 1985's 'My Ever Changing Moods' consolidated his new musical direction. No more guitar-led pub rock with angry young man-style lyrics. The young Mod had returned to the more thoughtful and melodic songs that had so inspired him as a teenager at soul nights.

Jam fans deserted him in droves as many new fans came on board and the commercial success of the Style Council would never eclipse that of the Jam. But many once-disillusioned now look back at the Style Council output with more favourable eyes than in the 80s.

And the 1990s solo Weller has regained his position as one of Britain's most revered artists with great success with his *Stanley Road* and *Heavy Soul* albums.

Weller's excursions into the R & B world didn't stop at blue-eyed soul, either. In 1997 he produced an out-and-out soul album for Carleen Anderson of the Young Disciples. Carleen, Bobby Byrd's niece, acknowledged Weller as a true soul master. The album, however, with its underproduced Stax-style wailers, and wistful ballads, was well received by the cognoscenti but didn't set the pop charts alight.

Norfolk-based DJ Ian Clark recalls: 'Paul Weller was into Northern Soul and still tips his hat to his soul influences. I've even sold him a few singles and albums, including Billy Butler's "Right Track" on an Okeh demo. He's also bought a few items off Ady Croasdell, who along with Tony Rounce DJ'd on one of the Jam tours playing 60s soul before the band came on stage.

'I remember standing in the DJ booth with Ady at Hammersmith Palais – he played the Miracles' "Ooh Baby Baby" as the Jam hit the stage,' Ian told *Manifesto* magazine.

In 1999 Weller is still a music icon and a name courted by stars like the Gallagher brothers of Oasis fame. A far cry from his talc-on-the-dance-floor antics at Woking Football Club's Northern Soul nights twenty-five years earlier . . .

Scotsman Kenny Burrell was among the thousands of soul fans captivated by a previously unheard-of Northern Soul stomper at Wigan Casino in the late 1970s. Legions of soul fans knew this instantly-danceable gem as 'Do I Love You' by Eddie Foster.

It was some years before the truth leaked out to DJs, collectors and Casino-goers. The record that was loved so much by Kenny and his fellow soul fans was actually a Motown stomper called 'Do I Love You (Indeed I Do)' by Frank Wilson.

Not only that, it was rumoured to be the rarest record in the world. And so began a frenzy among collectors and DJs that would result twenty years later in Kenny paying a mind-boggling £15,000 for an original copy of the record that had so captured his imagination as a youngster.

Frank Wilson, a much-respected Motown producer, was more used to playing a behind-the-scenes role in the Detroit label's success story. But he cut 'Do I Love You' with himself as the lead singer, and immediately had reservations about it.

Frank's singing debut was scheduled for release on 23

December 1965 on the US label Soul. It never saw the light of day, owing to a combination of Frank's U-turn and Motown boss Berry Gordy's lukewarm reception of his vocal efforts. A number of white promotional copies bearing the number 5-35019 were cut. Popular opinion is that all but two were destroyed. One copy is now neatly tucked into Kenny Burrell's record box. For the Dunfermline-based rare soul DJ and avid collector it is the fruition of a long-held ambition. 'I just had to have it,' he says. 'I probably paid over the odds to get it, but it was a take-it-or-leave-it price. I never lost any sleep over it beforehand, but I did some agonizing in the two or three days after I bought it.'

Mystique and rumour surround the real origins and route taken by the two known copies of 'Do I Love You' from the day they were cut to arriving in Britain, where both are now owned and loved by Northern Soul fanatics. Kenny's copy is believed to have come from the vaults of Motown via Detroit record collector Ron Murphy. He sold the disc in 1990 to Canada-based Martin Koppell, boss of the Goldmine CD label. Koppell's Northern Soul collection was legendary, and when news came that he was selling it off at Easter 1998, Kenny Burrell was at the front of the queue.

Yes, the Frank Wilson disc was for sale . . . for £15,000. Kenny had two years earlier drawn up a wants list of the 33 Northern Soul records that he most desired for his collection. The elusive Frank Wilson disc was among them.

Kenny recalled how the record excited him at Wigan Casino and still sends him into raptures even today. 'That record has everything. It is absolutely awesome. I can remember hearing it at Wigan Casino – I can't remember whether I knew it as by Eddie Foster or Frank Wilson – and I just loved it. When you are young you are very impressionable and I suppose nostalgia becomes more powerful when you are getting older.'

The demand caused by Wigan Casino, and particularly the championing of the record by Russ Winstanley, led to a UK release in 1979 for the Frank Wilson disc. Soul fans, including Kenny, picked up the official re-release for less than £2, but those like Kenny would only be happy when they owned the original US recording.

After a decade or so off the Northern Soul scene, Kenny came back into the fold in 1990 when he attended a soul night in Edinburgh. He said: 'I hardly knew any of the records that were being played. I realized that there was more to it than the Wigan top 50. I was hooked and I started collecting again.'

Kenny's rarities collection grew and grew to such an extent that he is now in great demand at all-nighters all over Britain. His record box, even without Frank Wilson, is one of the most valuable in the world (a fact which escaped the attentions of thieves who broke into his car, stole his jumper and simply dumped about £150,000 worth of records where Kenny found them the next day!).

In early 1997, Kenny phoned Tim Brown, Martin Koppell's partner in Goldmine Records. The Todmorden-based collector has the only other known copy of Frank Wilson, but refused to part with it. Said Kenny: 'It got to the stage where the price didn't matter – I just had to have it. When I heard Martin Koppell was selling his collection I was straight in there.' Kenny went to Tim's house in Todmorden to inspect Martin's copy. It was indeed a white demo in mint condition and the £15,000 deal was struck. Kenny was also captivated by Tim Brown's Motown acetate of Chris Clark's version of 'Do I Love You', but found himself somewhat bereft of spare cash after the Frank Wilson sale.

The Scotsman has no qualms about paying such a vast amount of money for a single 45, which now stays chained up in his record box whenever he takes it out with him. 'When I pick it up I get goosebumps just thinking about it. Records mean something to people. Not only is it a brilliant record, but it's the most valuable record in the world.

'I suppose you have to ask yourself is any record worth £15,000, but when these rarities turn up I'm a mug. I bought one for £15 last week that's every bit as good, but it's not as rare and not as famous as Frank Wilson.'

Kenny, who owns a double-glazing business, admits that he had to search his conscience before telling his non-soul-loving family he was shelling out the world record fee.

He said: 'My wife doesn't like the music at all, and the kids can't understand why a record that never got in the charts is worth so much. At the end of the day as long they are not deprived of anything it doesn't matter how much I spent.'

The £15,000 question is this: Are there any more copies out there?

DJ Chris King, who has compiled three CDs of rare Motown material and has extensive contacts in the USA, reckons there are more to be found. He believes there are at least five copies in circulation, three of which are in the States. One of them is owned by Berry Gordy Jr himself.

Chris said he had been told by his Motown contacts that the real reason the Frank Wilson single was dropped was because Gordy did not want his producers having successful recording careers. He wanted to keep them at Motown – in the background, writing and producing hits for his established artists. Chris doesn't think 'Do I Love You' is particularly rare: 'I think there are lots of copies somewhere. Motown would have pressed up hundreds of copies of it, maybe up to 1,000. Look at Linda Griner's "Goodbye Cruel World" – it was very rare then 1,000 copies turned up!'

If that happened with the Frank Wilson record, Mr Burrell would be entitled to feel a little peeved.

*Kenny Burrell's all-time Top Ten*

'They'll Never Know Why' Freddie Chavez
'If You Ever Walk Out of My Life' Dena Barnes
'You Don't Love Me' Epitome of Sound
'Just Another Heartache' Little Richie
'Queen of Fools' Barbara Mills
'Double Cookin'' Checkerboard Squares
'If You Ask Me' Jerry Williams
'I'm Coming Home in the Morning' Lou Pride
'Just Say You're Wanted and Needed' Gwen Owens
'Do I Love You' Frank Wilson

*Kenny Burrell's current favourites (from his own collection)*

'Sweet Temptation' Ward Burton
'You Just Don't Know' Ty Karim
'Who's Kissing You Tonight' Herman Lewis
'A Little Less Talk' Jerri Shaw
'Let's Try It Again' Gerri Shivers
'I Can Feel Him Slipping Away' Tobbie Bowie
'I'm Gonna Make You Love Me' Combinations
'I Just Can't Win' Mandells
'You Don't Know, Boy' Attractions
'Love's Alright' Jesse James

In the centre of the long, oblong-shaped reception room in Ian Levine's smart West London home is a table piled high with CDs – some in picture sleeves others with plain white covers with simple text recording who and what they are.

A five-foot-high silver Dalek stands guard over the enigmatic DJ-turned-producer's latter-day soul collection. Ian bristles at the mere suggestion that the Dalek could be anything other than a genuine BBC Dr Who prop. 'Of course it's an original BBC one. I got it at an auction some years ago,' he says. The question of authenticity is a good one, and an issue which we will return to on a different way very shortly.

He picks out a CD from a plain white cover and pops it into an expensive hi-fi system. From the two wall speakers comes a crashing Motown-derived stomper fronted by the distinctive voice of Detroit legend J J Barnes. The music is so loud conversation is impossible – the bass line thuds along and the beat is in the time-honoured Northern Soul on-the-fours fashion. It's uplifting, infectious and impossible to sit still. At the same time it sounds vaguely familiar, much in the way that an Oasis song can sometimes get you playing 'spot the Beatles track'.

Something in the backing track reminds me of Johnny Wyatt's 'This Thing Called Love'. Another element brings to mind Jimmy James's 'A Man Like Me'. These elements aren't really there, of course, but the music is so accessible and derivative of a thousand Northern Soul recordings that you would swear you had heard it before.

The song is called 'Talk of the Grapevine' and it sounds as authentic, crisp and immediate as anything that came out of the Hitsville studios in the mid-60s. Hang on a minute, though. Maybe it sounds a little too crisp for a 60s recording. There's something about the strings and the sound quality that suggests the 1990s rather than three decades earlier. Maybe it has just been remastered.

'If you like Northern Soul, how can you possibly not like this?' says Ian as J J Barnes's voice fades out. 'What on earth is wrong with this?' It's difficult to argue. The singer is the same J J Barnes who recorded 'Please Let Me In', 'Real Humdinger', 'Sweet Sherry', and a whole host of Ric Tic masterpieces which have been collected and loved by Northern Soul fans since the 1960s. You don't get much more of an authentic Northern Soul black American pedigree than old J J. A thought suddenly occurs to me.

'When was this recorded?'

'Which part?' asks Ian.

'The vocals.'

'1989.'

Ah-ha, part of Ian's commendable but ill-fated Motorcity

project where he signed more than 100 former Motown artists to his own label, made hundreds of recordings and lost a fortune.

'And the backing track?'

'Eight weeks ago,' Ian replies.

And the writing credits? Ian Levine and J J Barnes. Producer Ian Levine.

And therein lies the problem. Is this a genuine Northern Soul record worthy of being aired to the masses on the rare soul scene, or should it be consigned to the dustbin of 'tailormades' usually reserved for the worst examples of home-grown cover versions?

The debate is raging once again on the Northern Soul scene, just like it did in the 70s when Ian first began producing artists like the Exciters, L J Johnson and James Wells. On the one hand you have the purists who say 'This isn't Northern Soul. Northern Soul is 60s music made in the 60s by black American artists and producers.' Others say: 'This is a soul artists singing an original song. It sounds great. Who cares where and when it was produced?'

Soul fanzines, venues and the Internet have been buzzing with the cut and thrust of the debate over Ian's current productions which are now getting an airing on the soul scene mainly via his friend and record label boss Neil Rushton. The debate has sometimes become deeply personal, ill-tempered and out of all proportion to the alleged 'crimes' Ian is committing against the rare soul circuit.

Ian is heartily fed up with the sniping and downright nastiness his re-emergence on to the scene has brought. 'It sickens me. The people who should get the most out of recordings like this are too biased against me. If someone else gave me a recording like this I would love to play it.

'I'm not interested in records that sound computerized. I'm interested in records that sound right and lift you in the same way as the classics of the 1960s. It's a slightly cleaner, fresher version of Northern Soul, it's not sacrificing the musical integrity. If the critics thought it was something else they would love it, but because Ian Levine produced it they are not prepared to listen. If you don't like the stuff then fair enough, but judge it on its merits and not who made it.'

Ian is delighted with the finished product on the J J Barnes recording, and the dozens of others on which he is working. He accepts that no one has ever captured the tight, authentic sound of Motown's Funk Brothers apart from the legendary label itself. But new technology has meant that Ian now feels that the James Jamerson bass-line and the crashing drums that he produces today feel as close as anyone has ever got in recent decades.

He recently remixed his 1975 chart hit 'Reaching for the Best' by the Exciters, which he is happier with than with the original recording. 'When I went into the studio in the 70s you couldn't get the authentic Northern Soul sound. The Exciters sounded like a 70s record with a 60s beat. The more sophisticated technology has got, the easier it has become to duplicate the 60s sound. This J J Barnes track and the others have been made in a very clever way. Exactly how and where it was done isn't really that important.'

To make his point, he puts on another CD, this time an unissued Eddie Holman track, 'What Happened to Our Melody'. Once again it has a classic Northern Soul feel and Eddie's soul credentials cannot be questioned. But this is exactly the modern, recently-made track that has appalled and delighted people in droves on the Northern Soul scene.

In addition to classic artists, Ian has signed up some unknown black singers and taken them into the recording studio. One of Diana Ross's former backing singers, Rocq-E Harrell, has turned out the Levine-penned 'My Heart Keeps Beating Faster'.

Other releases via Neil Rushton's All-4-U label have included Pat Lewis's version of Gill Scott Heron's 'The Bottle' and 'Something New to Do' (Bobby Hebb); Brenda Holloway doing 'On the Real Side' (Larry Saunders); Ronnie McNeir's in-demand 'Lucky Number'. Then there's the unknown Tammi Lavette doing 'Tore Apart My Broken Heart' and the instrumental 'Soul A Go-Go' by the Watts 103rd Street Strings.

The upbeat publicity about the latter goes as follows: 'This caused mayhem at the Mecca when it got its debut play and it has since packed the dance floor at the Ritz, Keele, Blackburn etc.'

Another view is voiced by soul fans like Eddy Edmondson,

Andy Morris and Dave Watson. 'Levine's Home-Made Crap' is their assessment of his recent work. Their written attack on Kendal-based Eddy's website 'Soul Time' after Neil Rushton played Levine productions at the Ritz and other venues brought a furious and lengthy response from Ian.

Eddy is unrepentant: 'Can he not get it through his thick head. We don't want new made sounds. We didn't want them the first time . . . Soul Fox Strings, Wigan's Chosen Few, Ovations etc. We want to be left alone. We don't want to be on the telly, we don't want records in the charts, we don't want cameras in the venues.'

Ian Levine sees this attitude as insular and narrow-minded. It brings back unpleasant memories for him of the Levine Must Go campaign and he passionately believes that modern productions are the way to bring fresh blood on to the scene. Not that some want fresh blood at all, of course. 'The future is with these records like J J Barnes and Eddie Holman. You don't see many 19–20-year-olds at venues these days. These are the records that we need to serve the needs of the younger ones, to get new blood on to the scene without changing the basic northern sound,' he said. 'Why on earth can't someone else make records like this? I would be delighted to listen to stuff like this. The scene has got to move on, otherwise we will be left with 200 people in a club listening to stuff on the Shrine label [the rarest label of all time and a collector's dream].

'The reason the Shrine label releases are so rare is because they are shit. Compare the Shrine recordings to Groovesville and Mirwood, for instance. There is no comparison.'

Another reason Ian attracts his critics is his recent return to the scene after almost twenty years. The reason? Ian has set up his own production company to make a mammoth video documentary on the history of the Northern Soul scene. He has set about tracing and interviewing more than 200 people and artists around the world who have played major or minor roles in the Northern Soul scene.

Ian had initially hoped to make a three-hour video, but has been so overwhelmed with material and footage that it became a 10-hour epic. At the time of writing, Ian was having discussions with TV companies about a televised version.

Enter the critics once more: Levine is just out to make money out of the scene; Levine is doing it as an ego trip from his own perspective . . . It seems the guy can't win.

Ian by now is used to the attacks and insists that he has returned to the scene with the best of intentions. He has never stopped loving the music and never goes into anything halfheartedly. He says he wants to get it right and produce an in-depth documentary of the music scene that has given him so much pleasure (and career opportunities) over the years.

Ian said: 'I have traced and interviewed nearly 200 people – it's hardly about Ian Levine or my view of things. I've gone out of my way to be fair, and make sure that anyone who has done anything significant has got the proper credit they deserve. The film is not a Levine ego trip. It isn't about me, it's about the Northern Soul scene.'

Opinions come thick and fast about the new Levine productions. Kev Roberts, ex-Wigan Casino DJ and label manager of Goldmine Records, said: 'Firstly, I think the stuff that Ian has done recently are the best productions he has ever done. Secondly, I think it is bad timing. If we had had them ten or fifteen years ago I think he would have had a winner. The sad thing is that the majority of people who are on the scene today don't want to hear anything new, whether it's by Ian Levine or by Holland-Dozier-Holland.'

Record label boss Neil Rushton, who has issued Levine recordings through his All-4-U label, says soul fans shouldn't get too involved in the politics of who made it and where. 'The thing I don't like about Northern Soul is that some people always seem to be looking for an argument, even when there isn't one. I'm playing the Carstairs version of "Stick By Me, Baby". It isn't intended to replace the Salvadors', it's just another version. If you don't like it, fine. No one is forcing you to buy it. We might be covering other people's records, but I don't see why anyone should be worried about it. We are not trying to force anything down anyone's throats.'

DJ Richard Searling said: 'Ian means well, but you can't replicate the *Mona Lisa*. When he put out those things in the 70s, they were perfectly OK, but I never supported the Motorcity stuff. What he is doing is just blurring the memories.'

# 10

# I'll Never Forget You

*'I certainly don't feel forty-three. Dancing all night is like a good aerobics work-out. It keeps you fit and I get a buzz out of it.'*

When Lynn Shaw drops off her two young sons at her mother's home on a Friday night, it heralds the start of her regular soulful weekend. Lynn has been to an all-nighter every weekend for the last nineteen years ('And if there isn't one on, I'll turn a soul night into one by going back to someone's house afterwards!' she says).

The thought of just one weekend without living the Northern Soul lifestyle fills her with dread. Like many women, marriage, motherhood, divorce, and steady relationships have naturally all formed a large part of her life. But Northern Soul has never taken a back seat, and probably never will. 'I've never missed a single weekend since I was fourteen. If I don't do an all-nighter I feel soul dead,' said Lynn, from Nuneaton, Warwickshire. 'All your feelings and all your emotions come out on the dance floor.'

Lynn was introduced to Northern Soul while still at school in 1980. From there she progressed to local soul nights and then started to travel further afield to Wolverhampton, Leicester and Nottingham. She never made it to Wigan Casino owing to the fact that her lift didn't turn up, but got the all-nighter bug at Hinckley Leisure Centre after the Casino's closure.

It was on the soul scene that she met her first love and ex-husband Paul Shaw, and together they enjoyed the Northern Soul experience every weekend. Motherhood also didn't interrupt her outings thanks to her understanding mum. 'When the children were born my mum would look after them while we went out. I have never had any problems with babysitters. She would say I deserved to get a night out. Their dad was into it as well so we had a great time.'

Blonde-haired Lynn is also delighted that her two sons are starting to pick up on the rare music with which they have been bombarded since birth. 'I have always got the music on. When I put a tape on in the car my oldest one starts singing the words and the little one does the backing. It's so funny,' she said.

Lynn is now a familiar face at venues all over the country. Keele in Staffordshire, Winsford in Cheshire, the Ritz in Manchester, London's 100 Club, soul weekenders in Cleethorpes and in Great Yarmouth, are all on her list of regular haunts. She also achieved some fame when a camera crew followed her around for a Channel 4 documentary on the Cleethorpes soul weekender in 1996. That wasn't without its problems, as she has since encountered the odd bitchy comment about her 'superstar' status as TV spokeswoman for the Northern Soul scene.

Said Lynn: 'I suppose people get the impression that I think I'm "something". Perhaps it's because of the way I dance and the way I act. If they think that then they're judging a book by its cover.'

The girl *can* dance, too, having made the Cleethorpes dancing contest final. Her twists and turns maker her an instantly recognizable figure on the country's soul dance floors. 'Everyone has their own way of escaping from reality, and soul music and dancing is mine. I go out to enjoy myself and dance. The older I get the more comfortable I feel on the soul scene. I went around town the other week and felt so old and out of place it was awful.

'Everybody was drunk. Men don't respect you. On the soul scene you know men as friends before you get into a personal situation. I learn by soul music. You can go to a venue and tell someone you hardly know your problems and they will find the answer for you.'

Lynn's weekend routine usually begins on a Friday night

when she drops off the children at her mother's home. After her night out, she collects her sons the following day and spends a few hours with them before their father looks after them while she tackles an all-nighter. On Sunday night she picks them up.

'I never feel a bit guilty about going out,' said Lynn. 'If I ever went out with the girls around town I would end up with a hangover and wouldn't recover for two days. When I get back from an all-nighter and I've had a great night I feel ready to get on with life. It's my escapism and I can deal with things again.'

Lynn's favourite venue is the Winsford all-nighter and although she loves the traditional oldies she also loves the modern soul which is becoming a feature of two-roomed events. She has a theory about why so many diehard Northern Soul fans (usually men) refuse to accept the alternative modern sounds. 'The Northern stuff is a bit of a macho thing. When the 100 mph stuff is playing, the men feel masculine. It's all fast dancing and backdrops. A bit of a poser thing. If you put on a ballad or something slower they don't feel as strong. I think they feel a bit intimidated. Girls aren't bothered by all that. Some people aren't prepared to listen before they have a go.

'The modern stuff is keeping the soul going, and slowly but surely it's creeping into the main room, where the older ones who say they hate it are dancing to it anyway!'

Lynn, like many soul fans, realizes that any potential partner in her life will have to share her tastes in the music and lifestyle. 'All my boyfriends have always been on the soul scene,' she said. 'It makes it a lot easier. The music either hits you straight away or it never will. I always say to people, "If I have to explain to you what soul is then you are never going to understand."'

Lynn does not see herself retiring from the scene in the foreseeable future and is full of admiration for those in their late forties and older who are still keeping the faith. Her demanding weekend ritual does take its toll, however, and she has a ritual of eating bananas and drinking electrolyte and isotonic drinks to replace the energy lost through sweating and dancing. 'On Monday I'm fine, on Tuesday it catches up with me but by Wednesday I'm back to normal. If you know how much your body can take, that's fine.'

Ex-Wigan Casino-goer Káren Seddon, from Blackrod, near Wigan, chose marriage instead of a life devoted to soul music. When her husband died tragically twenty years later, leaving her and two teenage sons, she decided to regain her social life and was astonished to find a thriving Northern Soul scene.

A visit to a soul night at Chorley Town Hall rekindled her old interest in the music of her youth. 'I couldn't believe it was still going. I didn't know anyone there at all. It felt strange at first so I sat down for the first half a dozen records then I thought "Sod it" and got up to dance.'

It was there that she met Preston's Johnny Pearson, which started her on the road to a full-time return to the Northern Soul scene and club promotion, running monthly events at Preston Grasshoppers RUFC Club.

Her two now grown-up sons take a keen interest in their mother's nocturnal habits – leaving home late at night for an all-nighter and coming home at dawn – but have not yet been tempted to follow suit. They hardly bat an eyelid as carloads of 30- and 40-somethings arrive at Káren's home at daylight for a welcome morning brew after an all-nighter. The 'normal' world could be forgiven for thinking the roles should be reversed.

Káren was a ballet dancer as a youngster and had a chance of a Royal Ballet audition ('I chose Wigan Casino instead'). She has always kept herself in shape and feels that her regular swimming workouts keep her fit for dancing the night away.

Her current favourite venue is the Tony's Empress Ballroom all-nighter in Blackburn. 'I love it there. It's a bit of a dump and there's something about the smell that reminds me of the Casino.'

Káren is unbothered by age. 'I certainly don't feel forty-three. Dancing all night is like a good aerobics work-out. It keeps you fit and I get a buzz out of it. Northern Soul fans must have the strongest legs going. A lot of people have lost weight since coming back on to the scene.

'I'm really enjoying myself and why not? I have met people I haven't seen for twenty years and I have made so many new friends. For the first six months I knew the odd person and now I can go to any venue and know nearly everybody. From a single woman's point of view, where else can you go alone and feel completely at home? Where else can a single woman go and not feel threatened? If I went to the local pub or a nightclub on my own people would think I'm on the pick-up.'

The only problem that Káren now foresees is in personal relationships. 'I could never go out with anyone who isn't on the scene. I couldn't face having to explain why I stay out all night, the music and the people I know. It would be unbearable.'

Ex-Wigan Casino DJ Dave Evison, as a DJ, dancer and soul enthusiast, cannot see himself one day bowing out and leaving Northern Soul behind. He says: 'The whole scene is a drug. The drug is the music. I feel like a fish out of water in the local Tiffanys, and I don't really want a punch and a pint in my local pub. If I don't go out to a soul night I worry about what I'm missing. I think the scene has kept me young. I feel just as passionate about the scene as I did twenty years ago, I will know when the day comes that I feel old.'

Dave also has no qualms about his young son getting the Northern Soul bug. He said: 'I would feel far happier if he followed in my footsteps than if he got into any other musical genre, where there are far more opportunities for drug abuse and fighting and getting drunk. The Northern Soul scene is a far safer scene than any other all-nighter. It's a far friendlier and more respectable scene.'

Lester Wardle, a former Wigan Casino regular and current-day DJ, is one of the many 30- and 40-somethings who feel they have been given a second chance thanks to the 1990s Northern Soul revival. 'It's like being born again. I used to have depressions where I would go up to my bedroom and think about the most special time of my life, the Casino years. I can't believe it has come back now. I would like to keep going as long as I can, even with a Zimmer frame if necessary. Northern Soul will always be in my heart.'

When ex-teacher Martin Barnfather takes up position behind the decks at any soul venue in Britain, the crowd can predict only one thing: his unpredictability. Under his stage name of Soul Sam, a long-time Northern Soul DJ, Martin sticks to his creed of changing his playlist and moving with the times.

There's no chance of hearing the same tired oldies time after time with this guy. Promoters pay him, and the dancers come in numbers, to hear him play possibly the most varied and unique spot in Britain.

Sam may be a veteran DJ of a million all-nighters, but he is not resting on his laurels or his reputation. He is constantly seeking new tunes, whether they be from the 60s, 70s, 80s or 90s. And the rarer the better. He recently forked out a massive £2,000 for the ultra-rare Ernie Johnson single 'I Can't Stand the Pain', a sought-after item among the connoisseurs and record collectors, but relatively little known among many current soul fans. So can it really have been worth it?

'I can't think in a business way,' he says. 'I just like the record. I'm not in this for the money. You don't make money out of Northern Soul. I bought Ernie Johnson and two days later I sold the same amount, probably slightly more, in oldies. Rightly or wrongly, if I don't end up stony broke then I'm happy. I'm single and have no one to answer to. A wife wouldn't put up with what I do. I'm too selfish.'

Martin discovered his liking for soul in London in 1963 at a club called The Scene. He was getting fed up with the Mersey Beat sound and was overjoyed to hear things like 'Mocking Bird' by Inez Foxx. Checking the reviews and charts in *Record Mirror*, he avidly bought up all the current British releases on Stateside, London, and so on, and was rarely disappointed.

Never into the all-nighter scene at that time, he considered himself to have oddball tastes and found he loved records by the Incredibles, the Invitations, and Bobby Sheen, little knowing the same records were massively popular at the Twisted Wheel in Manchester. He began DJing in 1969 and enjoyed slipping in rare items like the Ikettes' 'Peaches and Cream' to audiences expecting pop music.

Fired up by visits to Blackpool Mecca in the early 70s – 'the best soul night ever up to about 1974, when they started playing disco' – he never went to Wigan Casino between 1974 and 1978, when he finally joined the guest DJ rota, but enhanced his reputation at first Cleethorpes Pier and then the Winter Gardens. 'The Pier between 1974 and 1975 was the best all-nighter for me. Personally, I thought Cleethorpes was better than the Casino – it played far more of a cross-section of music. Nobody was playing Simon Soussan tailormades or UK British pop with a Northern beat.'

Martin refused to go down the safe road of playing oldies, and kept on championing his new discoveries when he joined the Casino line-up. 'I've never been too bothered about the dance floor thinning out,' he says.

To his horror on his Casino debut, he found himself following Chris King on to the decks after King had played about a dozen of Martin's biggest sounds. He wasn't wrong-footed. 'What it enabled me to do was to play a dozen that had never been played before,' he said. Martin, or rather Soul Sam, became famous in the late 70s and early 80s for switching rather drastically to a more modern soul playlist. This alienated the 60s soul fans and oldies brigade, at a time when the scene suffered something of a split between the traditionalists and the modern soul/jazz funk fans.

Martin himself admits that maybe he went too far. 'On reflection, I got it wrong. I should have been playing 60s stuff alongside the modern things. The modern stuff went down well at Wigan and I went off at a tangent: I loved the modern stuff but maybe I should have played more across-the-board stuff.'

The North Wales-based soul spinner has never stopped DJing and liking black music and is now firmly back in the non-disco soul groove. His spot could range from the most obscure £2,000 1960s stomper to 70s 'floaters' to 90s items. He will also play oldies if the crowd demands it, but he refuses to be complacent. 'What I don't like about the Northern scene is that at certain venues you are obliged to play the same records,' he said. 'There aren't enough people that want to hear new records. Don't get me wrong, I still like to hear oldies, but I couldn't be a DJ if I had to play the same spot everywhere I went.

'The people that worry are the ones that won't listen to anything new. They are the ones that are just reliving their youth. They just want to hear the same old records. I sometimes wonder if they were ever into real music at all. For instance Drizabone's "Can't Take the Pressure" is huge, not because it's a great record but because it's played to death. There are many people on the scene who haven't got a mind of their own.'

Martin uses his plentiful supply of Northern Soul classic oldies to trade for newer items at venues around the country. Through his network of contacts like record dealers and collectors Johnny Manship, Tim Ashibende, Tim Brown and John Anderson of Soul Bowl he will be alerted to the latest 'finds'. One of them may play him a record down the phone, or Martin will take a trip down to scour their collections. A few plays by Soul Sam and a favourable dance floor reaction is often enough to elevate a record to cult status.

Martin is, however, reluctant to take all the credit for 'breaking' new sounds. One of his biggest current records, Chuck Holiday's 'Just Can't Trust Nobody', he has since discovered was played and virtually forgotten at the Stafford all-nighters in the mid-80s. 'You think you have found something, but there are always one or two people or collectors who will say they know it,' he said.

Martin continues to be impressed by the amount of material still being unearthed, and the open-minded nature of many Northern Soul fans. 'I thought certainly by 1980 that the Northern stuff was drying up. That was one of the main reasons I went into modern. It obviously hasn't dried up. Stafford was responsible for more mid-tempo records being played, and nowadays records that wouldn't have been played at all-nighters in the heyday are very popular. Things like Love's "Stormy Weather" would never have got played in the 70s.'

As the twentieth century fades away, the musical boundaries between the traditional Northern Soul sound and what is termed modern soul are being increasingly blurred. Some superbly soulful 90s tunes like Drizabone's 'Pressure' and Sean Oliver's 'You and Me' are crossing over from the modern rooms into the more 60s and 70s-orientated main rooms.

One man delighted with the intermingling of the two styles is London-based DJ Terry Jones. The long-time soul fan has a massive following for his 90s soul playlists, but his roots are firmly in 60s soul. Terry was captivated by the Motown sound via his elder sisters in the 60s, and quickly expanded his musical knowledge. He said: 'I couldn't get enough. I collected UK, US and any other versions of tracks I could lay my hands on. I also had this passion for great voices, which was the main reason the rest of the musical genre fell into place. Aretha Franklin, Jerry Butler, Chuck Jackson, Garnett Mimms and the like all ended up in my record boxes. I didn't really get into any of the nights up north at that time due to lack of funds. It was the lack of venues in London that really made me decide that something had to be done.'

In 1969 Terry went to the landlord of the Sebright pub in East London and suggested he try something different. Terry started DJing and put on a Tuesday night Motown night. East End girls came in force, which brought in lots of East End lads, and soon the Sebright was packed and predominantly a soul pub. It was through these Tuesday night events that Terry met many great friends, including Chris 'The Teacher' Forrest. After six years of success at the Sebright, the pub's boss acquired another hostelry about a mile away in Shoreditch. It was called the Norfolk Arms (later the Norfolk Village) and its Friday night events were to become the country's longest-running weekly soul sessions, lasting an incredible twenty-one years.

Terry found the invitation to be resident DJ at the Norfolk Village irresistible. He said: 'I couldn't refuse, with visions going through my head of creating a soul venue where my passion could be shared seven nights a week.'

The Friday sessions were the stuff of legends, and ran every week until 1996. Soul performers like Al Johnson, Alan Mason, Rick Webb and Odyssey all graced the venue, and the music policy varied from Vivien Reed and Corey Blake to Timi Yuro and Walter Jackson.

Said Terry: 'It fulfilled my personal dreams of getting legendary soul DJs like Richard Searling to come and play at my venues, and of course allowed me to indulge in my passion for playing *the* music to the masses. This pub really was at the forefront of real soul in London Town.'

For four years, Terry also ran his own pub called the Spreadeagle, which also hosted highly successful soul nights. Since then, he has been in constant demand at weekenders, all-nighters and soul nights up and down the country. His southern roots possibly make Terry more open-minded about what is acceptable at soul venues in the north. Old and new sounds sit happily in his playlist.

He said: 'It's not just new music that excites me, I am just as likely to find an old gem to play as I am a newie. I am glad that I am in the position where I don't get booked to play soul from one era, but from all eras and that gives me a lot of scope.

'Nobody discovers the music, we just bring it to people's attention. It may be "Save Your Love for Me" by Vivien Reed on Atco, "I Just Want to Fall in Love" by the Spinners on Atlantic, "Stormy" by the Supremes on Motown, or "Why Don't We Fall in Love" by John Valenti on Ariola. From 60s to 90s, they are there all the time.'

Terry believes that two-roomed venues have helped the music cross over between the Northern and modern rooms. 'A lot of 70s modern tunes are now being played in the Northern rooms, like Gloria Scott, Sidney Joe Qualls, etc., and it has made the Northern punters less sceptical about the music in the modern rooms. It also helps when respected Northern jocks like Richard Searling, Soul Sam and Bob Hinsley take tunes and play them in both rooms.'

Terry's quest for quality 90s soul and new release material will continue, with him optimistic about the future. He said: 'The music will never die. There is far too much talent about for anything final to happen. I am only apprehensive in so far as although the new talent is obviously out there, it is not so widespread as it used to be. There are bundles of quality soul records around in the 90s, you just have to dig a little deeper.'

*Terry Jones's all-time favourite soul tracks*

'The Love We Had' The Dells
'Ain't No Way' Aretha Franklin
'Try to Leave Me If You Can' Bessie Banks
'It's All Over Now' Annette Small
'How Can I Go On Without You' Corey Blake
'Save Your Love for Me' Vivien Reed
'Lighten Up' (70s version) Ty Karim
'Ask the Lonely' Four Tops
'The Turning Point' Jimmy Holliday
'It's an Uphill Climb to the Bottom' Walter Jackson

*Terry Jones's twenty modern soul favourites*

'Stay' Temptations
'False Faces' Temptations
'In and Out of Love' Patti Austin
'Here We Go Again' Aretha Franklin
'Save Me' Jerry Tombs
'Goodbye' Baby Lee
'Love Loan' Jeffree

'Watcha Gonna Do' Sherwood
'Love Don't Live' Michael Proctor
'Innerside' Shazz
'Déjà Vu' E Smooth with Latanza Walters
'Love for Love' Linda Tillery & Claytoven
'You & Me' Sean Oliver
'Floating On Your Love' Isley Brothers
'Your Love Keeps Working On Me' Joey Diggs
'Love's Mystery' Randy Crawford
'Pressure' Drizabone
'I Won't Let You Do That to Me' Luther Vandross
'Can't Help Lovin' You' Spinners
'Bed You Down' Kashif

DJ Dave Thorley is among those sticking with his contemporary outlook on soul music. Championing modern soul as much as the 60s rarities, Dave likes to push the boundaries of what is acceptable at Northern Soul events.

When he played a 1992 track by legendary Detroit house music performer/producer Frankie Knuckles at a recent Ritz all-nighter, the debate started up again about what is or isn't Northern Soul. The song in question, the album track 'It's Hard Sometimes', was well received by most of the Ritz crowd but created controversy among the diehard oldies fans.

Dave takes it all in his stride: 'I have kept my sense of humour and I always try to upset somebody when I'm DJing! It has great arrangement, swirling strings, and black vocals. It's a 90s Northern Soul record. Maybe it was just a step too far for the Ritz, but it has gone down a storm since. People are asking me to play it.

'I don't think we are too far away from going back to square one, an all-nighter where everything gets played in one room. I just want to keep it fresh. I go over to the States a lot now and I'm bringing back many CDs of current material which is as soulful as ever.

'The basic beat is still there, whether it has a garage feel or a funkier feel. If people want obscure stuff, some of these companies are only doing 1,000 or 2,000 copies. If the true premise of

271

Northern Soul is to go out and hear quality soul music that you don't hear every day in every club, then these things are still being made.'

Goldmine Records partner Tim Brown was immediately captivated as a teenager when he heard about a Blackpool-based DJ called Ian Levine who was going about buying up virtually every American soul record he could find. What a prospect, he thought. What a quest. To own virtually every soul record from the 60s and 70s, preferably on the original label. To have a home so full of these rare 45s that he wouldn't even know what all of them were, let alone sounded like.

So when he left school and began earning money, that's what Tim did. In the following years he would amass a collection of 30,000 singles that fit the Northern Soul criteria. ('I don't think there are that many more that we have missed,' he says.)

Almost thirty years of plundering record warehouses, junk shops, and record shops all over the USA by DJs, record collectors and CD company bosses have meant there can be few surprises left. But items still keep turning up – keeping true to Tim's maxim 'There's always something new – even if it's old'.

Said Tim: 'Many of the newer finds that are only just turning up now are severe flukes that didn't come out at the time. Now we are in the position of trying to find which singer's brother has a copy of a record that was never released, or some producer who has a record in his attic that he's forgotten about. We are on the level of having to dig very, very, deep nowadays.'

Tim's view of why English people have taken soul music to their hearts for decades when Americans didn't want to know is that 'The English person is more analytical than the average American. If something isn't commercially acceptable in the US, it isn't acceptable. We are more likely to look below the surface, to wonder why a record wasn't a success. It might have nothing to do with the quality of it.

'Look at Jerry Williams. For twenty years he thought that "If You Ask Me" was a total failure. Then he comes over here and sees the demand and the approval for it and suddenly he thinks "Maybe it didn't deserve to fail. Maybe I got a raw deal."

'The British DJ has done a lot to make the American artists realize what a treasure trove they're sitting on.'

Tim firmly believes nowadays that soul fans are more knowledgeable and aware of a record's background than they were in the 70s. He says it is easy with hindsight to criticize some of the 'poppy' dancers that plagued Wigan Casino for a couple of years, but they felt right at the time and no one then had the resources to research the origins of a single indefinitely.

'The perspective of time is all important,' said Tim. 'We know a lot more now about people like Gary Lewis and Tommy Sands, etc. There's a lot more integrity now. There's a demand now for genuine soul music, and I'm glad that it has come around that way. At the Casino, the demand was for records to keep the adrenalin level up right through the night. The pressure was on the DJs to play records at 80, 90 or 100 mph. Consequently there were a lot of records about that had the right feel and the right beat, but weren't soul. I never really thought that Wigan Casino was purely about 100 per cent black American soul.

'It was about young people having an insular scene of their own. It was about a scene that was not influenced by outside factors. Some of the British-made records like Nosmo King and "Footsee" were great dance records, but soul music they weren't. And the point is that no one ever questioned whether they should be played or not.'

One man who has had a long-standing love affair with the Northern Soul fraternity is Edwin Starr. Having played virtually every major, and minor, venue in the UK from the Twisted Wheel through Wigan Casino, Hinckley Leisure Centre in the 80s and Stoke's Kings Hall in the 90s, Edwin knows his English fans inside out.

And they know and love him – you are as likely to see the UK-based former Motown legend chatting to record dealers as you are to stare at him on a faraway stage. His performing career began in 1955 as a member of the high school band the Future Tones. They developed such a following that they were persuaded to go on a TV talent show called the *Uncle Jack Show*. They won it six times in a row, and from that moment on Edwin, born Charles Hatcher, knew what he wanted to do for a living.

A solo contract with Detroit-based Ric Tic records produced classics like 'SOS (Stop Her On Sight)', 'Headline News', 'Back Streets', 'Agent Double O Soul', etc. When Motown bought out Ric Tic, Edwin kept producing the hits in the form of '25 Miles', 'War', and the reissuing of his Ric Tic work also helped enhance his reputation in the US and abroad.

Northern Soul fans, however, always liked to look beyond the norm and once they had grown accustomed to dancing and listening to his well-known material, they were usually found raving about 'My Weakness is You', 'I Have Faith in You', 'Time', and his lesser-known outings.

When Edwin first came over to England to play live at the Twisted Wheel, he was immediately struck by the fans' knowledge of his music. He said: 'The people in the north of England are the most knowledgeable music people that you will ever find. I have often wondered whether there should be a *Mastermind* show on TV for Northern Soul people! They know virtually everything about the records; who recorded a disc, where it was recorded, who produced it, what date the session was done, even. There are people in that country who have absolute dossiers on every Northern Soul recording.

'Most major record companies still don't know that Northern Soul exists. They don't have a clue. They think we are talking about a handful of people in a little club somewhere in the northern part of England that's totally insulated. Those people that are into pop and disco and hip-hop are just following trends and fads. Eventually fads go away. Northern Soul has survived since the 1960s, and it will still be here come the millennium and beyond. It's like religion, and it's not necessarily a bad religion to be part of. It still surprises me today when I hear a DJ play a record at a venue that even I have never heard before.'

He still remembers vividly the first time he was asked to play live at a Wigan Casino all-nighter. When he was told he would be on stage at 4 am, his first reaction was *'What?* Who in the world would want to be up at four o'clock in the morning to see a show?'

He and his band were taken into the Station Road venue by a

side entrance and he was quickly won over by the famous Casino atmosphere. 'What struck me immediately was the heat in the building. Then all of a sudden I looked up and it looked like it was raining inside the building. It was pure condensation and sweat from people dancing. I said "Boy, this is my kind of place!"

'I went on stage at 4 am and came off at 6 am. It was wonderful. Everyone who came to Wigan came for one reason only – to hear the music and to dance. That's it.'

Edwin says he has no qualms about mixing with the crowds at his gigs because he has no illusions of being a superstar – 'I came up through the ranks and I didn't have the luxury of getting big-headed.'

As far as the dancing is concerned, Edwin was impressed and is still today impressed by the agility and enthusiasm of the Northern Soul crowd: 'In the US we had rock'n'roll and swing and jive, but I have never seen anything like Northern Soul dancing. Even today after all these years I still can't perfect it! The US doesn't have anything remotely near to Northern Soul dancing.

'Northern Soul is a group effort – everybody respects everybody else's space. It's like each person has their own individual interpretation of the music.'

Edwin is aware of the debt he owes to the fanatical British fans who have helped sustain his career long after America appeared to stop caring. 'I am sure that a great many of the artists would pay homage to the Northern Soul scene. It has allowed us to still have some place to be. Maybe we're not allowed to be on BBC Radio 1, in the national charts or recognized by our peers at musical awards etc, but the one legacy they can't take away from us is our Northern Soul legacy.'

Long-time Northern Soul DJ Ray 'Ginger' Taylor has his final 'gig' all figured out. Ginger has reserved a plot in the churchyard near his impressive seventeenth-century home on the edge of the Pennines for the day when he goes to that great all-nighter in the sky.

He also knows what he wants in his coffin – his treasured copy of his all-time favourite record, Billy Butler's 'Right Track' (on UK Columbia, demo of course). Such is the importance music plays in the life of the genial building firm boss.

One of the country's top Northern Soul DJs, Ginger's quest for the best and rarest soul sounds knows no bounds. It's an expensive business – with individual 45s frequently costing four-figure sums – but it has established his reputation as both a connoisseur and crowd pleaser.

Ginger has always lived in and around Todmorden, on the Lancashire/Yorkshire border. He gained his love of soul as a teenager, attending youth clubs and enjoying the diet of Motown and Atlantic records. He would later start DJing at youth clubs as his record collection and knowledge of soul music increased. By the late 60s he was very aware of the Twisted Wheel in Manchester, which was responsible for unearthing rarer imports like the Contours' 'Just a Little Misunderstanding', which still figures in Ginger's all-time top ten.

Trips to Burnley Mecca – where he would later land a DJing spot and preside over the much-respected Rose Room with his Ukrainian sidekick Eddie – led him to even more imports. A trip to the final all-nighter at the Wheel as a 16- or 17-year-old sealed his love of record collecting.

The growing reputation of the regular gigs at Burnley Mecca led to Mary Chapman offering Ginger and Eddie regular spots at the Cleethorpes all-nighters in the mid-70s, which were competing with Wigan Casino. It was then that the duo met John Anderson of Soup Bowl in King's Lynn, who would give them first pick of his latest imports. Ginger would later find himself added to the DJ rota at Wigan Casino towards the end of the Station Road venue's life.

After taking time out from the soul scene, like so many DJs, Ginger made his return behind the decks at a charity event in the late 1980s. He was quickly offered a spot by DJ/promoter Richard Searling at a Manchester soul night, and began collecting and re-buying hundreds of rare items which he had disposed of some years previously.

Now Ginger is a familiar figure in demand at events from the 100 Club in London to the Togetherness weekender in Fleetwood. The demands of his building business and a recent bout of ill health have curtailed his long-distance trips somewhat, but the father of two's popularity and passion for the music is undiminished.

Unlike some other 'elite' rare soul DJs, Ginger puts the accent on quality but plays to the crowd. Every promoter can tell tales of top-name DJs clearing the floor with obscurities, and when taken to task they will say something like 'It's not my fault this lot have no taste.' One such 'superstar' caused outrage at a North-West venue when the promoter asked him how he had managed to empty the venue. 'The further North you get, the thicker they get,' was his reply.

Ginger has no such arrogant airs. 'If they want me to play oldies, then I will,' he says. Left to his own devices, however, Ginger will put together a winning mix. He figures that in an average hour-long spot, he will play only 20–22 records. He therefore plans to play three or four current 'big' tunes, three or four 70s or modern items, three or four ultra rarities and a smattering of under-played or forgotten oldies.

He will even keep faith with records he dislikes if the crowd wants them ('I hate Nolan Porter "If I Could Only Be Sure",' he confesses). But the rarities are an important part of his set and need plenty of wheeling and dealing and plenty of cash to keep them coming.

In the same set, however, he may well play Martha Reeves' Tamla Motown recording 'No One There', Ruby Andrews' 'Just Loving You', or Timi Yuro's 'It'll Never Be Over for Me'. All of them are available for a few pounds for collectors. By contrast, the value of Joe Matthews' Wigan Casino monster 'Ain't Nothing You Can Do' on Kool Kat is shooting up because of its increased popularity via Ginger.

Stateside trips are not necessary for Ginger, as he has plenty of contacts in the UK, particularly with fellow Todmorden soulie Tim Brown of Goldmine Records.

To his frustration, Ginger finds that some items he sold for £100 up to twenty years ago like the Inspirations' 'No One Else Can Take Your Place' on Breakthrough are now priced at up to £4,000.

He recently re-acquired and then re-sold the Inspirations as part of the essential wheeling and dealing necessary to stay at the top. Ginger also off-loaded the Turbines' 'We Got to Start Over' on Cenco, another cited as one of the top twenty rarest records. Another recent acquisition, for a mere £800, was the Admirations' 'You Left Me/I Wanna be Free' on Peaches. Taking a chance on a record can be a gamble, but Ginger is used to weighing up the odds. He said: 'I have started looking at things a little differently. I don't see the point in having too many of the so-called big rarities because a lot of them are crap. I am more bothered about the quality and the condition of the record. I couldn't bear to have a £4,000 record in my box that's in poor condition.'

After paying out a tidy sum to re-acquire a copy of Joe Matthews' 'Ain't Nothing You Can Do' via Canada-based Martin Koppell, Ginger was in for a shock. He had parted with his original copy twenty years previously, when he used to scratch his initials 'RT' in the run-out-groove. Examining his new acquisition, Ginger found it was in fact his old copy, which he had sold for a tiny fraction of the 1999 price!

He found comfort in the rest of the deal, which brought him mega-rarities like the Nomads' 'Something's Bad' and Frankie Beverley's 'Because of My Heart'.

Can all this outlay really be worth it, when even the top DJs can earn less than £100 for a gig involving as much as a four- or five-hour round trip? Russ said: 'I'm a record collecting fool. I'm not business-minded enough. It's sheer pleasure to me, but it does piss me off that some of us DJs are not appreciated enough. But if the crowd is loyal to me then I hate letting people down. Without them and their enthusiasm and regular backing of me it wouldn't be the same.'

One area still exciting collectors and DJs is the amount of unreleased Motown material coming to light. Ginger was one of the DJs who pounced when DJ Pete Lowrie announced he was selling some of his famous unreleased Motown acetates which were literally recovered from skips after the label had moved its stores.

Ginger plumped for a 10-inch original studio acetate by Tommy Good called 'I Gotta Get Away', which he has since played to great acclaim on the Northern dance floors. It gave him great pleasure to own a unique disc from the legendary Detroit label, bearing the date it was recorded. Ginger also has, at the time of writing, a couple of dormant 'monsters' by Tammi Terrell and Carolyn Crawford which he is waiting to unleash on soul fans – again both Motown acetates acquired from Midlands DJ Chris King.

The unreleased studio tracks are becoming more and more important to the Northern Soul scene, says Ginger. 'I still get a great buzz out of hearing new rare records, but there aren't that many these days. I'm not saying it's drying up, but nowadays almost every one that I like is a studio acetate rather than an actual disc. But there are still many, many oldies that are worth reactivating.'

Looks like lots of money will keep changing hands . . .

*Ginger Taylor's Top Five soul sounds (May 1999)*

'I've Gotta Get Away'  Tommy Good
'Soul Sounds'  Harvey and the Jokers
'I Lost the Only Love I Had'  Joe Valentine
'What Price'  Nathan Williams
'Blessed With a Love'  Tranells

*Ginger Taylor's all-time Top Ten*

'Right Track'  Billy Butler
'You've Been Away'  Rubin
'Next In Line'  Hoagy Lands
'Just a Little Misunderstanding'  Contours
'I Am Nothing'  Al Williams
'I'm the One to Do It'  Jackie Wilson
'Stop Overlooking Me'  Cairos
'It'll Never Be Over for Me'  Timi Yuro
'Your Love's Got Me'  Satin
'The Drifter'  Ray Pollard

Midnight in Manchester. It's Easter Sunday and the city centre is sparsely populated with a scattering of people making their way home after a drink, a meal or a night at the theatre. Turn the corner into Whitworth Street West and you enter a different world. A massive queue snakes along the pavement for 100 yards in the darkness outside the Ritz ballroom, and it's getting larger by the minute as cars and minibuses pull into the rapidly filling NCP carpark alongside and disgorge their occupants.

It could be a scene from the 70s, but this is Northern Soul in 1999. Hundreds and hundreds of holdall-carrying soul fans wait in an orderly line up to three and four deep as the Ritz all-nighter prepares to open its doors. There are very few youngsters in evidence, and the gum-chewing soulies range in age mainly from the thirties to the late forties.

Running from just after midnight to 8 am, the all-nighters take place every bank holiday Sunday through the year and have become one of the highlights of the soul calendar. Former Wigan Casino DJ Richard Searling is the man who in 1993 instigated the Ritz events, regularly attracting up to 1,000 soul fans from all over Britain each time. For Richard, running the Ritz was a long-held ambition. The Manchester venue became famous in the 70s as an all-day venue run by Neil Rushton's Heart of England Soul Club.

The raised dance floor has gone, but the ambience, the balcony and the atmosphere remain the same.

Said Richard: 'We had an all-dayer there in the 80s with Ian Levine and Colin Curtis but we had so much hassle with the police due to Sunday licensing laws that it was not true. I always wanted to do all-nighters there. It's a great venue and we have never had a bad one.

'It has evolved from being more or less a revival event into something at the cutting edge of rare stuff. DJs like Soul Sam, Butch and Ady Croasdell have been coming up with rarer and rarer things and the reception has been superb. The clientele the Ritz attracts seem to be really up for it, and I think it will continue to flourish. I have never seen so much enthusiasm to embrace all aspects of soul music as there is now, and that can only be good.'

One of the highlights of the Ritz's history was when Motown

legends Kim Weston and Brenda Holloway appeared live on stage in 1998 at a special night devoted to the Detroit label. The two ladies were staggered by the adulation they received from 1,000 British soul fans.

Another frequently anticipated event is the annual Rarest of the Rare all-nighter, when only the rarest and non-predictable soul music is played. Attendances again don't appear to suffer even though the music may be unfamiliar to many.

Richard just wishes that the venue had a second room, which he feels would pull in another 300 or 400 people. Two-roomed events are becoming the norm on the Northern Soul scene, with a second room often playing modern soul.

That format has been successfully operated at the massive Togetherness all-nighters at the King's Hall in Stoke. Richard and partner Kev Roberts promoted the inaugural event in February 1997 and were astounded when 1,400 people turned up. The twice-yearly 10 pm to 7 am events now feature a mixture of old and new soul music and attract dancers from all over the UK.

Richard believes that modern soul is the perfect partner for rare soul. 'It has pulled in a younger crowd, and there isn't a lot of them in the main otherwise coming through. Some of the promoters are going towards house and garage, and that's disappointing. I've always been a great believer that music should be so soulful that people want to dance to it. House and garage is manufactured dance music.'

This being the Northern Soul scene, there is no shortage of critics of the success of the Togetherness events. 'Richard and Kev are just in it for the money' and 'They are trying to dominate the whole scene' are two common grumbles.

Richard says global domination is the furthest from their minds. 'We've paid our dues. We've spent many many years on the scene as DJs. We've travelled to the other side of the country to do a gig only to find the promoter has no money to pay us. We thought about teaming up to promote events ourselves and said Why not? What people don't realize is that it costs a lot of money to put on an event and promoters are taking a risk. They can lose money as well as make a profit.'

Kev Roberts admits that although he loves the music, he is in the Northern Soul business to make money. After all, no promoter wants to make a loss, despite what they might tell you. He said: 'I am a businessman and I love to promote things. I think Richard and I have paid our dues. I have worked for so many shoddy promoters who either didn't pay me or the equipment broke down or something. We like to do it right. Things have moved on. The sound system has to be right. The leafleting and marketing has to be right. People in their forties don't want to turn out just casually. They want to organize things in advance and pay by credit card and be sure they have got their tickets. Of course the hard-core Northern Soul fans are suspicious of us, but we didn't know we were going to make money when we started off the Togetherness events. It costs a hell of a lot of money to stage an event like that.'

He added: 'At the end of the day people just want to go out and have a good time. Some people have faded memories of the past – mine is very clear – but others don't. Organizers and people in the business seem to take it all too seriously.

'It always surprises me when people come up to me at an all-nighter and ask me for "Rescue Me" and "Needle in a Haystack". It still happens even today.'

The modern soul room at Togetherness has been a major success, drawing a different crowd from the main Northern Soul event, and ensuring an interesting mix of musical tastes and styles. Said Kev: 'Richard has always been into the modern soul and the scene has to move forward. Even in the main room, we are not just playing the same oldies all the time, although we get an abundance of requests for them. The trouble is, there isn't enough new blood coming on to the scene and in ten years' time we might be looked upon like the old rock'n'roll crew.'

The Togetherness soul machine has also produced a soul weekender, the first of which in 1998 attracted up to 900 soul fans to the Cala Gran Holiday Centre in Fleetwood. Another is planned for September 1999.

More than 25 DJs in two rooms and a live performance by Brenda Holloway with a top-class band kept the dancers entertained during two all-night sessions, two afternoon sessions and a farewell evening party. An on-site FM station churned out non-stop sounds during an orgy of soul for the benefit of the music fans staying in luxury caravans.

The right venue and the right facilities are something that Richard feels strongly about. 'You can't get away any more with the spit-and-sawdust type places. There's a definite need for the venue to be of good quality.'

It's 2 am as Brenda Holloway bounds on to the stage to tumultuous applause from the 900 or so Northern Soul fans. Wearing an ankle-length gold-sequined dress, she beams with genuine surprise and appreciation at her reception. It's thirty-three years since Brenda, now a grandmother of seven, toured with the Beatles as an up-and-coming soul singer. Now she is enjoying her 'second career' in the late 1990s, courtesy of her British fans.

As Brenda goes through her routine with the accomplished Snake Davis band on stage at the Togetherness soul weekender in Fleetwood, Lancs, she is experiencing the peculiarly British music enthusiasm for black American 60s music. 'I can't believe it. It's almost unreal,' she reflects later. 'When I come here it's like going back to the 60s. There's nothing like this anywhere else in the world.'

Brenda, one of the most underrated Motown vocalists ever, was born in Atascardo, California, in 1946. In 1964 after being spotted by a Motown talent scout she became the label's first West Coast signing. She immediately found herself among the greatest hitmakers of the day ('I felt like I was in Disneyland').

But despite her immense talent and powerful voice she did not enjoy the same commercial success as her illustrious stablemates like the Supremes, the Four Tops, and Marvin Gaye.

Her first single for Tamla, 'Every Little Bit Hurts', reached number thirteen in the US charts and was later covered by the Spencer Davis Group. The Smokey Robinson-penned 'When I'm Gone' made it to twenty-five the following year, and, criminally, the sublime 'You've Made Me So Very Happy' only reached thirty-nine. The latter, co-written by Brenda, was later turned into a major smash by Blood Sweat and Tears.

Sadly, her career petered out and Brenda set about raising her four daughters. In 1987 she joined many other ex-Motown artists in recording for Ian Levine's Motorcity label. That label's output posed no threat to the pop charts and Brenda thought her singing career was effectively over.

Then in the early 1990s British soul fan Peter Whitney visited her at home in Los Angeles and told her about her cult following across the Atlantic. In particular, her unissued 1966 recording of 'Reconsider' (also known as 'Think It Over Before You Break My Heart') which had found its way into the hands of Northern Soul DJ Peter Lowrie during a trip to the States. The side was massive in the all-night clubs in Britain and had revived interest in her plentiful recordings.

'I had forgotten recording "Reconsider" but when Pete played it to me it started coming back,' said Brenda. 'Pete told me about the Northern Soul scene over here and I must admit I was a bit dubious about what he said.

'I was doing nothing but raise children, so I thought I would come over and see for myself. The fans over here know more about the music than the artists themselves. It's unbelievable. There's one guy in Los Angeles who we consider to be a collector but the knowledge the British fans have is amazing. They know everything.'

In 1998 Brenda did a number of major gigs in Britain, often with backing tapes, but notably with a live backing band at the soul weekender. She is now experiencing the kind of adulation that her peers on the other side of the Atlantic find hard to fathom.

'In America unless you have a record in the charts people forget about you. They are as fickle as that. In America and Hollywood things are constantly changing. They are stuck on youth and they have a very short memory. In the US the 60s stuff has really caught on with the Hispanics and we have oldies stations which are pretty big, but it would be impossible for one artist to draw a crowd, unless it was a major act like the Isley Brothers.

'The English have their own tastes and they know good music from bad music. When something is good it's good for ever. 60s music is at the core of today's music. Everything that's going now has grown from that. The scene over here is even better than Peter told me. I have to pinch myself to see that I'm not dreaming.

'And I'm delighted that I've been able to do "You Made Me So Very Happy" the way I wanted. People always remember the Blood Sweat and Tears version, but for the first time this weekend I have been able to perform it properly the way I wanted it to sound.'

As for England, her ambitions lie with more live dates and hopes of a recording contract. 'I have never known fans with the kind of passion that they have over here. The English have got the master tapes and the demos so there's virtually nothing left in America.

'God gave me a talent and I'm not going to waste it. In the last six years I have learned a lot about myself. When I was alone I used to think, "Is this it?" I didn't like me. A few years ago the children wondered if the Brenda Holloway I used to be was a made-up lady. Now they know she's real.'

Brenda Holloway is indeed very real to her fans as she responds to the cries of 'encore' after a storming set with the inevitable 'Reconsider'. Quite appropriate considering the song has, thanks to the fanaticism of her knowledgeable English Northern Soul fans, been probably the single most important factor in reviving her career.

As the revival in Northern Soul's fortunes in the late 1990s continues, a whole plethora of small clubs are running regular soul nights. Apart from the major 1,000-capacity venues which have become essential regular gathering points for the country's rare soul fans, there are dozens of smaller clubs run for little or no profit by music enthusiasts who should be old enough to know better.

One small event is the monthly soul night run at the Grasshoppers RUFC Club in Preston, Lancs. The 350-capacity venue has attracted a strong and loyal following since it opened in November 1997 and its monthly Friday 8 pm to 1 am events are now a permanent fixture of the north-west soul scene.

The events are run by the 'dynamic duo' of Johnny Pearson and Káren Seddon, who decided on their return to the Northern

Soul scene that there was a gap in the market for a soul night in the Preston area. Then one night Johnny, a professional DJ, was hired to entertain a school reunion party at the Grasshoppers. He kept being asked for some of the more commercial Northern Soul sounds – 'Ghost in My House', 'Out On the Floor', 'Skiing in the Snow' etc, and saw what a great reaction they got on the dance floor.

He and Káren decided it would make a great soul venue. The pair met the club committee, who were reluctant at first owing to the Northern Soul scene's drugs reputation from the 1970s, but eventually agreed to a trial run. Johnny set about hiring the DJs and the sound system, and Káren's job was to promote the event.

At that time, and with Johnny working weekends, she had little choice but to travel around alone distributing flyers at other soul events and spreading the word on the Grasshoppers event.

Káren said: 'I was sometimes doing three or four venues in one night – I could go to Chorley, Horwich, and Burnley in the same night and I didn't know anybody.' Johnny gratefully acknowledges the work she puts in: 'It's brilliant having a woman involved in the club and Káren is out there every weekend talking to people, making friends, talking to the women, and getting people along to the Grasshoppers.'

The opening night came and Johnny and Káren and assorted helpers turned up at 4.45 pm to set out the tables and chairs and rig up the sound system. 135 people paid their £3 each to get into the first Grasshoppers event. As well as local DJs, Johnny and Káren had hired the ex-Wigan Casino 'Soul Twins', Stuart and Neil Brackenridge as the main attraction. They felt that Preston had always supported an oldies-based music format and this was the policy on that opening night.

The extremely nervous promoters decided it had been a satisfactory but unspectacular event. Although they and the crowd were happy with the event, they felt that a lot of customers were not the regular soul crowd. In a word, they felt that some of the visitors were 'handbaggers' – a mischievous term applied by soul fans to female punters in particular who turn up to events not really sure where they are and dance around their handbags (considered totally uncool on the Northern Soul scene).

Johnny and Káren set about attracting more 'real' soulies through making the music less commercial, and more attractive to current rare soul fans. Regular mentions on Richard Searling's weekend show on Jazz FM, newspaper write-ups and word of mouth led to attendances rising and the customer profile changing. 'As the music policy changed, the handbaggers dropped off and we started pulling in more of the proper soul fans,' said Káren.

Top DJs like Ginger Taylor, Chris King, Neil Rushton, and Steve Whittle have all helped pull in customers to the Grass-hoppers and by the first anniversary there were 350 attendees. Apart from the inevitable knockers – the pair received a nasty letter very early on saying it would never work and a couple of less-than-complimentary write-ups in fanzines – their foray into club promotion has been well received.

Káren's game-for-a-laugh approach has also helped put the club on the map. She once dressed up as a French maid to present a DJ with a birthday cake and at the anniversary burst out of a giant box wearing a white basque and suspenders (the blokes are still talking about that). Now the club's free lollies are legendary and popular with punters and their children at home. 'It pays to have a gimmick,' says Káren.

Johnny said the music policy was mainly 60 per cent oldies, 40 per cent newer material and cross-over material. But he insists on one thing – that the last two records are always the famous Casino enders: Tobi Legend's 'Time Will Pass You By' and Dean Parrish's 'I'm On My Way'. Johnny is not bothered about the format of the records that are played, unlike the elitist view taken by some bigger clubs. He said: 'I'm not fussed if it's vinyl or CD – it's what comes out of the speakers that matters. Ninety per cent of the girls on the soul scene don't care what label a record is on, that's just a blokes' thing. The girls want to dance and have a good time and that's all that matters.'

'We are making money now, but that is just an added bonus for us,' said Káren. 'When I stand on a chair and see everybody enjoying themselves on the dance floor, that's when I get the biggest buzz.'

Lowton? Where on earth is Lowton? That was the question on most soul fans' lips when news filtered through that a trial soul night was being staged in February 1996.

Some years later there aren't many Northern Soul fans around the country still in the same state of ignorance. Soul music has put Lowton, a small town between St Helens and Leigh, firmly on the map of great nights out.

Acclaimed by many as the venue for Britain's finest soul night outside of an all-nighter, Lowton Civic Hall was facing an uncertain future in 1996. Wigan council had spent lots of money on the building and it wasn't making a profit. When Wigan-based soul fan Kev Murphy was asked by a long-time friend on the council to suggest someone who might want to put on an event at the civic hall, he didn't put himself in the frame. After numerous phone calls and inquiries, he and friend Steve Connor could find no one prepared to take it on. So after a meeting with the council, they decided to promote a soul night themselves at three months' notice.

**SOUL**

NAKED MUSIC NYC - PINNAE - JAMES GRIER - CHANTE SAVAGE - DEJA VU - TERRY GORDON - CHARLES MANN - DYNELLS - MARK IV - TRUE IMAGE - NATURAL FOUR - ANDRE LEE - MARY J - DAVINA - DAYBREAK - PATTI AUSTIN - PAGES - DESINY'S CHILD - PREMIER - SHIRLEY KAROL - TERRY CALLIER - RONNIE McNEIR - UJIMA - ERICA YANCY - TURNPIKES - 21ST CENTURY - PURPLE MUNDI - ARETHA FRANKLYN - SEAN OLIVER - PHIL PERRY - CHANNEL 3 - ESSEX IV - BARBARA ACKLIN - CONNIE LAVERN- GATIN - ELUSION - BLACKSMITH - KEITH WASHINGTON - TARAL TOWA TEI - ELEMENTS OF LIFE - GEORGE BENSON - SIDNEY JOE QUALLS - ARTHUR PRYSOCK - JEFF PERRY DAVID SEA - SMOOTH - BRIAN McKNIGHT - SAM DEES - ADRIANA EVANS - ANTHONY HAMILTON - JUANTA DALEY SPARKLE - TAMMY HERT - GENE CHANDLER - ROBBIE DANZIE - NANCY WILSON - TEMPTATIOS - SOLO - SOUL FLAVAS McFADDEN & WHITEHEAD....

**ModeRn SouL 70's 80's & 90's**
**FRIDAY 12 MARCH 1999**          **8.30pm - 1.00 am**
*PUSHING BACK THE MUSICAL BOUNDRIES !*
THREE YEARS AND NOW ESTABLISHED AS ONE OF THE BEST 70'S 80'S AND 90'S SOUL NIGHTS IN THE COUNTRY

**Soul Central**
no boundaries with a total 'across the board' policy new releases - x- over - 70's monsters - rare grooves essential 80's upfront 90's floorfillers and more !
THE SOUL CENTRAL HAD MARCH MOTIVATORS !

**BAZ MALEEDY - STEVE CONNOR**
**FLANNY and special guest**
**'Tall' PAUL HAWKINS**
what an incredible venue this is - with the north wests' top Jocks and special guests bringing a new flavour to our traditional soul clubs - Remember Northern Soul was borne out of new releases and classics - Is this the future? try it you just might like it!................... top sounds - great new sound system - large NEW wooden dancefloor - brilliant atmosphere !

**soul central at Lowton room II - the monthly Friday, modern soul night you just can't afford to miss !**

brought to you by the:
**MODERN SOUL COLLECTIVE**
A CO-OPERATIVE OF NORTH WEST SOUL DJ'S AND PROMOTERS STRIVING TO BRING QUALITY AND VALUE BY PROMOTING SOUL NIGHTS WITH A DIFFERENCE - WORKING TOGETHER TO PROVIDE BETTER VENUES FOR SOUL MUSIC IN THE NORTH WEST
*ACCEPT NO SUBSTITUTES !*

**TWO NIGHTS FOR THE PRICE OF ONE**
LOWTON CIVIC HALL, LOWTON Nr WIGAN TEL (01942)672971

Kev recalled: 'We had loads of flyers printed and spread the word about this new soul night. Most people didn't know where Lowton was. We built up the interest and we got 500 in on the first night.'

The Lowton Civic Hall events generally run from 8.30 pm until 'only' 1 am, but pull in soul fans from all over the country. Their regular date of the second Friday in the month is now firmly established in the minds of Northern Soul fans, and occasional live acts and special events running until 4 am have secured Lowton's reputation as a top venue.

An ever-changing line-up of the country's best DJs and a varied music policy quickly put Lowton on the soul map. Its capacity of 700 has been reached many times, and the development of a second, smaller room playing the best in modern soul has brought in even more new faces.

Lowton has even experimented with a third room, and an all-nighter in February 1999 was another sell-out event. More such events are planned. The promoters have become more ambitious as the soul nights have gone from strength to strength. Soul vocalist Tommy Hunt has made several appearances singing to backing tapes, but the venue has also seen top shows from Jerry Williams and Eddie Holman, complete with live backing bands.

Kev puts the success of the Lowton events down to giving the punters what they want. They asked for a second room featuring rarities and connoisseurs' 45s, and got it. They asked for a modern soul room, and got it. 'We listen to what people say and try to give them what they want. When you do that you know it's going to be right. We still work as hard at promoting it now as we did in the beginning.'

Soul fans attending the first anniversary found themselves with the usual line-up of top DJs and a live performance by Tommy Hunt, for the normal £3 admission price.

Kev says that that night figures high up on his list of great memories from Lowton. He said: 'We didn't tell anyone he was turning up. He came on at 12 o'clock and he was awesome. People came up to me and said, "How on earth have you done this for three quid?" That's the sort of thing that makes it all worthwhile.

'I'm not in it for the money. People think it's a great big money spinner, but we are not making a fortune. These events cost money, and we've lost on them too.'

Kev and Steve are always looking to make changes, and surprised everyone when they changed the format and brought in top rare soul DJs Kenny Burrell, Andy Rix and Carl Fortnum for the third anniversary. The music was up front, rare and moved away from the oldies-based sounds in the main room.

Said Kev: 'We went out of our way to change the music policy. People were ready for a change and it went brilliantly. When you pick DJs of a certain calibre you know they are going to do the job for you. We are always looking forward.'

Another successful venue which enjoys a loyal crowd is Tony's Empress Ballroom in Blackburn, which has been running monthly all-nighters since 1991. Promoter Little Scotty of Wolverhampton says: 'Blackburn tends to be a big happy family. It's enjoyable, soulful and friendly.'

At the other end of the scale, the Keele University all-nighters have been pulling in up to 1,000 punters since 1988. The traditional main hall with its massive dance floor plays host to Northern Soul fans only about four time a year, but they are eagerly awaited events. Organizer Neil Clowes has also shown he is keen to move with the times by adding a second room which attracts a different dance-oriented audience.

And for those who find an all-nighter too short, there are always the annual Cleethorpes soul weekenders. Ady Croasdell is again the man in charge, and the Friday-to-Sunday June events even attract mums, dads and children. After a couple of loss-making years, the weekenders are now a guaranteed sell-out and an eagerly anticipated part of the Northern Soul calendar. The event was immortalized by a Channel 4 documentary in 1996.

Live acts from the USA, like Doris Troy, Al Wilson, Little Ann and Bobby Hutton have all entertained up to 1,000-strong crowds at the mammoth events. Two all-night sessions and major daytime events have brought soul fans from all over Europe to the annual gatherings. Ady said the international flavour was an important part of the special atmosphere as fans from countries including Spain, France, and Germany were entertained by up to 20 DJs.

The arrival of the Togetherness Weekender in Fleetwood in September leaves Ady unflustered: 'I'm not bothered by the competition. We are always a sell-out anyway,' he said.

Also making a return to promoting Northern Soul events is none other than Chris Burton of Torch fame. His occasional all-nighters at Trentham Gardens in Stoke have been ambitious, featuring up to three rooms and live acts including Rose Batiste, the Flirtations, and an ambitious event featuring the Dells live on stage. 'I never thought that twenty-six years on, Northern Soul would still be happening,' said Chris. 'Promoting events has always been my love, and I hope that I can bring something back to the scene that is missing. The crowd are unique. I am not into all the negative crap and politics that exist, and I will wait to see what the next year brings.'

Northern Soul's profile in the media has never been higher since the 70s. Hardly a week goes by without one magazine or other doing a feature on the '70s scene that refuses to die'.

In 1998 there was a plethora of media forays into Northern Soul, including a 30-minute Granada documentary celebrating twenty-five years since the Wigan Casino all-nighters began. Radio 2 got in on the act with a six-part Wednesday night series on the music and personalities associated with the scene.

You may be forgiven for thinking that all soul fans were delighted at the raised profile given to their music and their scene. Not a bit of it. Just like the 70s, some resented the intrusion and misconceptions which they felt the media brought with them. After the Radio 2 series, *Soulful Kinda Music* editor Dave Rimmer spluttered in his fanzine's editorial: 'The opportunity to be constructive, informed and entertaining has been passed up again by the mainstream media. There were so many factual errors . . . and the choice of music! I listened faithfully every week hoping it would get better, until the fourth show. By the end of the show I had heard "Footsee", "Under My Thumb" and various other pieces of drivel that were played.

'The first show had a member of Soft Cell (David Ball) as a

guest. Why? I don't remember seeing him at a niter in the last year, so what relevance does he now have to the Northern Soul scene?'

And so it went on, echoing the 70s when all the media hype drove away almost as many people as it brought in.

It goes to show that times don't change. Northern Soul fans still want the scene to remain their exclusive property, unsullied by outside influences. If the media does make its occasional foray into an all-nighter, soul fans would like their scene to be portrayed in an accurate and contemporary way.

One enigma that has remained largely unanswered is this: Why should the music of 60s black America strike such a chord with predominantly white, working-class youngsters in north-west England? DJ Richard Searling has an interesting theory about why this exciting form of black American music should have such an effect. 'In the 60s, although the music was made by black performers, it was white controlled in most cases. The blacks tried to control their own destiny but in the 60s they were basically being used. Apart from Motown, I think that because of that white control there was a definite thread to the white culture over here.'

Many American blacks thought that Motown was 'too white' and had 'sold out' its soul roots. And a much-respected 1960s producer involved with many cult Northern Soul recordings shocked top DJs this year during a visit to Britain when he described their taste in music as 'pop soul'. Pop soul! Us! Surely not!

DJ Ian Levine sums up: 'Northern Soul gave people a purpose in life. If you worked from Monday to Friday in a launderette or something you spent your whole week living for the weekend. When the weekend comes you have your music and you are the centre of attention. You feel part of something, you feel important.

'Les Cockell was a road sweeper in Yorkshire, but at the weekend, he was a DJ at the Twisted Wheel. He was *somebody*. That's what Northern Soul gives you.'

# 11

# Soul Self Satisfaction

*'Ironically, we live in the United States, birthplace of soul music, yet we still discover men and women who would rather listen to pop music crooned by white artists...'*

Thirty years ago the only way to keep in touch with Northern Soul happenings was via word of mouth or by having a hastily produced flyer shoved into your hand in a darkened venue. Now the scene has gone truly international and hi-tech, and soulies are just as likely to surf the Internet and chat to fellow soul fans on the other side of the globe as they are to look up an advert in the latest fanzine.

One of the most impressive websites devoted to Northern Soul comes from the unlikely source of Israel. Yoni Neeman set up the 'Soul Of The Net' site in early 1997. A full-colour photo of a soul act greets surfers, and soulies will find a veritable treasure trove of Northern Soul facts, figures and opinions all lovingly compiled by a 40-year-old soul fanatic.

Yoni's top 40 takes viewers through a guided tour of his current favourite sounds, with potted critiques and background information to appeal to the trainspotter in all of us. And if you don't know the track he is raving about, a click of the mouse brings it to life through your computer's speakers.

Reviews of CDs and videos, and biographies and discographies can occupy soul fans for long enough to result in vast Internet call bills. Yoni lists four main reasons for his hi-tech labour of love: 'Trying to give back some of what I get out of soul music; wanting to help all who record, reissue and promote soul music today; wanting to get in touch with like-minded soul fans and broaden my knowledge about soul; making a site I would love to find on the net myself.'

Yoni spends several hours a week maintaining and updating the site (http://www.cet.ac.il/personnel/yonin/index.htm) in his spare time. 'It doesn't cost me anything, because the disk space is kindly given to me by the company I work for, the Center of Educational Technology.' He finds that he gets as much out of the site as he puts in, thanks to the vast knowledge of soul fans around the globe. If he compiles a discography he immediately receives comments and additions so the discography becomes very accurate and extensive.

'Due to the site I get too much music and info coming in – I am drowning in a sea of tapes, but I like it. Also one of the most exciting things about it is getting messages from people who were involved in the music business themselves, who are surprised to see soul music treated so seriously and lovingly on the net.'

In its first year, Yoni's site received 22,200 visits. It now averages about 100 a day. His great regret is that there is no Northern Soul scene at all in Israel. He has to content himself with trips to the UK to share nights out with like-minded music fanatics.

He said: 'When I discovered the UK Northern scene, it was bliss finding all these people who liked 60s soul as much as I did. I can't say I've become a part of the scene though. I can't dance that northern dance very well, and I do listen to a lot of the non-northern 60s/early 70s soul, for example deep soul, and some funkier stuff.

'However, when I'm in the UK I try to go to at least one Northern event, and I think it's just a wonderful scene, so different and better than everything else that goes on in other clubs. And I'm thankful for all the rare records unravelled by Northern Soul DJs. I guess most of the sounds would have died without being heard if it weren't for the UK's Northern Soul scene.'

His discovery of Northern Soul is a far cry from the normal story related by most of his contemporaries from the North of

England. As a young boy in the 1960s Yoni lived in Cyprus and he found himself drawn to the musical tastes of his older brother. He takes up the story: 'I've been a total soul freak for almost thirty years – yes, that means from 1968 when I was just ten, I was living in Cyprus then, and my first idols were the Stones and the Dave Clark Five, but soon after that my older brother Bin found a US Army radio station that was broadcasting from Turkey, where we heard for the first time James Brown, Wilson Pickett, Sam & Dave etc., who really blew our minds. The DJing style helped too, superbly fast, with lots of jingles, puns on the lyrics, etc; some of the first soul records we ever heard were "Nobody But Me" – Human Beinz; "Shake a Tail Feather" – both by the 5 Du-tones and J & B Purify; "Boogaloo" – Tom & Jerrio; "Lovers' Holiday" – Peggy Scott & Jo Jo Benson; "Apples Peaches Pumpkin Pie" – Jay & the Techniques; "Sweet Sweet Lovin'" – Platters; "Say I Am" – Tommy James and the Shondells (I consider that soul music); "Little Latin Lupe Lu" – Mitch Ryder.

'All great happy stuff with a dash of Northern Soul before anyone knew what that was. With such exciting music in abundance, my interest in mainstream rock groups grew weaker, to the bewilderment of my peers who were just starting to get into rock and pop music.

'After a year in Cyprus my family moved back to Israel. Although Bin built a 50-metre cable antenna on the roof of our building, we could not receive that US Army station any more, except for a few summer nights. But we found other radio stations that played even better soul music. While in London, Radio 1 was playing a boring top 40 playlist, you would not believe what rare soul gems were played by government-owned stations of almost every Middle East state, from which Bin and I got a real soul education.

'We had a good 50-metre antenna, and it paid off; little by little we discovered the right programmes to listen to for soul. There were many "pop music" programmes in the stations of the area, no special soul show, but when you said "pop" in those days, there was usually a regular dosage of soul. Usually there were uninterrupted music programmes, no DJ, no introduction of the songs, and we were sitting there, taping the good stuff and trying to sort out who's singing what.

'We started buying records too, not so many at first, since as young kids there was not a lot of money to be spent. We bought the Israeli releases of Otis Redding, Wilson Pickett, James Brown, Sam and Dave LPs. Also a lot of European compilation LPs. No 45s though; there were almost no singles in Israel, just a few EPs. Gradually we learned through the radio and through records about Solomon Burke, Etta James, Arthur Conley, Clarence Carter, Johnnie Taylor, James Carr, and got a better knowledge of Motown, although southern soul was always the predominant soul style in our residence. But from the beginning, there were some records on our tapes that we could not find in the record stores in Israel; a few of the first of those mystery songs were: "Bar B Q" – Wendy Rene (we couldn't even guess the title – we thought she was saying something like "I like a party too"); "Mr Soul Satisfaction" – Timmy Willis; "Get Down With It" – Bobby Marchan; "Sister's Got a Boyfriend" – Rufus Thomas; "The Funky Judge" – Bull and the Matadors; "It Takes a Whole Lotta Woman" – Jerry Combs and the Mannix; "Tomorrow" – Lonnie Youngblood; "Tired of Being Nobody" – The Valentinos.

'And LOADS of others. It took Bin and me years of searching, but by now we've found, I'd say, 98 per cent of those early radio mystery tunes, mainly on 45s, some of them on compilations. This was great fun, because when we found a record, the joy was double – we not only had it, but we got to know who it was by! There are still some mysteries to this day though. Some of them are presented in audio in the "wants & mystery page" in my website.

'On those early radio days there was also a lot of stuff that I later re-encountered as Northern Soul. Bin and I knew nothing about that scene until around 1980, but we knew and loved "Sweet Sherry" – J J Barnes; "Just Because of You" – Rocky Roberts & the Airedales; "Just Ain't No Love" – Barbara Acklin; "You Gotta Pay the Price" – Gloria Taylor; "I Spy For The FBI" – Jamo Thomas; "What Can a Man Do?" – Show-stoppers; "Soul Self Satisfaction" – Earl Jackson. We got all of these from the radio. And on compilation records we bought we discovered "That's Enough" – Roscoe Robinson; "I Can't Please You" – Jimmy Robins; "60 Minutes of Your Love" – Homer Banks. So when Bin and I made a pilgrimage to England in 1982, having heard rumours about this strange Northern Soul phenomenon, it blew our minds that these English people were dancing to those tracks by the hundreds and thousands. Until then we were under the impression that the whole world had forgotten about (or rather, had never known) this old soul music. Yes, the 70s were a great period for us musically, learning so much about the music through listening to the radio and buying (cheap) records, but it was tough emotionally to be so isolated. So the first time I saw a soul 45 for sale for 50 quid, I was actually overjoyed, not thinking about the negative financial consequences this would have on my own budget – no more cheap records, but recognition at last.

'For the last couple of years I've had an urge to help start a soul/Northern Soul scene in Israel. I've met some other people in Israel who are into soul (I mean, what we call soul music, not that current crap), we've had a few events, but we are still too few. Hopefully the Israeli Northern Soul Movement will gather some momentum.'

*Yoni's top 10 Northern Soul faves*

'Can We Talk It Over'  L Allen
'Because of My Heart'  Frankie Beverley and the Butlers
'Just Because of You'  Rocky Roberts and the Airedales
'A Lot of Love'  Homer Banks
'Lucky to be Loved by You'  Emanuel Laskey
'My Heart Cries for You'  Porgy and the Monarchs
'I'm a Fool (I Must Love You)'  The Falcons
'Friday Night'  Johnnie Taylor
'I Can't Please You'  Jimmy Robins
'There's That Mountain'  The Tripp

Another massively popular Northern Soul website is run by ex-pat Mick Fitzpatrick from Germany. Currently running at

20,000 visits a year, the Night Owl Northern Soul Club contains a wealth of information and personal stories from soul fans from all over the world.

Mick, a former Wigan Casino regular originally from Nelson, Lancashire, set up the site in 1996. Colourfully illustrated and containing dozens of sub-sites to visit, the Night Owl contains everything from chat rooms to record wants. It has been reviewed in Q magazine and has even made Virgin's music top 10 sites. 'It has had a lot of media coverage and I have made many friends worldwide because of it,' says Mick. 'It takes too much time to maintain, but it is a labour of love so I don't give a toss. I'd do anything to keep the scene going.'

Mick, who is in the army in Germany, says the benefits of running the site for himself and other soul fans have been enormous. Canadian soul fans have now teamed up because of it ('I doubt these people would have met up without my site,' he said). Old mates have rediscovered each other, he finds he can now get hold of virtually any track he wants, he has received invitations to visit people all over the world, and he has even landed writing jobs on Italian and Spanish soul magazines.

'I got a mate a job from someone I met via my site; it has brought me offers of work, and it lets people at the other end of the world know what tunes were played at the last do in the UK. The benefits are enormous. I could go on and on,' said Mick. His site can be found at http://members.tripod.com/mickfitz.

Stefano Oggiano, of Milan, Italy, is just one of the growing band of continental soul fans who are fascinated by the British Northern Soul scene. 'Here in Italy the Northern scene is growing slowly but constantly: there are soul clubs in Genova (Black Trefoil) and in Rimini (Right Combination). Up to date most of the aficionados are Mods or former Mods but things are changing. We have organized well-attended (250 punters) soul nights and all-nighters in Milan, where I live, and in the North of Italy (Liguria). Now you can find Kent and Goldmine CDs in some record shops and soul fans can listen at home to their favourite tracks and discover new ones.'

Stefano discovered the music in 1995 when he picked up a

copy of Kent Records' *For Dancers Only*. 'I was immediately captured. Now I collect both CDs and singles, and I am always amazed at the quantity of records to unearth,' he said.

In 1997, Stefano started a fanzine called *La Pelle Nera* ('For connoisseurs of Soul'), Italy's only magazine about 60s and 70s rare soul. Contributors include Joe Moran of the Dublin Soul Club and Mick Fitzpatrick of the 'Night Owl' website. He is also involved in a weekly radio programme called *Soul Machine*.

'For the future we are planning a big event with DJs from UK and Europe; unfortunately we don't have much money but our enthusiasm will help,' he said.

*Stefano's current favourites are:*

'This is the Thanks I Get' Barbara Lynn
'Make Sure' Dells
'Crying Clown' Eddie Parker
'Look at Me Now' Ethics
'Seven Doors' VI Campbell
'What Good am I?' TSU Tornados
'The Way I Love You' Continental 4
'That's the Price You Have to Pay' Brenda & The Tabulations
'Here She Comes' Tymes
'Let Me Try' Odds & Ends

Listeners to radio station PBS 106.7fm in Melbourne, Australia, are treated to the dulcet tones of ex-Twisted Wheel DJ Vince Peach. Liverpool-born Vince was introduced to the world of Northern Soul all-nighters in the early 60s. That was at the Room At The Top in Wigan (preceding the famed Casino events by a good few years). The Twisted Wheel inevitably followed, along with a lifetime's devotion to soul music.

Vince moved to Australia in 1982 and set about trying to convert the natives to the British taste in soul music. He started a Northern Soul scene in Melbourne, and while DJing in Sydney for 'Agent 00 Soul' he met ex-Wiganers Andy and Fiona Nevin, who boast having bought part of the famous Wigan Casino dance floor. It still adorns the kitchen floor of their former home back in England.

Vince is also in regular contact with Pete Fowler, formerly of Chorley, Lancashire, who runs Perth soul events. Now he has a weekly radio show *Soul Time*, on air since 1984, and a host of new friends.

Northern Soul all-nighters in Melbourne are every week at Little Reata's from 11 pm to 7 am and a Double O Soul weekend takes place every month, with Friday and Saturday all-nighters. The main DJs are Vince himself and guests including Ady Pountain, Maria Orlvic, Craig Bayliss, and Frank Driscoll.

Vince also DJs at Sydney soul nights, national soul week-enders, and 'anywhere else they play Northern Soul'.

Said Vince: 'The Aussie soul scene is good. There are native DJs in Melbourne, Sydney, and Adelaide, all in their early twenties. The scene in all three cities is made up of Mods and scooterists, a few ex-pats, and the curious, who it must be said do get into the sounds.

'The club and music scene in Oz is well into black music, mostly funk related and modern R & B, hip-hop and the like, and Aussies do like to party.'

The only drawback to being a soul fan in Australia is the vast distances involved. Northern Soul fans are renowned for their enthusiasm and willingness to drive several hours to the right venue. But in the sprawling continent of Australia, a car journey can take *days*.

A salutary tale reaches the author, of an ex-Brit who drove for three days to reach a soul weekender. Arriving at the event, weary and in need of some stimulation, he overindulged in substances of a dubious nature and spent the first all-nighter wandering about talking complete rubbish to total strangers. He then 'crashed out' for the next two days, missing the rest of the weekend's activities, and finally recovered in time for the three-day drive home! Who said we get older and wiser?

When Canadian resident and ex-pat Les Thomas logged on to the Internet on his new personal computer, he was astonished to find a goldmine of information and contacts not only all over the world, but surprisingly close to home. Les says the history of

Northern Soul in Canada, is pretty recent history, but its roots stretch way back to places like the Twisted Wheel, Wigan Casino, Blackpool Mecca, Stafford and the London 100 Club. He recalls: 'Having been away from "The Scene" for many years, the dying embers were rekindled about two months ago. I had to make a couple of trips home to the UK within a few months of each other. Once I was back among my old mates the inevitable question was asked, "Want to go to a Northern do?"

'As I needed some cheering up, off we went to Lowton Civic Hall. It was like stepping through a time warp. I was a 38-year-old teenager, the old sounds, that same old feeling, I could still dance, absolute magic!

'Another night at Rylands, another at Lowton and one at the Carlton, one of my old stomping grounds, and I was on cloud ten never mind nine. I arrived back in my adopted home of Canada loaded down with as many Goldmine and Kent CDs as I could cram into my bags, and promptly stuck five at a time on the CD player and hit the random button and started dancing like a loony around the living room.

'The wife said "Bloody hell, I haven't seen that for years." The kids laughed their heads off. They're still laughing!'

For Les, it all started back in about 1970.

## The Soul of the Net

### Welcome to Yoni's Home of Soul Music

Bringing together 60's soul, northern soul, deep soul, funky soul, southern soul, 70's 80's 90's - any kinda soul as long as it's REAL

Bookmark this page and visit it again soon. The Soul of the Net is a home for Real Soul Music on the net: discographies, information, trivia, CD, vinyl and video reviews, and links to all other soul sites I know of. Hopefully it will keep expanding and include more of everything as time goes by.

'Well, it didn't take long did it, to Whitchurch to the all-dayer, Nantwich Cricket Club (big marquee, dancing on grass), the Pendulum (dancing on paving stones), my first all-nighter at the Carlton in Warrington.'

Then came the advent of the Wigan Casino all-nighters and an even bigger circle of friends. He got in with the crowd from Crewe, Rhyl, Blackpool, free coaches to the Mecca, Reading, Walsall. He particularly remembers Little Scotty running around the Casino with a phone attached to his pants pocket telling people, 'It's for you.' ('Was this the invention of the mobile phone?' wonders Les.)

Marathon weekend sessions began at Samantha's in Sheffield on Friday, Blackpool and Wigan on Saturday, and ended in Stoke or Whitchurch on the Sunday.

Highlights for Les include starting the Cheshire Soul Club at Northwich's Morgue with some mates, and low times trouble with the tax man and Cheshire Constabulary. Settling down to marriage and made redundant himself, his wife found a job in Canada and the Thomases emigrated.

Les says that despite emigrating to the virtually soul-free country of Canada, the music was still with him, bubbling under the surface. On his occasional record-hunting missions, he found the odd bargain like the Undisputed Truth's 'You've Got the Love I Need' for 50 cents on Canadian Tamla, and the Velvet Satins' 'Nothing Can Compare to You' for 25 cents on red General American.

Then came the trips home to England in November '96 and January '97. Suddenly, says Les, 'I'm born again, love it, find out I can get my hands on Northern Soul CDs from Marty Koppell's record shop in Toronto. I'm in heaven, well almost – there's still nowhere to go to hear the stuff as it should be heard, at a million decibels and with a dance floor to pound away on.'

All that changed with the arrival of the family computer and Internet access. Suddenly Les found he had fellow soul enthusiasts as near as thirty minutes' drive from his home.

In May 1998 Alun Bell, formerly of Preston (an ex-Blackpool Mecca regular), Mick Taylor from Doncaster (ex-Wheel), Kev Cox from Reading (ex-Stafford and the 100 Club in London),

Tom Powers from Guildford (ex-100 Club), and Les himself put on probably the first ever Northern Soul night in Canada at Fathers Pub in Toronto.

Said Les: 'After that, we got a few nights at the Duke of Gloucester and have since moved to what has become our regular venue, the Rancho Relaxo in Toronto. It is a strictly amateur night as we are the DJs and only Tom and Kev had ever done any before, but the music is great, oldies and Motown stuff, lots of dancing and Guinness. As well as a few more old ex-pat soulies and our wives and girlfriends we have managed to attract a young crowd of Mods who are getting right into it.

'I'm back on cloud 10 and have started buying vinyl again, only now I can afford to get more than one at a time. I really enjoy the DJing, I should have started doing it years ago, I might never have been made redundant. The scene in Canada is just beginning, but if things keep on rolling along like they have the last twelve months, who knows where it'll be in a few years? Regular all-nighters? You never know!'

*Les Thomas's Top Ten Northern Soul sounds*

'A Quitter Never Wins' Williams & Watson
'Soul Time' Shirley Ellis
'I've Been Blessed' Bobby Taylor
'My Weakness Is You' Edwin Starr
'Love You, Baby' Eddie Parker
'Mr Creator' Apollas
'Just Another Heartache' Little Ritchie
'Love a Go-Go' Stevie Wonder
'Hopes Dreams & Tombstones' Jimmy Frazier
'Time Will Pass You By' Tobi Legend

Exiled Yorkshireman Mick Taylor, now living in Canada, was stunned when his 19-year-old son got on to the Internet. Mick found the British-based Soul Source site, then the Night Owl site, where he chatted to a lad from Wigan living not far away from him, wanting to get together.

They did, others joined them and eventually there were five

soul fans 'sharing drinks in each other's basements'.

Mick takes up the story: 'Unknown to any of us, there has been a strong Mod scene in Toronto for some time, with scooter clubs etc. So I'm playing all my old stuff, and they all show up one night, and they love it! Motown, Atlantic plus Kinks, Spencer Davis, Small Faces, the Rolling Stones, Pretty Things, etc.

'Now we have a regular following of 80–100 people who come out to every do; we've been asked to do scooter rallies in the summer (we did a New Year's Eve bash and went down a bomb!) So I'm getting a second crack at being a teenager and loving every minute of it!'

Sunday/Monday May 2nd/ 3rd, 12.05-8.00am

A RITZ SPECIAL EVENT ALLNIGHTER

**Rare Rarer Rarest**

OF THE RARE PART (5)

A STUNNING NIGHT of ALL THE VERY BEST OF ALL THE VERY RAREST in Northern Soul from the UK's top DJs!

Featuring: Richard Searling, Bob Hinsley, Soul Sam, Ginger Taylor, Chris King & Kenny Burrell. Special guests: Ady Croasdell, Butch, Keith Money and Andy Rix.

The Ritz, Whitworth Street, West, Manchester.
Admission £8 (CFOS Members), £10 (Member's Guests)

**Ritz ALL-NIGHTER**

Another well-used website is 'Soul Source', set up by Mike Hughes in early 1997. Mike, originally from Llandudno in North Wales, grew up with the backbeat of Northern Soul playing throughout his early life. He graduated from local venues to the major venues like Blackpool Mecca in 1976, and kept up his UK soul pilgrimages until he was posted overseas by the army in 1980.

When he conceived the idea for Soul Source, there were only about half a dozen sites on the web devoted to the rare soul scene. Mike said: 'These sites, especially "The Old Soul Music Home Page", gave me a bit of inspiration and as I had done a bit of knocking around with computers and most of all still have the "love of soul" in me, the thought of putting a site together that would be informative, worthwhile and most of all soulful grabbed me.

'It started off small but took off quickly thanks to many of the soul on-line community. Pete Smith of Hastings was and still is a regular contributor and played a big part in the early days.

'The idea behind Soul Source is for it to be a source for soul. Information on the soul scene in the past has depended (like a lot of underground scenes) on word of mouth or by monthly mags. As the Internet is ideal for getting and giving information, it is a handy way of keeping in touch with the soul scene.

'The Internet now allows soul fans to grab instant information and soul injections – need to know what was played at last 100 Club all-nighter, when is the next Lowton, want to listen to that £500 plus sound, what articles are in the latest issue of your favourite mag, interested in what new records that New York vinyl dealer has in, fancy a bit of a memory trip with a video of Wiganchat with your old mate who now lives in Australia – yeah it's all possible through the web.'

Mike says putting 'Soul Source' together and throwing it up can take up a lot of time, but it's an excuse for him to work with one of his passions. 'The thought of people visiting the site and finding it both enjoyable and useful also gives me a bit of a buzz, the sharing, receiving, passing on of soul stuff is just a good enjoyable thing to do and whilst not a substitute for being away from the hub of the scene it helps ease the ache.'

The site is now currently receiving around 300–400 visits per week. Mike found that at first a lot of visitors were ex-pats, but nowadays it's quite a mixture. They range from people actively involved in the UK scene, young people from countries like the USA, members of the strong German scene, Scandinavia, and also from a lot of the more mainstream Soul fans.

Mike sees the future holding great potential for Northern Soul on the Internet, as in the last couple of years there has been considerable development. He says the sound and video quality has improved 100 per cent and as technology continues to march onwards, the sharing and enjoyment of soul material will increase.

Sherry Loewinger is a founder member of the group the United Soul Club of America, which is dedicated to promoting Northern Soul in its country of origin. Sherry, of Alameda, California, said: 'Ironically, we live in the United States, birthplace of soul music, yet we still discover men and women who would rather listen to pop music crooned by white artists. Perhaps Northern Soul demands an acquired taste. Nevertheless, when an individual eventually receives a "soul injection", one remains addicted for life.'

The Californian acquired a taste for the rarer side of soul music after being indoctrinated via standard Motown and Stax material aired at Mod dance nights in California. Sherry takes up the story: 'My obsession with vinyl collecting commenced with the purchase of "Sweet Soul Music" by Arthur Conley on Collectibles, a label specializing in reissued products. At that particular time, I never considered the idea of pursuing original-label 45s, dismissing such a hobby as too time-consuming and beyond my expertise. Ultimately, reissues and bootlegs no longer interested me and almost instantly, I found myself only searching for genuine 45s and albums. Slowly, I abandoned the search for commercial, top 40 tunes and yearned for the more obscure and rare sounds. Northern Soul officially entered my life.

'During my journey, I encountered a group of young and devoted soul enthusiasts, who identified themselves as the United Soul Club of America. Established in 1983 in Los Angeles by fellow Americans Mike Kenyon and Dave Thomas, this society stands as the oldest and longest-running Northern Soul association in the United States. Their main priority involves reintroducing the brilliant Northern sounds back into the United States.

'Sifting through hundreds of record boxes week after week comprising mostly country & western 45s, the founding members relied on intuition to determine whether or not a particular record qualified as a Northern record. No handbooks, record guides, or Internet sources appeared during the early 1980s; as a result, their search required a trial-and-error lesson involving the right tracks, labels, artists, and producers.

'Within a few years, the United Soul Club of America arranged their first all-day event to introduce their latest acquisitions to a crowd raised primarily on Motown hits. Noting the positive reaction received by the Los Angeles crowd, the members of the club opted to relocate to the Bay Area in order to share their vast record collections, extensive knowledge, and pure love for the music with the rest of California. In 1996, I proudly joined the ranks as a member of the United Soul Club of America.'

Sherry says one of the joys of being a white person enjoying soul music in America is when hunting for records. 'As over-zealous American record collectors, a largely satisfying experience occurs when strolling into a dusty and antiquated record shop owned by an African-American family and watching the surprise emerge on their faces. Caucasians that parade and shop in a district catering to a mostly black population strikes most of the residents as unusual. However, what completely astounds the storeowners is the adoration and respect that we each hold for the artists and the songs created. The songs which were never aired on the commercial radio stations, never reached the mass population of the United States, and thus never landed a spot on the Top 40 Billboard charts. The tunes which lingered in the old and dilapidated record boxes, rarely acknowledged due to the strained race relations occurring in the United States during the tumultuous decade of the 1960s. Thirty years later, a few white 20-somethings storm through their community shops, exhibiting a great enthusiasm towards their merchandise. We obviously do not possess the power to transform the politics of our society. However, we attempt to provide an opportunity for these unknown but fabulous tracks to gain the fame they originally failed to receive, yet deserve.

'Currently, our society organizes the only proper Northern Soul all-nighter in the United States, exclusively playing original 45s, in the tradition of the British scene of the 1970s. We hosted our first true all-nighter in January of 1998 in Santa Clara, California with a fair amount of attendees. We realize that Northern Soul will not overwhelm our country in an overnight fashion; yet, the prospect of converting at least one person into a "soulie" piques our interest. As a matter of fact, it only encourages us to try harder. As more people learn about Northern Soul and grow more acquainted with these sounds, our scene can only advance stronger and more united. As Chuck Jackson would say, "Good things come to those who wait!"'

Ex-pat Pete Fowler, now living in Perth Australia, found the Internet invaluable in discovering fellow soulies in that vast continent. Regular Northern Soul nights in Perth and contact with soul fans in Melbourne and Sydney led to him organizing and running the first ever national soul weekender in Adelaide in October 1998.

Pete, a former Wigan Casino regular, originally from Chorley, Lancashire, emigrated to Australia in 1992. The Northern Soul scene seemed a distant memory until a friend returned from the UK with the Goldmine CD *The Wigan Casino Story*. Pete was in heaven, and immediately set about collecting other Goldmine compilations and even dusted off his old vinyl record collection.

He also decided to check out the local scootering scene as a way of finding if there was any interest in Northern Soul. A Lambretta spare parts stockist in Perth gave him some contacts and Pete found out that a group of scooter enthusiasts occasionally held soul nights.

Kicking off at a small venue in Perth in around August 1996, the local soul nights gradually moved more and more towards out-and-out Northern Soul events. By March 1998, they had become a permanent fixture at the Irish Club in Perth and soul fans were celebrating the venue's first anniversary.

Said Pete: 'They were there for one thing only, dancing to Northern Soul and for the camaraderie and friendships that have long been associated with the scene.

'In any expatriate environment the camaraderie would exist, but it seemed to be a quantum leap more noticeable at the Irish Club than it used to be in the UK. All of a sudden my phone book was overflowing with names, and invitations to barbecues were getting out of hand.

'I had made a hundred new good mates overnight and they were all clearly as thrilled as I was at being a part of the scene again. There were hour-long phone calls discussing B sides, tapes arriving through the door every week, and shirts, badges, CDs, and car stickers all being made.'

Pete had also been keeping in touch with fellow soul fan Craig Bayliss in Melbourne, and through him got to hear about Vince Peach's radio show in that city. Vince was also promoting soul nights in Melbourne area with Frank Driscoll. Through them, Pete learned about the Sydney soul scene being enthusiastically promoted by Maria, Alex and Chrissie.

One day over a beer, Pete and his friend Andy Dean, an ex-Casino and Leeds Central regular, talked about how it would be great to unite the soul scenes happening in the three cities. From that germ of an idea, the Adelaide national soul weekender was born.

At 7.30 pm on 24 October 1998, it all came together as scores of soul fans travelled across Australia to enjoy the scene many of them thought they would never experience again.

Adelaide scooter boys Mark Howlett and Eddie Holland got the first all-nighter under way at the start of a mammoth week-end in two venues.

Pete recalled: 'The ulcers, blisters and calf muscles had hardly any time to mend when it was Sunday noon in the Crown and Anchor and we were up and running again. The consensus was that, having travelled so far, rather than chill it down a bit, we would go for another full-tilt session and postpone recovery for the flights home.

'As expected, most of the Adelaide crowd stayed home, leaving around sixty interstaters to rip into another twelve hours of Northern Soul. By the time Ady Pountain rounded off with Esther Phillips's stirring ender "Just Say Goodbye", everyone was knackered but totally elated.'

The second national weekender was being organized as this book went to press, with even more interest from ex-pat soulies down under.

*Current Irish Club favourites are:*

'You Should O Held On' 7th Avenue Aviators
'You Got the Love I Need' Undisputed Truth
'It'll Never be Over For Me' Timi Yuro
'I'm Gone' Eddie Parker
'Baby, Don't You Weep' Edward Hamilton
'Baby, Baby, Don't Waste My Time' Gladys Knight

The Berlin soul community recalled on the Night Owl website how the Germans are 'keeping the faith' in their own way:

Northern Soul reached Berlin in 1985. There were little parties in smaller clubs as well as big events in the Stadthaus Bocklerpark. The latter twice a year. Music policy was a mixture of 60s Northern oldies, Motown, 60s Northern newies and rare Modern Soul.

The Allnighters were well visited by a well mixed audience, so also people who weren't Mods got in touch with this music. A small Northern Soul community formed consisting of fans, dancers, collectors and DJs. But after the German unification the whole nightlife changed place as well as musical taste. Now the former East Berlin centre with its small clubs was the place to go. The clubs were too small to dance to Northern Soul, very expensive to rent and totally occupied by the rising Hip Hop, Urban Soul and of course Techno movements.

Apart from the Northern Soul community nobody seemed to be interested in Northern Soul any longer. A decrease from over 2000 who once visited the Stadthaus to less than a hundred. Although a highlight in the history of Northern Soul in Berlin occurred in June 1991 when Mark Forrest arranged the first German soul weekender.

Three top-DJs from UK (John Buck, Gary Spencer and Mark Soulie) and five German DJs were at the turntables.

Unfortunately, apart from the members of the Berlin Northern Soul community hardly anybody showed up. A financial disaster for Mark but nevertheless a great experience for all who were there. Shortly after that the 'old' Stadthaus Bocklerpark DJs gave up, one even sold her records, and it got silent on the scene. Then in 1995 three guys (Micha, Olivier, Costa), called the Farfisa Imperium, tried something new.

In opposition to the rising Easy Listening movement they played strong Farfisa-organ dominated instrumentals in spite of the soft Hammond-organ ones. In addition French Beat, Garage Punk, Psychedelic, R & B-orientated Northern Soul could be heard. The aim of this team is not to change to a classic Northern Soul event but to cultivate a mixture of high-quality rare 60s music to show there is something beyond Beatles and James Brown.

In spring 1996 some new players showed up. Four men (Stefan (Screaming Jay), Hannes, Hermann (Jean-Luc), Olaf (Magic Shoemaker)) and one woman (Katja) out of the former Northern Soul community met by chance and decided that it was time to reactivate Northern Soul on their own. Fortuna presented the nearly perfect room . . . an adjoining room of a theatre located in the centre of Berlin. The room called Roter Salon has a bar, tables and chairs along the walls, a wooden dance floor and a very 60s stylish ambience. The first event was a success, so we arranged a regular monthly appearance.

Since winter 1995/96 there are also occasional venues in small clubs, sometimes with the participation of one or two of the Roter Salon DJs.

**LA PELLE NERA**
*FOR CONNOISSEURS OF SOUL*
N. 6  ESTATE 1998 - L. 5.000

*Personal Top Tens*
*Hannes Rosenhagen*

'What Condition My Condition Was In'  Betty Lavette
'The Things I Do for You'  Linda Martell and the Angelos
'Girl Across the Street'  Moses Smith
'Shing A-Ling'  The Cooperettes
'It's Written All Over My Face'  Marva Holiday
'Love's Gone Bad'  Chris Clark
'Earthquake'  Bobby Lynn
'Opportunity Street'  Bobby Lynn
'No More Tears'  Bessie Jones
'Stop and Take a Look at Yourself'  Shalimars
'I Can't Escape From You'  Richie Adams

*Katja Metzner*

'A Little Togetherness'  The Younghearts
'7 Days Too Long'  Chuck Wood
'The End of Our Love'  Nancy Wilson
'Stronger Than Her Love'  The Flirtations
'Stop Her on Sight'  Edwin Starr
'I'm Ready for Love'  Martha and the Vandellas
'Earthquake'  Bobby Lynn
'If That's What You Wanted'  Frank Beverly and the Butlers
'You Turned My Bitter Into Sweet'  Mary Love
'Gettin' Mighty Crowded'  Betty Everett

*Stefan the B*

'You Can Count on Me'  Sammy Davis Jr
'Sign On the Dotted Line'  Gene Latter
'You Got Me Where You Want Me'  Larry Santos
'This Thing Called Love'  Johnny Wyatt
'Earthquake'  Bobby Lynn
'Don't Pretend'  The Belles
'Don't Let Him Hurt You'  The Chansonettes
'Stop, Leave My Heart Alone'  Two People
'Love is Like an Itching in My Heart'  The Supremes

### Kay

'I Can't Help Loving You' Paul Anka
'Peanut Duck' Marsha Gee
'Sunny' Bobby Hebb
'Eddie's My Name' Eddie Holman
'Too Much of a Good Thing' The Shirelles
'City Lights' Jerry Nailor
'Black Power' James Coit
'The 81' Candy and the Kisses
'Pay to the Piper' Chairmen of The Board
'Long After Tonight is All Over' Jimmy Radcliffe

### Micha Wangeov (Farfisa Imperium)

'The Chaperone' La Brenda Ben
'Hit and Run' Rose Batiste
'69 Tears' Big Maybelle
'Don't Freeze on Me' Jessie Mac
'We Love Each Other' Ruby Rowe
'Any Way You Wanta' Harvey
'My Man Don't Think I Know' Gwen Dawis
'Together' Bobby Star
'Money' Barrett Strong
'Make It One For My Baby' Obeira Martin
'I've Done You Wrong' Kip Anderson

### Alex Brassel (Agent OO Soul), Düsseldorf

'I'm Coming Home in the Morning' Lou Pride
'She'll Come Running Back' Mel Britt
'Little Darling' The Flirtations
'The Drifter' Ray Pollard
'Dearly Beloved' Jack Montgomery
'Spinning Top' The Orlons
'Earthquake' Bobby Lynn
'Mr Creator' Valerie Simpson
'Too Late' Williams & Watson
'I Remember the Feeling' Barbara Lewis

Nick James, formerly of Boston, Lincs, set off for his first all-nighter at St Ives in 1976 aged just fourteen and a half. Now he finds himself running soul nights in his adopted home of Copenhagen, Denmark!

Nick says: 'The Northern Soul scene is something we should all treasure no matter who is doing what. We still have this great music and always will so keep it going. In 1987 I moved to Denmark. In 1991 I attempted to set up a club as I wanted people to hear music that could give them something, but it took till July 1998 when our club finally got a home in Copenhagen.

'The scene is very good and people travel long distances every month, with an age range of eighteen to thirties. They all love it, and I love to see them enjoying it as I did at their age, and I still do today. It is a wonderful experience to see the scene grow over here. The two clubs who set it up are Back Street and the Spinning Cat in Malmo.

'Many thanks to Ste Livesey, who flies over from England to play with us, and Roy Parkin my partner in this.

'My passion will die with me and every time I see a cheap ticket to England I usually come home to get filled up with Northern Soul. And people think I am nuts but who cares?'

*Nick James's Favourite Sounds*

'I Was Born to Love You'  Herbert Hunter
'I Travel Alone'  Lou Ragland
'My World is on Fire'  Jimmy Mack
'Don't Depend on Me'  Fantastic Johnny C
'Our Love is in the Pocket'  Darrell Banks
'Love Factory'  Eloise Laws
'Of Hopes and Dreams'  Jimmy Fraser
'They'll Never Know Why'  Freddie Chavez
'Get It off My Conscience'  Lovelites
'Love, Love, Love'  Bobby Hebb

Sweden too has its Northern Soul fans and a group of Swedish DJs have selected their top ten favourites.

*Magnus 'Munken' Rems*

'Gotta Right to Cry'  Otis Leavill
'I Ain't Going Nowhere'  Leroy Barbour
'Crook His Little Finger'  Ann Heywood
'Nothing Can Compare to You'  The Velvet Satins
'You're Everything'  The Showmen
'That Girl'  Porgy and the Monarchs
'Come Back'  Ken Williams
'Do You Love Me, Baby'  The Masquerades
'Wherever You Where'  Bud Harper
'You're the Dream'  Roscoe Shelton

*Robert Baum*

'Sleepless Nights'  Paris
'The Sweetest Thing'  Channel 3
'Village of Tears'  Ben Zine

'Lonely For You, Baby' Sam Dees
'Say Something Nice to Me' Bobby Kline
'I'll Never Forget You' The Metros
'I Love You' Otis Leavill
'Pyramid' Soul Bros. Inc
'Sweet Thing' Billy Kennedy
'Dearly Beloved' Jack Montgomery

*Fredrik 'The Snake' Ekander*

'They'll Never Know Why' Freddie Chavez
'Love Factory' Eloise Laws
'A Little Togetherness' The Younghearts
'Too Late' Williams & Watson
'I've Got to Find Me Somebody' The Vel-Vets
'Ain't No More Room' The Kittens
'6 by 6' Earl Van Dyke
'This Love-Starved Heart of Mine' Marvin Gaye
'You've Been Leading Me On' The Steinways
'I Wanna Give You Tomorrow' Benny Troy

*Richard Karström*

'Please Let Me In' J J Barnes
'The Who Who Song' Jackie Wilson
'Uptight' Nancy Wilson
'I Shall Not Be Moved' Barrino Brothers
'So Soon' Donnie Elbert
'Chain Reaction' Celestrals
'Changing by the Minute' Darrow Fletcher
'Picture Me Gone' Madeleine Bell
'I Only Get This Feeling' Dee Irwin
'At Last (I Found a Love)' Marvin Gaye

*Dave Deacon*

'Looking at Tomorrow' Chubby Checker
'Love Runs Out' Willie Hutch

'Let Our Love Grow Higher'  Eula Cooper
'Lighten Up'  Larry Atkins
'You Just Can't Walk Away'  Dean Courtney
'I Still Love You'  Four Larks
'Time's A-Wasting'  Fuller Brothers
'Ain't No Soul'  Major Lance
'Crying Over You'  Duke Browner
'Just As Much'  Kris Peterson

# 12

# It'll Never Be Over For Me

*'I haven't seen a packed carpark like this since Wigan. This place looks amazing.'*

The revival of the Northern Soul scene has meant different things to different people. The unique atmosphere surrounding the scene has ensured the loyal support of many an original soulie, delighted at the opportunity to meet up with old friends in a familiar environment, and relive experiences which had seemed almost certainly confined to the past. However, the music and lifestyle which first appealed to the youthful fans of the 60s has found many new followers in the 90s.

A relatively new face on the scene, Barbara Davies of Colwyn Bay in North Wales, relates here how she first became involved with Northern Soul in the early 90s, and what it means to her today:

Fist clenched, I pounded the dough, wishing that it would magically turn into the man I had recently loved and lost. Baking was therapeutic. As Gladys Knight's 'Just Walk In My Shoes' echoed my own pain and anguish, my tears turned the once elastic dough into a globule of sticky stuff.

> Just walk in my shoes, this hurt inside is too much for me
> Just walk in my shoes and you'll see the love that used to be

Flour dusted the kitchen floor as I danced feeling every morsel of that song. I delivered my body willingly and gratefully to soul. My world became bearable for at least four minutes. I danced my way to open the door of my somewhat sad-looking council maisonette. Older sister Jayne had no sooner crossed the crumbling threshold when she began to accompany Gladys in full voice (Gladys had no reason for concern).

Jayne explained that this was a good old northern soul track, and later took it back to her house since it belonged to her. Farewell Gladys – once again I have loved and lost all in a week.

Perhaps I should have been cheered at the prospect of a Friday night out on the town? The thought of a whole evening spent in Yates Wine Lodge filled me with abhorrence; it had never been my thing. That night I was groped I was mauled I was pushed I was sickly pisst I was home by ten thirty.

Weeks passed and November brought news of a cold, dark and dank winter to come. I scanned the local Wigan rag. No luck – the economy suffered and the prospect of finding work was as bleak as the weather forecast. Spirits down and all hope abandoned, I glanced at the entertainment section: *Northern Soul night to be held at Wigan Cricketers.*

Holy Cow! How could this be? Was this so? Why, the Casino was long dead. 'Jayne, Jayne, get your coat!'

That night at the Cricketers I pledged my soul to a master that was neither male nor female. A master who knew all, felt all, and could depict the strongest of human emotions through lyrics. Love, hate, guilt, jealousy – yes, that too. My master was soul music, and to that I would commit my heart.

I met people, so many people, I instantly loved them, and vowed friendship to my fellow soulies. My world changed, and slowly my heart began to heal, slowly.

I look upon those early days now, seeing things as clear as day. My naivety met by my desire to love would bring hurt and betrayal as I have never known. When a lover betrays you it is the fault of human passion. When a friend betrays you it brings a hurt that kills a part of your soul.

My first all-nighter at Blackburn Tony's Empress Ballroom, and clad in black leggings I stood at the edge of the dance floor and paid homage to my god, like a servant of unquestionable loyalty. The sounds of Bobby Paris and 'I Walked Away' filled the room:

There's nothing colder than goodbye.

My feet danced and my tears fell. Head down, I danced away the misery I felt inside. Bobby must have felt as I did for his lyrics told my story. They somehow brought me back to life, and for the first time I felt I was not alone.

From then on my hunger grew into something that could not be controlled, my need to wallow in soul was stronger than my own life force. Weekdays were of no consequence to me, night time was for living and day time for the dead. The intensity of Northern Soul and what we call the scene controlled and manipulated my mind to such an extent that I was no longer my own person. I was isolated from the outside world and what it had to offer – work, communication and family I cared nothing for. I gave my home, my time, my emotions and my every waking thought to the people of Northern Soul. However, a time came when I realised that all people – friends and lovers too – show human weaknesses.

I got no trust in my fellow man,
'cos he lies with his lips and he hurts with his hand

Tony Clark's lyrics are so true to form and originate from a favourite of mine; I wonder why it is that the lyrics so often ring true? The joy of Northern Soul has brought so much to smile about, and now some eight years later I look back and realize I have taken control of it and not the other way round. I am still devoted to my music, yet I am now the master. There are so many other pleasures in living, working and achieving – my love of music complements these, and allows me to have it all.

I'll keep on holding on.

*

The legend on the back of the guy's T-shirt just about summed it up: 'So Much Soul, So Little Time'.

The irony isn't lost on any of the onlookers at the all-nighter at the King's Hall in Stoke. You would think that ten hours of non-stop ear-battering music would be enough for any rational person. But these are Northern Soul fanatics, and that simple logo on the T-shirt is very apt when you consider that so many people are enjoying their second bite of the cherry of the music which gave them so much pleasure in their younger years.

How many years do we have left in us to keep up this frantic pace? How many years before relationships crack under the strain caused by one partner frequently disappearing to soul venues? How many years before the knees start to seize up and refuse to glide you around the dance floor like they used to? How many years before the scene dies forever?

All these thoughts occurred to us as the Blackpool posse made its pilgrimage to the Torch revival all-nighter at the King's Hall, Stoke-on-Trent.

Getting ready for the hour and a half's journey from Blackpool that night, the old familiar feelings start to flood through you as you pack your holdall. Two changes of shirt, deodorant, the compulsory packet of chewing gum, a bottle of Lucozade and mineral water to attempt to smuggle in past the door staff, cash for records/CDs, and a spare pair of pants for the morning.

Tonight as we travel down in Mojo's car to Stoke, the experience is such a throwback to the 70s that it is almost comical. 'The stereo's not working, so I've brought this,' said Mojo apologetically, plonking a tinny little portable cassette player on the dashboard. Motown rarities start to squawk out of this 70s-style cassette recorder and we all smile to ourselves. Instant nostalgia.

Making up the foursome with me and Mojo are Mark Isles and Kim Turner, also former Casino boys. Part of the attraction of Northern Soul is the way it brings people together, and despite the fact that six months previously I had never even met Mojo or Kim (Mark was an old athletics club pal from years ago but neither of us knew about our 'soulful' past), I feel like I have known them all for ever.

Part of the all-nighter experience is getting ripped off at motorway service stations, so we keep with tradition and stop off en route on the M6. It is only 10.30 pm and the night is still young.

Having been relieved of several pounds for what we all agree is probably the most awful cafetiere of coffee ever made, we sit chatting, smoking and reminiscing in a virtually deserted restaurant. Deserted, that is, apart from a party of pensioners who look weary and keep glancing across as we talk ever more loudly about music, life, love and various misdemeanours committed since the Torch opened its doors in 1973.

We are variously aged between thirty-nine and forty-three; we are all proud dads, boasting seven kids between us, and six wives/ex wives, and we are all what could be described as Respectable Family Men approaching middle age. Yet as we sit there turning back the years, you realize nothing much has changed.

We are still adventurous, passionate and filled with youthful enthusiasm for the music that has shaped our lives. And thanks to running, football, swimming and hour after hour of energetic dancing, we are fortunate enough to be (almost) as fit as we were two decades ago.

After half an hour of chewing the cud, we can stand the wait no longer. The Torch revival is beckoning. The few miles to Stoke pass quickly and soon we are into the baffling one-way system. Having been to another all-nighter only two months previously at the same venue, I assure Mojo I know the way. After several laps of the town centre and much swearing, we decide we are totally confused. Suddenly, just as the abuse aimed in my direction is reaching fever pitch, we spot the narrow turning leading to King's Hall. 'Thank Christ for that,' someone says, thinking we would be spending the next eight hours circumnavigating Stoke listening to Mojo's tiny cassette recorder. But the ordeal is not over yet. A large pay-and-display carpark opposite the King's Hall is jammed full. It's 11.30 pm and it's obvious that no pub-goers are coming out to reclaim their cars – all these vehicles belong to the 'soulies' crammed into the nearby all-nighter. Two of us leap out and shoot off to different corners of the carpark, seeking a parking spot for Mojo to guide his car into. We spot one, but the situation is complicated by the arrival of more carloads of soulies with the same intentions. Finally he manages to outwit the others, and as they take a wrong turning he screeches into the one available space between about 200 cars and turns off the engine.

We all grab our holdalls and march off through the fine, crisp winter night towards the massive grey-brick building that is the King's Hall. In another town it would be the town hall. Here it is a dark two-storey concert venue which dominates the immediate neighbourhood.

Weaving through the closely parked cars, minibuses and coaches, we can see light shining from the venue's entrance and fall into step behind half a dozen other soul fans.

'I haven't seen a packed carpark like this since Wigan,' said Mojo. 'This place looks amazing.'

After a short orderly queue (thank God it *wasn't* Wigan!), we enter the brightly lit foyer and hand over our £10 admission tickets. The swing doors in front of us open to reveal what our souls have been searching for – the excitement, companionship and energy of a Northern Soul all-nighter.

As the eyes slowly become accustomed to the darkness, it is clear the King's Hall's concert room is virtually a replica of Wigan Casino's main room. Its vast oblong dance floor, almost the size of a football pitch, sways with hundreds of bodies. Along two edges of the dance floor are rows of chairs and tables (yes, it is permissible to sit down occasionally!), every one of them occupied.

On the raised stage at the far end of the room, DJ Richard Searling is selecting the rare soul sides to entertain the crowd. Seeing the former Wigan Casino DJ in a venue like this sends shivers down the spines of us former Casino-goers. A glance upwards confirms there is indeed a balcony ringing the floor. Soul fans can be seen milling around upstairs, enjoying the sights, the sounds and atmosphere.

Our pace quickens as we make our way along the edge of the crowded dance floor to the front left-hand corner of the stage. This, we agree, will be our base for the night and we dump holdalls and coats behind a table in the certain knowledge that everything will still be intact when we come to collect it later.

Clutching an old vinyl Kent album I'm trying to sell, I hit the floor. Richard is playing the Tempos' 'Countdown Here I

Come'. 'Possibly one of the most uplifting pieces of Northern Soul,' he shouts, and no one disagrees. The numbers on the dance floor swell as the falsetto voice comes in over swirling strings: 'Just like a guided missile, my love is heading for you, baby . . .'

I look around the dance floor; Mark, Kim and Mojo have also wasted no time working up a sweat. Already the place is buzzing, clapping punctuates each record, shirts and dresses are stained with sweat and brows are being mopped. This is heaven to a Northern Soul freak. An atmospheric venue with 1,000-plus like-minded fanatics. And then it dawns on you. This could be 1977, 1987 or 1997 . . . it makes no difference here. Northern Soul's fans' demands and needs have not changed in three decades. Great music, a good dance floor, good company, somewhere to buy and sell records, and a soft-drinks bar is just about all we need.

Couple that with the same shuffling, gliding, stomping and spinning dancing style and the timeless music of the Torch, and this could just as easily be 1972. Our bodies may not tell us so, but that's what it *feels* like.

Some of us may not even have been into Northern Soul twenty-five years ago. Some of us may have been at primary school. Some of us may hardly have been to a Northern Soul venue *since* 1972. But none of that matters tonight. This is a mass celebration in time-honoured fashion of the great musical output of black America in the 1960s.

Tonight is a Torch revival event and is co-promoted by Midlands-based DJ Kev Roberts, who also runs the twice-yearly events Togetherness at the same venue with Richard Searling.

The Togetherness success story started in February 1997 and is based on the main hall playing Northern Soul, and upstairs, along the King's Hall's winding corridors and stairs, another smaller room playing Modern Soul.

Tonight, however, the Torch revival is in one room only, and the 9 pm–7 am opening hours cunningly draw both the more 'casual' soul fan and the diehard all-nighter goers. More than 1,000 punters have responded, and the upstairs bar and balcony seats are opened to cater for the overflow.

At 1 am Colin Curtis is the host DJ and is in brilliant form, keeping the knowledgeable crowd on the dance floor with Torch classics. Looking around, there is no denying that Northern Soul fans in the late 1990s come in all shapes and sizes.

Ages range from the twenties to the fifties, with the average punter probably in his late thirties/early forties. He will probably be dressed in loose-fitting trousers or jeans, and polo shirt or vest. Or maybe chinos and a shirt worn outside the trousers. Or maybe no top at all, and just a pair of old jeans reserved specially for the rigours of a Northern Soul all-nighter. Oh, what the hell, there is no such thing as an *average* soul fan these days.

The 'uniform' of the Wigan era – singlet, baggy pants with beer towel, and shiny brogues – has long since gone. In Stoke you can stand in one spot and admire the dancing of a muscular guy in his thirties wearing a singlet and a flat cap on backwards. Next to him is a sober-looking bald-headed guy, maybe fiftyish, in black T-shirt and slacks. Then there's a Rastafarian dancing next to a girl in her twenties wearing only a bikini top and cycling shorts. Near the woman in her forties in a sensible cool flowing dress, there's a jeans-wearing skinhead dancing topless apart from a pair of braces. For every skinny, athletic-looking bloke there's a guy who in any other setting would look like a portly middle-aged man. For every curvaceous, youthful-looking woman in tight jeans there's a mature woman with a more ample figure. For every clean-shaven young man with curly locks there's a balding, moustached punter.

None of this matters one jot, other than to paint a picture to the outsider that you cannot clone a Northern Soul fan. Whether you are twenty-five or fifty, built like Kate Moss or Dawn French, or dance like Michael Flatley or Mr Blobby, *nobody gives a toss*!

And maybe that's the heartwarming beauty of being a Northern Soul fan in the 1990s. The youthful insecurities, the cliquishness that sometimes existed, the competitive edge on the dance floor that became almost aggressive – all that has now gone. Most of us are now happy with what we are and who we are, and with age have hopefully learned more tolerance.

The pure joy, (yes, *joy*) of being able to live, relive, and soak up the underground scene we all love brings a bond that does not exist in any other music movement. Dancing is at the core of the scene, and always will be, but no longer does it matter if you can do a suicidally fast spin followed by backdrop, splits and a handstand in the break of Lou Pride's 'I'm Comin' Home in the Morning'.

Sure, there are still some cool-looking and age-defying movers out there, but the majority glide around with the minimum of effort, never missing a beat and mouthing the words to the floorshaker currently on the turntable. One drawback of the age range is that it's impossible to play Spot The Drugs Squad, which used to provide hours of amusement at Wigan.

At the Casino the 'squad' were usually considerably older than the normal punter and would have that fish-out-of-water look that would alert any law-breakers quicker than you could say 'Got any gear?' Now the drugs squad detectives, even if they were interested, would probably look more like your son or daughter. Times change.

Back in the King's Hall, the sounds go on and on, and the numbers continue to swell. We are all working up a sweat on the dance floor and I buy Mojo a pint of lager before the bar stops serving alcohol. In a darkened corner of the main hall and outside in the lit passageway, the record dealers are plying their trade. What was once an exclusively vinyl domain is now being increasingly eaten into by the CD market. Rare vinyl is still, and always will be, the mainstay of the Northern Soul scene, but the 24-tracks-for-£10 CD market is booming. Nowadays, boxes of rare 45s marked 'Northern Soul oldies', 'Rare British issues', or 'Current biggies', or '70s soul', sit happily alongside rows and rows of compilation CDs.

Punters crowd around the tables bearing sought-after soul treasures, flicking through lovingly cared-for import singles.

'How much for this, mate?'

'£50.'

'I'll give you £40.'

'Sod off.'

'All right, I'll give you this' – producing another rare 45 – 'and £30.'

And so on.

CDs are much easier to negotiate a deal over. The prices are all marked: £6, £10, £15. More and more punters are selling their vinyl collections (very profitably, too) and re-acquiring the same sounds on CD. OK, the purists may not approve, but the convenience, longevity and cheapness of a CD compilation of tracks that might otherwise cost you literally hundreds of pounds to own is very attractive to many soul fans.

In the midst of all the bartering and to-ing and fro-ing from the main hall to the entrance hall, the doormen look on bored. This is probably the easiest night's wages they will earn. No one appears drunk, no one fights, no one throws up over anyone's girlfriend. The bouncers look on bemused as soul fans of all shapes and sizes and ages stay up until dawn listening to the obscure offerings of otherwise long-forgotten American artists.

The laid-back attitude of the bouncers is entirely appropriate and appreciated by the soul crowd. Cash-strapped soulies take empty bottles with them to the toilets to fill them with tap water. The odd can of beer or Lucozade is smuggled in, but there is no paranoia about getting caught, beaten up and thrown out in the 1999 soul scene. The bar is doing a roaring trade in soft drinks anyway, now the licensing hours have expired, and the queue for tea, coffee and snacks is constant all night long.

In the gents the entertainment continues, with guys of all shapes and sizes in various states of undress. In the centre of the lavatories there is a bank of back-to-back sinks in a manner that reminds me of my primary school days. Holdalls are scattered around as guys grab fresh shirts, spray on the Lynx (whatever happened to Brut?), and splash water on their faces before rejoining the fray on the dance floor.

In the corner a tall, gaunt guy in his thirties is doing karate kicks and stretches while his fellow soul fans continue their ablutions, hardly giving him a second glance. If you weren't just a little bit eccentric, you wouldn't be here.

Handshakes and words are easily exchanged as you try to edge your way back towards the door, but almost inevitably a familiar face appears, flushed, and eager to chat.

It's the same story in the corridor skirting the whole length of the main hall. In this cool and well-lit environment, small groups of fans gather chatting. You try valiantly to make it back to the dance floor, but between the Blackpool lads, the Chorley lot, and the Preston lot, there are many possible delays as you edge your way back slowly but surely towards the darkness of the all-nighter.

At 3.30 am the floor is still rocking. Martyn 'Mr Torch' Ellis has returned to do his first DJing spot for donkey's years, Dave Evison is playing a mixed set of Torch oldies and the heat and condensation builds up nicely again.

Everyone is on the dance floor now, and most people I spot are now on their second shirt. The beat goes on and the memories come flooding back . . . Mr Flood's Party's 'Compared to What', Steve Karmen's 'Breakaway', Harold Melvin's 'Get Out', the Superlatives' 'I Still Love You', the Younghearts' 'A Little Togetherness'.

An hour later, the crowd has thinned out and the diehard all-nighter-goers are in their element. Alert, overheated and gum-chewing dancers stake their claim on their part of the dance floor. It's at this point you start to notice the best dancers, marvel at the enthusiasm of the 'veterans' who are still giving it their best shot, and realize you are becoming so wrapped up in the music and the event that you have forgotten there is a world outside the sturdy walls of the King's Hall. A glance outside the doors confirms that it is still and deathly quiet in the winter darkness.

But while the non-soul-obsessed world sleeps, the ten-hour marathon for nocturnally inclined dance fans continues. The crowd's appetite for the music is insatiable. A great majority can name the title, artist and label of every record played and the DJ who thinks he can get away with playing a sound already played earlier will be swiftly taken to task.

It's 6 am and the dance floor is thinning out noticeably as DJ Kev Roberts comes on to do his spot. He reads the mood perfectly and throws in some non-Torch material to broaden the musical content. Odd corners of the dance hall contain some weary-looking faces and some couples are starting to grab their coats and drift off home.

But not the Blackpool posse. Mojo is driving, and Mojo is

having a great time and isn't going anywhere. Taking a rare breather from the dance floor, he comes across to our table and takes a swig of water. 'Might as well stay to the end,' he says, wipes his brow and disappears.

The old legs are starting to turn to jelly as Keith Minshull takes over for the last hour, but he plays solid oldies and the odd 70s stormer to keep everyone's attention.

Finally, to the strains of Jimmy Radcliffe's 'Long After Tonight is All Over', we drag our tiring bodies to the toilets to get towelled down and changed for the long journey home. An old familiar feeling drifts in as the lights go on and the all-nighter ends. 'Where the hell has the last eight hours gone?'

The bored-looking doormen now look even more under-occupied, nodding goodbye as we file out. An enterprising promoter is standing by the reception desk handing out flyers for a soul event somewhere or other as we stumble out into the winter darkness, ears ringing from the loud music.

It seems the nearby carpark is still full to overflowing, with subdued-looking soulies sitting in the driving seats of their cars. Where they used to be Ford Cortinas, Hillman Imps and Morris Minors, there are now posh Rovers, top-of-the-range Fords, and solid-looking people carriers. Many soulies have taken advantage of the overnight lifting of parking restrictions to leave their vehicles on double yellow lines. There's not a police car in sight as hundreds of soulies file out quietly.

Mojo's car is still intact, as are the contents of our unattended holdalls (as we knew they would be). During the hour and a half drive home to Blackpool, the post-mortem on the night begins.

'Chuffed to bits they played "Mr Flood's Party".'

'What was that one that Minshull played towards the end? . . .' and so on.

After we have cruised through Stoke, north up the M6 and to the end of the M55 for what seems like an age, a momentous thought occurs to Mojo. 'Bloody hell, we've come all this way and we haven't stopped at a single traffic light.'

The four of us ponder this important piece of information and agree that he is right. From that point on, the last three miles home becomes a nerve-jangling ordeal. Will the lights stay at green all the way home? Will we be forced to stop? Will Mojo ignore the red light anyway just to prove it can be done? Yes, folks, this is a carload of mature family men at play on their way home from an all-night dance venue. Boys will always be boys.

It's daylight now at almost 9 am as the car pulls up outside my house, which is still in darkness with the curtains closed. Obviously my wife and two young children are still in bed. It's now 12 hours since we set out and it feels crisp and cold in the morning air. Suddenly all thoughts of tiredness disappear as the debate in the car begins.

'Fancy going to the next Lowton soul night, lads?'

'There's always Golborne.'

'How about Blackburn?'

'The Ritz?'

'Give you a ring next week.'

Yes, soul boys will always be soul boys.


*David Nowell's all-time favourite Northern Soul sounds (I think)*

'You Didn't Say a Word'  Yvonne Baker
'Countdown Here I Come'  The Tempos
'A Case of Too Much Lovemaking'  Gloria Scott
'The Panic is On'  Roy Hamilton
'If That's What You Wanted'  Frankie Beverley
'The Pieces of My Broken Heart'  Gladys Knight
'I Never Loved Her Anyway'  Jimmy Beaumont
'What Kind of Lady'  Dee Dee Sharp
'It'll Never Be Over for Me'  Timi Yuro
'What About My Love' Johnny Taylor

# Useful Information

Togetherness all-nighters/weekenders: 01909 515150
Keele all-nighters: 01782 814110
Cleethorpes weekenders: 01858 465780
Tony's Empress Ballroom Blackburn all-nighters: 01902 652214
100 Club all-nighters: 0171 636 2622
Lowton Civic Hall soul nights: 01942 493795
*Manifesto* magazine: 01452 300894
Trentham Gardens, Stoke all-nighters: 01543 304022
Soul Essence Weekenders, Great Yarmouth: 01525 370250
King George's Hall, Blackburn soul nights: 0161 877 1004

*The Strange World of Northern Soul* (video, CD and booklet
 by Ian Levine): 01543 304022 (£39.99)
Kent Records: 0181 453 1311 (web address:
 www.acerecords.co.uk)
Goldmine Records: 01706 819280 (web address:
 www.firstnet.co.uk/goldsoul)

Night Owl Northern Soul Club: www.nightowl.co.uk
The Soul of the Net: www.cet.ac.il/personnel/yonin/index.htm
Soul Source: www.http://soulsource99.cjb.net

**Books used for research:**

Clayson, Alan, *Beat Merchants* (Blandford)
Davis, Sharon, *The Motown Story* (Guiness)
Gordy, Berry, *To Be Loved* (Headline)
McAleer, Dave, *Beatboom, Pop Goes The Sixties* (Hamlyn)